American Psychology-Law Society Series

Series Editor
Ronald Roesch

Editorial Board
Gail S. Goodman
Thomas Grisso
Craig Haney
Kirk Heilbrun
John Monahan
Marlene Moretti
Edward P. Mulvey
J. Don Read
N. Dickon Reppucci
Gary L. Wells
Lawrence S. Wrightsman
Patricia A. Zapf

Books in the Series

Trial Consulting
Amy J. Posey and Lawrence S. Wrightsman

Death by Design: Capital Punishment as a Social Psychological System
Craig Haney

Psychological Injuries: Forensic Assessment, Treatment, and Law
William J. Koch, Kevin S. Douglas, Tonia L. Nicholls, and Melanie L. O'Neill

Emergency Department Treatment of the Psychiatric Patient: Policy Issues and Legal Requirements
Susan Stefan

The Psychology of the Supreme Court
Lawrence S. Wrightsman

Proving the Unprovable
Christopher Slobogin

Adolescents, Media, and the Law
Roger J.R. Levesque

Oral Arguments before the Supreme Court: An Empirical Approach
Lawrence S. Wrightsman

Oral Arguments before the Supreme Court

An Empirical Approach

Lawrence S. Wrightsman

OXFORD
UNIVERSITY PRESS

2008

OXFORD
UNIVERSITY PRESS

Oxford University Press, Inc., publishes works that further
Oxford University's objective of excellence
in research, scholarship, and education.

Oxford   New York
Auckland   Cape Town   Dar es Salaam   Hong Kong   Karachi
Kuala Lumpur   Madrid   Melbourne   Mexico City   Nairobi
New Delhi   Shanghai   Taipei   Toronto

With offices in
Argentina   Austria   Brazil   Chile   Czech Republic   France   Greece
Guatemala   Hungary   Italy   Japan   Poland   Portugal   Singapore
South Korea   Switzerland   Thailand   Turkey   Ukraine   Vietnam

Published by Oxford University Press, Inc.
198 Madison Avenue, New York, New York 10016

www.oup.com

Oxford is a registered trademark of Oxford University Press

Library of Congress Cataloging-in-Publication Data
Wrightsman, Lawrence S.
Oral arguments before the supreme court :
an empirical approach / Lawrence S. Wrightsman.
   p. cm.—(American Psychology-Law Society series)
Includes bibliographical references and index.
ISBN 978-0-19-536862-8
1. United States. Supreme Court—Decision making. 2. Oral pleading—United States.
3. Forensic orations—United States. I. Title.

KF8748.W752 2008

347.73'72—dc22   2008004248

9 8 7 6 5 4 3 2 1

Printed in the United States of America
on acid-free paper

To my son,
Allan Jefferson Wrightsman

Series Foreword

This book series is sponsored by the American Psychology-Law Society (APLS). The APLS is an interdisciplinary organization devoted to scholarship, practice, and public service in psychology and law. Its goals include advancing the contributions of psychology to the understanding of law and legal institutions through basic and applied research; promoting the education of psychologists in matters of law and the education of legal personnel in matters of psychology; and informing the psychological and legal communities and the general public of current research, educational, and service activities in the field of psychology and law. APLS membership includes psychologists from the academic research and clinical practice communities as well as members of the legal community. Research and practice are represented in both the civil and criminal legal arenas. The APLS has chosen Oxford University Press as a strategic partner in publishing because of its commitment to scholarship, quality, and the international dissemination of ideas. These strengths will help the APLS reach our goal of educating the psychology and legal professions as well as the general public about important developments in psychology and law. The focus of the book series reflects the diversity of the field of psychology and law, as we publish books on a broad range of topics.

This is the second book on the Supreme Court that Professor Lawrence Wrightsman has contributed to this series. In *The Psychology of the Supreme Court*, Wrightsman provided readers with a compelling and thoughtful analysis of how the nine Supreme Court justices behave both individually and as a group in reaching decisions that can affect all Americans. In *Oral Arguments before the Supreme Court: An Empirical Approach*, he continues his focus on the Supreme Court but turns his attention to the role that oral arguments play in Supreme Court decisions. He traces the history of oral arguments from the time of John Jay and the beginning of the Supreme Court to the present-day Roberts Court. Challenging the notion that oral arguments play an insignificant role in decisions, Wrightsman provides a careful and detailed analysis of the transcripts of oral arguments and shows that oral arguments are central to the decision-making process. Suggesting that values and attitudes of the justices do matter, Wrightsman finds, for example, that justices tend to ask more questions of the losing side in ideological cases than in cases in which ideology is not a factor. His analysis also reveals that Justice Roberts has created a more relaxed atmosphere for oral arguments, one that appears more receptive to advocates than that of his predecessor, Justice Rehnquist.

In *Oral Arguments before the Supreme Court*, Wrightsman continues the study of the personality of justices that he began in his previous book. In a fascinating application of the Five Factor theory of personality, he uses his analysis of oral arguments and other information to identify justices who each exemplify one of the Big Five: Justice Scalia (Extraversion), Justice Breyer (Agreeableness), Justice Souter (Conscientiousness), Justice Kennedy (Openness to Experience), and Justice Thomas (Negative Affectivity). His discussion of the basis for his characterizations of the justices provides insight into their approach to cases and the psychology of their decisions.

In the concluding chapter, Wrightsman presents psychological research and his perspective on an issue that may become a pressing one before the Court—whether to allow televised oral arguments. Congress is currently considering a bill that would permit the televising of oral arguments, a move that is likely not supported by the Supreme Court justices.

Professor Wrightsman has once again provided an insightful book about the Supreme Court and how nine individuals reach decisions in often complex and controversial, ideological cases. This book is of value to social scientists, as it provides a model for understanding the dynamics of judicial decision making from an empirical perspective. It will also be of interest to advocates who may appear before the Supreme Court, as it will provide them with incisive pointers on what types of questions to expect from the various justices and, most important, how to avoid making the classic mistakes that advocates have made in the past.

Ronald Roesch
Series Editor

Preface

Of the three branches of our federal government, the judicial branch is arguably the most secret. For example, the justices of the Supreme Court decide
in secret which cases to resolve, they meet in secret to take a preliminary vote,
the opinions are drafted in secret, and not until their decision is announced is
the public privy to their actions. But one step in the decision-making process
is open to the public: the oral arguments. Despite its transparency, the process
of holding oral arguments has been challenged. Some critics—and even a current justice—believe that the exercise is useless in the overall process of decision making, as justices' minds have been made up before this step.

　In this book, I challenge that conclusion. The viewpoint of this book is
that oral arguments are a significant part of the Supreme Court's decision-
making process. Justices have an opportunity to test the limits of claims made
by advocates in their briefs; furthermore, the argument procedure provides an
opportunity for justices to sense the strength of feelings held by other justices
and even to try to persuade their colleagues as they question the advocates.
The requisite nature of oral arguments was illustrated in a case that came before the Court on October 19, 2007, Medellin v. Texas. It was a case of major
significance as it was a death-penalty case. But even more, it asked whether
the President of the United States, on his own, could order a state court to
follow a decision by the International Court of Justice that foreign nationals
on death row in the United States—in this case, one Jose Medellin—can obtain counsel from their native countries. The comments and questions from
the justices were so frequent and heated that Justice John Paul Stevens, ever
gracious on the bench, told the Solicitor General of Texas that he would like

to hear the six points in the advocate's argument "without interruption by my colleagues." Chief Justice Roberts did something that was unprecedented: he gave each side 15 minutes extra time to argue their case; scheduled for an hour, the oral argument lasted an hour and a half. By the end, the justices had directed 122 questions or comments to the petitioner's attorney and 93 to the respondent's.

Granted, not all cases draw this intense interest from the justices. Nonetheless, each oral argument provides a window into the justices' thinking and even their unique personalities. In short, a study of the oral arguments lends understanding into the workings of the Court. Only a few books have studied the oral arguments from an empirical perspective, and this is the first book by a psychologist to do so. One may question how decision making by the Court can be studied empirically, given that much of its behavior occurs behind closed doors. However, conclusions can be drawn from analyses of transcripts of the oral arguments and the eventual decisions, all of which are part of the public record. In this book, the following empirical questions are asked and answered:

- Do some types of advocates win their cases more often than others?
- Do members of the so-called Supreme Court bar (i.e., advocates who specialize in appellate advocacy) do better than first-timers or attorneys from state attorney generals' offices?
- Do justices "telegraph" the way they will vote through the types and frequency of questions they ask advocates from each side?
- Did the change in leadership of the Court, from that of Chief Justice Rehnquist to Chief Justice Roberts, have an effect on the atmosphere of questioning by the justices?
- Does each justice have such a distinctive style of questioning that he or she can be identified on a transcript of oral arguments that doesn't give the name of the questioner?

In addition to supplementing empirical knowledge about oral arguments, this book provides a distinction between two types of cases, thus helping us to understand the dynamics of judicial decision making. For years scholars have been asked to choose between two models—the legal model, which argues that justices use reasoning and precedent in making their decisions, and the attitudinal model, which proposes that justices are strongly influenced by their own values and attitudes. This book classifies cases as ideological or nonideological and demonstrates empirically that the justices treat these two types of cases differently, in how often their eventual decisions are unanimous, how long it takes to resolve the case, the degree to which they follow the position of the Office of Solicitor General, and lastly, but most relevant to the focus on oral arguments, whether the questioning during oral arguments predicts the outcome.

The Supreme Court is going through a period of transition. After a record-setting 12 years with the same nine justices, the term that began in October 2005 was headed by a new Chief Justice, and in February 2006 a new Associate Justice came aboard. The term completed in June 2007 saw a major shift in decisions involving significant ideological cases, such as those on abortion, sexual discrimination, and school desegregation.

Further changes in the composition of the Court will mean that its processes will continue to receive scrutiny. This book is an attempt to provide one set of guideposts for studying the decisions of the Court.

Acknowledgments

In a variety of ways a number of people have helped me prepare this book, and it is my pleasure to acknowledge their significant contributions. Three students at the University of Kansas—Sarah Thimsen, Jacqueline Austin, and Erin Vernon—did empirical Senior Honors theses on Supreme Court decision making. Not only their findings but also their questions and insights are reflected in the pages of this book. Furthermore, three research assistants—Jerry Nguyen, Ashley Hirschorn, and Brie Padgett—did much of the nitty-gritty work, including such important matters as counting the numbers of words uttered by advocates before they were interrupted by a justice during oral arguments. I am indebted to them for their diligence and responsiveness. Cindy Sexton once more solved many problems related to the production of the manuscript and was always willing to go the second mile. Professor Ronald Roesch, Senior Editor of the American Psychology-Law Society series of books published by Oxford University Press, has once more been encouraging and enthusiastic in his response to my ideas and my chapter drafts.

Any errors in the book, despite the efforts of all these people, are mine.

Contents

Oral Arguments before the Supreme Court

1

Oral Arguments: Are They No Longer Essential?

Side by side with the great name of [Chief Justice] Marshall should be placed that of Daniel Webster. The arguments of one were as necessary as the decisions of the other.

—S. W. Finley (1979, p. 70)

Oral Arguments as a Window on the Justices' Activities

The oral arguments before the Supreme Court provide the public its only opportunity to view the justices as they decide important cases. Yet some would say the oral arguments are only window dressing. The purpose of this book is to examine the role that oral arguments play in the decision making of the Supreme Court.

In recent years more than a million people have visited the Supreme Court building annually. With luck, they actually get to see the Supreme Court justices in action—with a lot of luck, that is. The Supreme Court typically holds its oral arguments only on Monday, Tuesday, and Wednesday mornings from 10 A.M. until noon. Otherwise, access to the justices is off limits, unless a visitor is fortunate to spot one in the cafeteria located in the basement of the Supreme Court building. (Every working day Justice Harry Blackmun would eat breakfast there with his law clerks, and Chief Justice John Roberts has been seen having lunch there occasionally.) The public is not allowed to visit the justices in their offices, in contrast to members of Congress, and, in fact, the portion of the building that houses the justices' chambers and their conference room is closely guarded.

So what chance does a visitor have of seeing the justices at work? It is slim. Oral arguments are held on only 14 weeks of the year, spanning from early October to the latter part of April. The possible number of such hours each year is 84; compare that with the number of hours the building is open, from 9 A.M. until 4:30 P.M. each Monday through Friday (holidays excluded). Furthermore, although the building's courtroom is massive, most of its 350 seats are reserved for members of the Supreme Court bar, guests of the justices, the media, the law clerks, and families of the advocates and their clients. Typically, only about 50 seats are available for the public on a first-come, first-served basis, which means the requirement of standing outside for several hours to obtain a seat.

A Variety of Cases, a Variety of Oral Arguments

Watching an oral argument in the three-story courtroom is a memorable experience. The marshal calls the session to order, and the justices enter through the massive curtain and take their seats (each chair is of a different height and designed specifically for that justice). A journalist recently recounted his impressions:

> This week offered the last oral arguments in the Court's current term, and on Monday I went to see and hear what the nine justices do.... Like a New Yorker who has never been to the Statue of Liberty and a Washingtonian who has never visited the White House, I've managed a career in political journalism without attending an oral argument before the Supreme Court....
>
> Attending the Supreme Court may be better than going to church insofar as you can't attend the Court in your gym clothes. The Court's hearing chamber may be the last best place to experience authentic decorum anywhere in America. Cell phones? They even forbid reading material. As the moment to begin arrives, a clerk instructs, "Remain absolutely silent." The best yet: "If you find yourself falling asleep, you are free to leave the courtroom." A somnolent 7-year-old in front of me was admonished twice.
>
> The Court is not wholly immune from the compulsions of popular culture. When they entered the chamber, one felt the presence of celebrities. They sit beneath a large suspended clock, with Roman numerals. Its sweeping second hand is visible to the attorneys who have 30 minutes to make their case. As the 10 A.M. start approached, the room fell from murmurs and whispers to still silence. (Henniger, 2006, p. A14)

For tourists at the Court on a particular day, a case may be arcane, or it may deal with something perfectly understandable. For example, visitors for the two cases argued on Tuesday, February 28, 2006, witnessed the oral argument in *Marshall v. Marshall,* a case that had captivated the national news media because it involved a dispute between Anna Nicole Smith, a former *Playboy* model who in 1994 married an 89-year-old wheelchair-bound Texas oilman, and her deceased husband's son. (The visitor might even have spotted Ms. Smith, who was in the audience.) The conflict centered on $88 million from J. Howard Marshall's estate. Anna Nicole Smith, listed in the Court proceedings as Vickie Lynn Marshall, her real name, had sued her husband's son, E. Pierce Marshall, over the estate—estimated to be worth as much as $1.6 billion—after the elderly Marshall had died a year after marrying the 26-year-old Smith. The Supreme Court agreed to hear this case not because of its titillation value but because it involved a conflict between probate law and bankruptcy law.

The typical visitor might be surprised at the procedures and format of the oral arguments. They differ from jury trials, which are within the common knowledge of most citizens. The relevant parties to the case are called the "petitioner" and the "respondent" (or, the "appellant" and the "appellee"), rather than the plaintiff and the defendant, as in a trial. The petitioner and respondent may or may not be present, only as observers (both Anna Nicole Smith and E. Pierce Marshall were). Attorneys for each side are limited to 30 minutes unless the Court grants extra time prior to the hearings. Petitioners' attorneys may reserve part of their time for a rebuttal, which they may give at the end of the hour, but respondents' attorneys are not granted this privilege. If the federal government has an interest in the outcome of the case, an attorney from the office of the solicitor general may be allocated a portion of one side's 30 minutes of oral argument (usually 10 minutes). These government attorneys appear formally dressed in their nineteenth-century garb—swallow-tail coats, striped pants, and vests—and all the other attorneys are expected to be soberly dressed. (When Warren Burger was chief justice, he was offended by the inappropriateness of one advocate's necktie.)

Those visitors attracted to the *Marshall v. Marshall* session because one of the litigants was a former *Playboy* model probably expected a more sensationalistic discussion than that of the usual oral argument before the Court. While the questions did not linger at that level, there were sporadic exchanges that reflected the florid facts of the case. Kent L. Richland, a Los Angeles attorney who represented Vickie Lynn Marshall, began his presentation by saying, "This is a bankruptcy case." The facts of the case were the following: first, after a 45-day trial (in which Vickie Marshall testified for 6 days), a jury for a Texas probate court unanimously determined that Ms. Marshall was entitled to nothing from her husband's estate beyond the $6 million in gifts that had been bestowed upon her while he was still alive. (She had claimed that he promised her half of his estate and that he had established a trust reflecting this, but that his son had "suppressed or destroyed" the document and cut her out of the inheritance.)

Then a federal bankruptcy court in California intervened, after she declared bankruptcy there. That court ruled that Ms. Marshall was entitled to $449 million, plus $25 million in punitive damages, because of E. Pierce Marshall's alleged fraud in dealing with her inheritance. Next, a federal court in California reduced the amount to $88 million but supported the claims of fraud. Finally, the Ninth Circuit Court of Appeals reversed that decision, ruling that the federal bankruptcy court in California should not have intervened in a decision made by a Texas probate court. Thus, as the loser in the lower-court decision, Ms. Marshall appealed to the United States Supreme Court and became the petitioner in this case.

The highest court in the land receives between 8,000 and 9,000 petitions a year—in the term ending in the summer of 2007 it was 8,857—but agrees to decide only about 70 to 80 of them. (In the vast remainder, the decision of the lower court remains in effect.) The Court decided to act on Vickie Marshall's petition because of ambiguity about the boundaries between the state and federal courts, especially when it comes to matters of probate. Is there a "probate exception" that bars federal bankruptcy courts from deciding a case that, at the same time, is being administered by a state probate court? Even though federal bankruptcy courts have broad discretion, they have tended to avoid matters involving domestic relations and probate, on the assumption that state courts are better able to decide them.

But the visitor to the Court that day who chose to observe the oral arguments probably did not know the background of the case. When the oral arguments for *Marshall v. Marshall* began, visitors found the attorneys and justices immediately entangled in a dialogue on whether bankruptcy courts have jurisdiction to decide such matters as probate of wills. The colloquy between the justices and Ms. Marshall's attorney was sprinkled with puzzling legal terms—"tort claim," "inter vivos estate," "probate exception," "in rem jurisdiction"—and obscure references to past cases. It was only when the respondent's time came to speak that the justices referred to the parties in the suit. For example:

Justice Stephen Breyer: "I thought that the case simply held that because your clients had interfered with an effort by J. Howard [Marshall] to give quite a few million dollars to Vickie Marshall—because of that interference, they had committed the tort of inter vivos interference with a gift, and they had to pay damages. Now, they did say a lot of things by way of what the evidence was. Indeed, they did say, as you point out, that your clients forged three pages of the will. But that was simply evidence of their bad intent, and it did not invalidate anything in the probate proceeding, as I read it. Now, what have I said that is not right?" (*Marshall v. Marshall* transcript of oral argument, p. 28).

Later Justice David Souter challenged E. Pierce Marshall's attorney by concluding, "That's all she is saying as I understand it....As I understand her cause of action, it can proceed on the assumption that the will is valid, the trust is valid. 'Just give me the money that I would have had'" (p. 39). But the dialogue was not without its moments of humor. Justice Antonin Scalia asked Ms. Marshall's attorney if his position wasn't more extreme than necessary: "Do you have a lesser position...that might cause you to win?" (p. 6).

From the viewpoint of experienced observers of the Court's oral arguments, E. Pierce Marshall's attorney (G. Eric Brunstad, Jr., a Yale law professor) got pummeled with questions from a variety of justices, not only Breyer and Souter but also Justice Ruth Bader Ginsburg and Chief Justice John Roberts. Based on the extent and nature of the questions one would predict that the justices would rule in favor of Anna Nicole Smith. And they did, unanimously, 2 months later. In actuality, the Court did not award her any money, but ruled that a federal court in California could deal with her case, saying that the federal court did have the authority to resolve disputes over estates. The case was returned to the Ninth Circuit for more hearings. But the final dispensation of the case is incomplete, because of a combination of several unexpected events: first the death of E. Pierce Marshall in June 2006, then the death of Smith's 20-year-old son 3 months later, and finally, and perhaps most unforeseen, the death of Anna Nicole Smith, at the age of 36, in February 2007 which led to a dispute over the paternity of her recently born daughter.

The second case that day likely held less interest for many visitors but had much greater implications for the public at large: it dealt with a challenge to Vermont's law that put limits on political candidates' spending (three appeals were consolidated into one for the oral arguments: *Randall v. Sorrell, Sorrell v. Randall*, and *Vermont Republican Party v. Sorrell*, 2007). And if a citizen arrived on another day, he or she might observe oral arguments on two cases involving an interpretation of a seemingly obscure federal law or the degree to which the tax code could be applied to a specific action. The variety of cases handled by the Court in a given term is truly stunning; the justices need to make themselves knowledgeable on topics ranging from death-penalty statutes to detainees' rights, from copyright laws to the Confrontation Clause of the Constitution.

The Oral Argument: In Diminished Regard?

Regardless of how fathomable the nature of the case, visitors can watch the justices quiz the advocates, each of whom usually gets only precious moments to make his or her argument before the Court. Questions may come at a fast and furious rate; before John Roberts was appointed chief justice, he argued 39 cases before the Court, and for one of these he later counted 150 questions directed at him in 30 minutes! Each of the justices has his or her distinctive manner of speaking and questioning, a topic described at length in Chapter 5.

The oral arguments not only provide the public an opportunity to see the Court in action but may also receive (depending on the case) attention from newspaper, television, and radio journalists and columnists. (In recent terms the Court has held oral arguments on between 70 and 80 cases, but typically only about a fourth of them receive coverage in even the major media.)

In actuality, most of the Court's work is done behind closed doors. These activities include conferences to decide which cases to take, discussions and tentative votes on cases, and the drafting and revising of opinions, concurrences, and dissents. Without the publicly accessible oral arguments, almost everything about the Court's activities would be secret. Given that, why is the oral argument held in less than highest regard?

Some would say that oral arguments played a vital part in the Court's decision making 200 years ago but have since diminished in importance. Others view them as useful but dispensable if necessary to do so. Two types of actions by the justices bring into question whether the justices themselves consider the oral arguments an essential part of the steps the Court goes through in deciding its appeals. First, several occurrences during the term that began in October 2004 caused a justice to miss oral arguments. The more serious of these was Chief Justice William Rehnquist's thyroid cancer, which forced him to be absent from the oral arguments in 44 cases. He was receiving treatment and unable to attend any of the arguments made between the first of November and early March, as well as the conferences in which these cases were discussed and preliminary votes were taken. Despite his absence he assigned himself the task of writing the majority opinion in four of these cases (*Muehler v. Mena, Tenet v. Doe, Pace v. DiGuglielmo,* and *Van Orden v. Perry*). Also, Justice John Paul Stevens was not present for the oral arguments in two important eminent-domain cases because inclement weather shut down the airport in Florida from which he was returning to Washington, D.C. (He was, however, presumably there for the conference discussion and votes on these cases.) Being the senior justice in the majority in one of these cases, he assigned himself the task of writing the Court's opinion in *Kelo v. City of New London*. This decision emerged as arguably the most controversial one of the whole 2004–2005 term, because it permitted the city of New London, CT, to apply the eminent-domain principle from the Constitution's Commerce Clause and take over several residents' homes in order for a private developer to build a hotel and conference center on their land.

Perhaps these absences are not crucial; after all, the missing justices could later listen to audiotapes or read the transcripts of the oral arguments. But a second kind of occurrence reflects the fragile status of oral arguments. In 1981, when William Brennan and Sandra Day O'Connor were both on the bench, the justices had overburdened themselves by accepting too many cases for review and decisions. Justice O'Connor made a proposal to her colleagues that they dispense with oral arguments for recently accepted cases and decide them on the basis of the briefs and other written materials. Chief Justice Burger and Justice Rehnquist, then an associate justice, both endorsed the idea, as they zealously sought efficiency in the Court's procedures. Some justices had mixed reactions, however; Justice Lewis Powell responded, "I could agree with Sandra's proposed change [but] my only concern is that we might abuse this privilege. I believe in the utility of oral argument, and also in the symbolism it portrays for the public. Accordingly, if the rule is changed, I would hope that we could use this option sparingly" (Biskupic, 2005, p. 120).

Justice Brennan was adamantly opposed to Justice's O'Connor's proposal. He wrote: "Dear Chief: I could *not* agree to Sandra's proposed change....I expect my reaction is influenced by my New Jersey experience [and] the [past] practice of the [state's] highest court in deciding almost all cases on briefs without oral argument. The low quality of final judgments was traced directly to that practice...Thus the New Jersey Supreme Court rule [now] requires oral argument of every case granted review....I feel so strongly about this that I must publicly dissent if the rule is changed" (Biskupic, 2005, pp. 120–121, italics in original).

The rule was not changed in 1981, and the justices who participated actively in the discussion of this proposal are no longer on the Court. Since the time of Justice O'Connor's proposal the Court has severely reduced the number of cases it agrees to decide, so there is no longer the backlog that generated her suggestion. But the value of the oral argument remains in dispute, as Chapter 2 illustrates in detail.

Why the Decline?

If it is true that oral arguments have declined in importance, why is this the case? One reason stems from the fact that 200 years ago the Court had no written briefs by the parties, no amicus briefs by others who were interested in the outcome of the case, and a limited trial record. The justices *had* to rely on oral presentations. And they were fortunate, during the first 50 years of the Court's operations, to have very talented advocates make these oral presentations. The quality of advocacy before the Court during the first third of the 1800s, when the Court began to deal with important constitutional questions, was outstanding. The era of John Marshall as chief justice, from 1801 to 1835, "witnessed some of the most celebrated advocates and oral arguments in the Court's history" (Frederick, 2005b, p. 1). Some recent justices, in contrast, have demeaned the quality of advocacy before their bench; these criticisms will be described in detail later in this chapter.

The Court's beginning was rather haphazard. Apparently during the constitutional convention in Philadelphia in the summer of 1787, the Framers spent little time on the federal judiciary; "no debate whatsoever is recorded on the extent or nature of its jurisdiction" (Holt, 2005, p. 12). The Constitution certainly gave no details about its practices and procedures. In the decade after the founding of the Republic, membership in the Supreme Court was not held in high regard. John Jay resigned as the first chief justice in 1795 to become governor of New York, and Alexander Hamilton declined the offer to replace him. Five years later, when Oliver Ellsworth resigned as chief justice, President John Adams sent Jay's name to the Senate, without his knowledge, as a replacement, but after he was confirmed by the Senate Jay declined because he felt that the Court lacked the dignity and authority to achieve its goals. (He also disliked, understandably, the circuit-riding responsibilities of the position.) John Rutledge resigned his position on the Court to become the chief justice of a state court, the South Carolina Court of Common Pleas.

As Frederick (2005a) has noted, more as a matter of expediency than one of considered judgment, the justices in 1791 specified that those seeking action by the Court should follow the practices of the courts in England. There, written filings were quite brief (perhaps only a few sentences). "By longstanding tradition, advocates at the King's Bench presented their material orally to the court. Advocates in England routinely read aloud to the members of the court the opinions from which the appeal was taken, before proceeding into the relevant facts, points of law, and authorities on which their cases were built. Judges had little or nothing to prepare in advance but would sit listening patiently for days as advocates presented the two sides of the case" (Frederick, 2005a, pp. 382–383).

While this activity seems tedious and inefficient, it should be recognized that in the Supreme Court's early years the Court had few cases to decide and met for only a few weeks each year. In its first 10 years it only decided an average of five cases per year, and most of those dealt with treaties and admiralty law (Casto, 1995). It was not until 1796 that the appellate docket began to surface. One of the primary responsibilities of each justice, of which there were only six when the Republic began, was to ride circuits. That is, 6 months of the year, each justice served as a judge in an "inferior court"—what we would now call a district court judge. He would preside at trials along with the local judge. This required extensive and arduous travel by the justices (Freeman, 2006). They complained about this responsibility not only because of the travel but also the impropriety of the same individuals serving as both trial judges and appellate judges in the same cases. Over the next century, Congress only gradually reduced these duties. It was not until 1891 that the creation of the courts of appeals fully eliminated the justices' circuit-riding responsibilities (Baum, 2007). Even now, each justice is assigned to a relationship with a specific circuit. Justices process emergency appeals from their assigned circuits, sometimes making an initial ruling but sometimes passing the appeal to the entire Court. The day after Justice Samuel Alito was confirmed and sworn in, he was assigned the Eighth Circuit.

Given their circuit-riding duties, the early justices met as a Supreme Court briefly in February and again in August. Since few cases came before the Court during these formative years, the oral arguments for a particular case could extend over several days. Frederick has observed, "Very little is known about the course of arguments in the 1790s, but notes available from a few cases indicate that, although they occasionally asked questions of counsel, the justices mostly listened to the advocates' presentations for hours without interruption" (2005a, p. 383). Only when the advocates said they were finished did the chief justice end the oral argument.

Frankly, the Court lacked the prestige of the other two branches of the federal government. The place designated for its location was never developed; when the seat of government moved from Philadelphia to Washington, D.C., the Court was forced to use an impoverished room in the Capitol building, converted into a courtroom, and the justices had no offices. When the Capitol was renovated in 1808 and 1809, the Court spent a term holding its sessions in a local tavern (Peppers, 2006). The proceedings of the Court drew little attention except when prominent statesmen argued cases and "the moment they sat down, the whole audience arose, and broke up as if the Court had adjourned" (McGuire, 1993, p. 13).

After John Marshall became chief justice in 1801, some things changed. The most talented attorneys in the country began to appear before the Court with regularity; some represented private individuals or organizations, others appeared in their capacity as attorney general of the United States. Roger Taney, later to become chief justice, argued numerous cases before the Court while he was attorney general in the Jackson administration. These advocates' arguments clearly made a difference in outcomes, and the presence of outstanding advocates, in the words of Justice Samuel Miller, was "a sufficient guarantee that the matter was well considered" (O'Brien, 2000, p. 257). Furthermore, oral presentation was "a major form of communication in early nineteenth-century American culture. Oratory was high art; listening to lengthy speeches was an established social and intellectual activity" (White, 1988, pp. 203–204). Members of Washington society, dressed in their finest clothes, filled the small courtroom for oral arguments (Urofsky, 1993).

Chief Justice Marshall took full advantage of the talent before the Court; he encouraged extended arguments, established no time limits, and sometimes enabled a single lawyer to speak for 2 or 3 days (Severn, 1969). He was appreciative even of those advocates and arguments he rejected, because they helped him analyze the issues in the case. In the words of his colleague, Justice Joseph Story:

> He was solicitous to hear arguments and not to decide causes without hearing them....And no judge ever profited more by them. No matter what the subject was, new or old....buried under the mass of obsolete learning, or developed for the first time yesterday–whatever its nature, he courted argument, nay demanded it. (Severn, 1969, p. 174)

Among these advocates, the most recognizable names today are those of Francis Scott Key and Daniel Webster. The latter argued a number of momentous cases, including *McCulloch v. Maryland* in 1819. In this decision the Court unanimously upheld Congress's power to incorporate a national bank. The opinion of Chief Justice Marshall borrowed heavily from the oral arguments by the advocates who argued against the efforts of the state of Maryland to try to tax the Bank of the United States. His decision established broad powers for the federal government at a time when the individual states struggled to maintain their power and autonomy. Relying on what Webster had said, Chief Justice Marshall concluded that Congress had powers grounded in the Necessary and Proper Clause of the Constitution for dealing with the "crises of human affairs," thus establishing the doctrine of "implied powers," which became the basis for controversial decisions by the Court 150 years later on a right to privacy.

While far less important than the *McCulloch* decision, the case in *Dartmouth College v. Woodward*, argued within a month of *McCulloch*, produced from Daniel Webster a level of oratory that impressed, touched, and influenced the justices. At issue was the legality of an action by the legislature of the state of New Hampshire. The college had been started by missionaries as a charitable organization to Christianize the Indians. In 1769, before the founding of the Republic, the King of England had granted to the college's trustees and "their successors forever" a charter that permitted them to establish the school, appoint its staff, and make its rules and regulations (Severn, 1969). Half a century later, the clientele had changed, and the college was in financial distress. The state legislature thus abrogated the Dartmouth College charter in order to replace the board of trustees with its own. The effect of the legislature's action was to convert a private institution into a public one. The New Hampshire Chief Justice of the Court of Common Pleas, William Woodward (thus "*Dartmouth College v. Woodward*"), directed that the charter and records be turned over to the new trustees, who began a new school. As a result, the original trustees sued Woodward to get the records back.

Webster, who was a graduate of Dartmouth and only 36 at the time, told the Court that the state law altering the charter violated the contract provision of the U.S. Constitution. He argued the following:

> Sir, you may destroy this little institution. It is weak. It is in your hands! I know it is one of the lesser lights in the literary horizon of the country. You may put it out. But if you do so, you must carry through your work. You must extinguish, one after another, all those great lights of science which, for more than a century, have thrown their radiance over our land.
>
> Dartmouth is, Sir, as I have said, a small college and yet, there are those who love it. (Severn, 1969, p. 179)

Webster's oratory won the day; according to contemporary accounts, several justices were brought to tears, and Dartmouth remained a private institution, as it is today.

The case of *Gibbons v. Ogden*, argued in 1824 by Daniel Webster and William Wirt, dealt with Congress's right to regulate commerce versus a state's claim to exclusive power over the use of its navigable waterways. The New York state legislature had granted Aaron Ogden an exclusive right to operate steamboats in the state, but his former partner, Thomas Gibbons, received a federal license to do so, putting him in direct competition with Ogden. Lower courts had ruled in favor of Ogden, who had claimed that the competition had destroyed his monopoly on steamboat service. Did the federal government have power to regulate such commerce?

The oral arguments for *Gibbons v. Ogden* encompassed 20 hours spread over 5 days. In keeping with the distinguished quality of the advocates, the audience included most of the leaders of Congress, who came down to the basement of the U.S. Capitol building (where the Supreme Court then met) to hear the presentations. The Court, in an opinion written by Chief Justice Marshall, ruled that Congress did have the power to regulate commerce within the states, and its power limited the power of states to regulate transportation within their own borders if a state's law conflicted with federal regulations. Daniel Webster again was successful; he won almost all of the major constitutional cases he argued. (However, he did not win all his cases before the Court; a tabulation of 170 cases that he argued between 1814 and 1851 found him winning slightly less than half [Finley, 1979].)

Although his name is not as well known as Daniel Webster's, the case can be made that William Pinkney was the most prominent advocate in the early 1800s—for example, he argued more than half the cases in the Court's 1814 term (Shapiro, 1988). The previously described case of *McCulloch v. Maryland* was argued over 9 days and featured six distinguished advocates, including Webster and Pinkney. Justice Joseph Story described Pinkney's argument in that case as the greatest speech he had ever heard, saying, "His eloquence was overwhelming. His language, his style, his figures, his arguments were most brilliant and sparkling" (Hobson, 2005, p. 56). Chief Justice Marshall, who witnessed oral arguments for 34 years, called Pinkney the greatest man he had ever seen in a court (Shapiro, 1988). One reason that Pinkney is not so well known today is that he did not leave any written record of his arguments, in contrast to Webster, who transcribed his arguments and made them available to the public (Shapiro, 1988).

But Pinkney had his idiosyncrasies, and his behavior often descended into *ad hominem* attacks; Frederick describes him as follows:

> William Pinkney…was a clothes horse, dressing in the latest fashion in his court appearances. At times, he was known to speak in court wearing amber-colored doeskin gloves. (This is the kind of fashion accessory that likely would draw some comment if any advocate felt emboldened to do it today.) Even with his foppishness, however, Pinkney was an advocate of the first rank. The problem was, he knew it—and he made his opponents know it too. For all his brilliance, Pinkney was prone to insulting his adversaries in the courtroom, sometimes with unfortunate results. He once disparaged Daniel Webster in court, whereupon Webster invited

Pinkney to a room in the Capitol, locked the door, and put the key in his pocket. What ensued has not been recorded for posterity, but the next morning Pinkney appeared in court and tendered a very courteous apology to Webster. On another occasion, Pinkney said in open court of Luther Martin, at that time the attorney general of Maryland, that "he would not long trespass on the patience of the Court, which had been already so severely taxed by the long, though learned argument of the Attorney General—whose speech, however, was distinguished by these two qualities, that of being remarkably redundant, and remarkably deficient." (2005b, pp. 4–5)

Despite his quirks, Pinkney was recognized by the Court as exceptional; upon his sudden death in 1822 of exhaustion, the justices adjourned the Court proceedings as a mark of their profound respect for him, and they wore black armbands for the rest of the term. The procession of 200 carriages that accompanied his body to its grave had never been seen in Washington before (Shapiro, 1988).

Representatives of the government were also among the leading advocates. Walter Jones, who was attorney general for the District of Columbia, argued more than 300 cases before the Court between 1801 and 1850, apparently a record (Douglas, 1980). Often representing the federal government was another distinguished advocate, William Wirt, who was attorney general of the United States from 1817 to 1829. In that capacity he presented 39 cases to the Court, but during the same period he argued 99 appeals before the justices as a private practitioner! As Frederick (2005b) has observed, Wirt viewed the work as attorney general as an intrusion, was frequently gone from Washington, and often failed to see the interest of the United States when it clearly was present.

What made these and other advocates of the early 1800s so successful? What can we learn from the techniques and skills of lawyers 200 years ago that are applicable today? Some things differ, but some remain.

First, they prepared extensively. For example, William Wirt worked both day and night, preparing his oral arguments, so that his family members came to refer to his exhausted state as his "annual Supreme Court sickness" (Frederick, 2005b, p. 7).

Second, most of them were forceful intellects, brilliant lawyers, and incisive debaters. Stephen Vincent Benet's play *The Devil and Daniel Webster*, made into a four-star movie in 1941 starring Walter Huston as the Devil ("Mr. Scratch") and Edward Arnold as Webster, was based on the common saying back in the 1800s that Webster could argue the devil out of his due. The knowledge possessed by these advocates was extensive, and they could think effectively on their feet. Interestingly, Webster was fond of using a kind of hypothetical question to pose to the justices, a tactic similar to what the justices now inflict on advocates. (Chapter 4 gives some contemporary examples.) Webster's questions would ask the justices to consider the outer limits of the other party's position, thus indicating the possibility that if the justices found for the other side, they were initiating movement down a "slippery slope" that could lead to unforeseen consequences. For example, in the *Dartmouth College* case described earlier, Webster raised the possibility that if the Court found the action of the New Hampshire legislature to be constitutional, it would introduce the possibility that all private colleges throughout the nation could come under the control of the state.

These advocates also used close textual analysis, forcing the justices to focus on the meaning of specific terms. Frederick has provided an example:

> In *McCulloch*, Pinkney compared the use of the term "necessary" as it appears in the Necessary and Proper Clause with its use in Article I, Section 10 of the Constitution, which provides that "No State shall, without the consent of Congress, lay any imposts, or duties on imports or exports, except what may be *absolutely necessary* for executing its inspection laws." The Necessary and Proper Clause does not contain a modifier of "necessary" with the word "absolutely." Rather, it authorizes Congress "to make all Laws which shall be necessary and proper for carrying into Execution" the powers of the general government. As Pinkney argued, there was "no qualification of the necessity. It need not be absolute. It may be taken in its ordinary grammatical sense. The word *necessary*, standing by itself, has no inflexible meaning; it is used in a sense more or less strict, according to the subject." Chief Justice Marshall's opinion picked up on that theme; it is "impossible" to compare those two provisions "without feeling a conviction that the [Constitutional] convention understood itself to change materially the meaning of the word 'necessary,' by prefixing the word 'absolutely.' This word, then, like others, is used in various senses." (2005b, p. 10)

These advocates were also a central part of the political life of the country. Daniel Webster was a member of Congress from New Hampshire and later from Massachusetts, a senator from Massachusetts for 20 years, and secretary of state twice. William Pinkney was U.S. attorney general and ambassador to Great Britain and later to Russia. In the year that he argued *McCulloch v. Maryland* with Webster and Wirt as his co-counsel, he was elected to the U.S. Senate from Maryland. As McGuire has noted, "These men were leaders, not only of the bar but in American politics more generally" (1993, p. 16).

Given their immersion in the country's politics, it is understandable that many of these early advocates were able to understand the sympathies of the justices and accommodate to them in their arguments. Those who worked in the nation's capital formed a close-knit collegial community. When John Marshall was chief justice he made arrangements for all the justices to room at the same boarding house in the brand new (and undeveloped) capital city (Rosen, 2007). Some litigators before the Court also stayed there. It is likely that comments and gossip shared as they broke bread together would make the justices' biases known throughout the city.

As talented as Chief Justice Marshall was in establishing the courts as a co-equal branch with the executive and legislative ones, these lawyers provided a constituency that was necessary to develop the Supreme Court's institutional vitality (McGuire, 1993). The distinguished historian of the Court, Robert G. McCloskey, describes this group further:

> An essential element of that constituency, though by no means the whole of it, was the American legal fraternity, or as it has been called, "the inner republic of bench and bar." In these early days lawyers were already occupying the pivotal position in American political affairs that they have occupied ever since. And they tended to reinforce the Supreme Court, partly no doubt because they represented the affluent "haves" who would profit from the stable, nationalized structure Marshall was building, but partly too because their training had taught them to esteem the rule of law which Marshall and his associates stood for. It was not only that men like William Pinkney and Daniel Webster vindicated Marshallian doctrine with the magic of their oratory in formal argument before the supreme bench; they and their lesser colleagues also helped, in letters, in conversations, in appearances before lower courts, in state legislatures, and in Congress, to generate the atmosphere of consent that made Marshall's achievements possible. (1994, p. 47)

The Shrinking Oral Argument: From 5 Days to 1 Hour

Toward the end of Chief Justice Marshall's long tenure on the bench, the Court became less enchanted with the prolonged nature of each oral argument. As his replacement, Chief Justice Taney (Francis Scott Key's brother-in-law) complained that an advocate "introduced so much extraneous matter, or dwelt so long on unimportant points, that the attention was apt to be fatigued and withdrawn, and the logic and force of his argument lost" (Frederick, 2005b, p. 11). Justice Story, who served from 1811 to 1845, could be seen to be writing during the presentations; the attorneys doubtless assumed he was taking notes on their memorable arguments, but according to his son and biographer, he was composing poetry (Frederick, 2005b). One bit of his verse remains good advice to counsel almost 200 years after it was penned:

> Staff not your speech with every sort of law,
> Give us the grain and throw away the straw...
> What's a great lawyer? He who aims to say
> The least his cause requires, not all he may. (Mauro, 2004d, p. 8)

In 1833 the Court suggested that the advocates provide "printed arguments," but this rule was not mandatory, and so the practice of submitting briefs only gradually became standard.

But there was another reason for the length of oral arguments, and, inferentially, their impact, being reduced: the Court's workload increased. It handled 98 cases in 1810 but 253 in 1850. By 1845 the Court was devoting 99 days a year to oral arguments. In comparison, for the term that began in October 2007, it allocated only 39 days for them. And, of course, in 1845 the justices had circuit-riding duties as well.

In 1849 the Court became more restrictive, establishing two firm rules: no counsel would be permitted to participate in oral arguments unless he had first submitted a printed abstract of points and authorities, and second, each side was limited to 2 hours of oral presentation, unless the Court granted further time. By 1911 the time was reduced to 1 1/2 hours per side; by 1970 it was 30 minutes per side, as it remains today. (On rare occasions, for special cases, the Court makes a prior arrangement for extended time, as it did twice during the October 2005 term, in the cases of *League of United Latin American Citizens v. Perry*, dealing with redistricting in Texas, and *Hamdan v. Rumsfeld*, dealing with the rights of detainees to civilian trials.) Is the typical length of 30 minutes for each side adequate? Longtime Chief Justice Rehnquist felt that it was; the "present rules for oral argument are about right....A good lawyer should be able to make his [sic] necessary points...in one half hour" (Rehnquist, 1987, p. 274). I will evaluate the issue of the appropriate length of oral arguments in the concluding chapter.

Changes in the Advocates

Other changes have occurred: no longer, of course, do only white males appear before the Court, as was the custom two centuries ago. Currently, to argue a case before the Supreme Court, one first must be admitted to the Supreme Court bar. Applicants must be sponsored by two current members of that bar, who swear that the applicant has been a member of good standing of the bar of the highest court in his or her state for at least 3 years. Once admitted, counsel can file briefs and argue before the Court, although nowadays "most join simply for the prestige of being a member of an elite bar" (Cushman, 2001, p. 79).

These rules evolved gradually, and the Court was not prepared when the first African American applied to be admitted to the Supreme Court bar. In 1865 John S. Rock did so; it was only 8 years after the notorious *Dred Scott* decision had labeled members of his race as "beings of an inferior order, and altogether unfit to associate with the white race" (Shapiro, 2005). In fact, Rock was granted admission to the Supreme Court bar as several justices in the *Dred Scott* majority watched, and "the faces of the older members of the bar present in the courtroom on that day were knotted in rage" (Shapiro, 2005,

p. 1). Rock, who had a successful career as a physician and dentist before he passed the bar examination in Massachusetts, was 40 years old at the time. Sadly, he caught a severe cold on his trip to Washington for the ceremony, his health deteriorated rapidly, and he died during the next year.

The first woman to seek admission to the Supreme Court bar was Belva A. Lockwood, in 1876. The Court's reaction to her was also less than welcoming. Chief Justice Morrison Waite told her:

> By the uniform practice of the Court from its organization to the present time, and by the fair construction of its rules, none but men are permitted to practice before it as attorneys and counselors. This is in accordance with immemorial usage in England, and the law and practice in all the States until a recent period. (Shapiro, 2005, p. 3)

In fact, only 3 years before, this same court, in the case of *Bradwell v. Illinois*, had upheld a lower court's ruling that a state bar could refuse to admit a woman. But the genius of Belva Lockwood was, according to her biographer, to accept temporary setbacks but make plans to overcome them (Norgren, 2007). She used her contacts, including President Grant, to seek redress from the U.S. Congress (Stansell, 2007). In 1879 Congress passed a law stating that "any woman who shall have been a member of the bar of the highest court in any State or Territory or of the bar of the Supreme Court of the District of Columbia for the space of three years, and shall have maintained a good standing before such court, and who shall be a person of good moral character, shall, on motion, and the production of such record, be admitted to practice before the Supreme Court of the United States" (Shapiro, 2005, p. 4). A remarkable person, Ms. Lockwood was the first woman to run a full campaign for president of the United States—in 1884 and again in 1888. She received more than 4,000 votes—all, as Pillard observed, "from men, of course" (2005, p. 14). After Ms. Lockwood was admitted to the Supreme Court bar in 1880, at the age of 50, she argued her first case before it, a commercial law case. She went on to argue several more cases, including one in 1906, in which she represented the Cherokee Indian tribe, that she won, leading to a $5 million dollar award to her clients. (She was 76 years old at the time.) By the time she died in 1917, women had been admitted to practice law in all but four states. But it was not until 1972 that the office of solicitor general hired a woman lawyer (Pillard, 2005). In recent terms, about 15% to 20% of the advocates arguing cases before the Court are women (Pillard, 2006).

The Decline in Quality of Advocacy and the Reemergence of a Supreme Court Bar

The twentieth century saw many changes that led to what some saw as a deterioration in the quality of advocacy before the Court. For example, the relative ease of transportation and the spread of population across the width of the continent meant that no longer were most of the advocates those public figures who spent their working lives in the nation's capital. Increasingly, advocates appearing before the Court were less experienced. For example, the attorney who represented the respondent in the monumental *Brown v. Board of Education of Topeka* (1954) case was an assistant attorney general for the state of Kansas who had never before argued a case before *any* type of appellate court (Wilson, 1995).

It is also true, however, that the first half of the 20th century saw some eloquent advocates before the Court. John W. Davis argued 140 cases between 1913 and 1954. No longer a household name, 75 years ago he was considered the best trial attorney in the country. He was president of the American Bar Association, a member of Congress and solicitor general of the United States, an ambassador to the Court of St. James, and in 1924 the Democratic Party's candidate for president (he lost to Coolidge). Justice Oliver Wendell Holmes, Jr., once said that he tried not to listen to Davis's oral arguments so that he would not be overly influenced by their sheer "beauty" (Cole, 1997). Ironically, in his last oral argument before the Court, Davis represented South Carolina, the losing side, in one of the school segregation cases combined into *Brown v. Board of Education.*

Another excellent advocate during the first half of the twentieth century was Bruce Bromley. According to Justice William O. Douglas, what made him so effective in his appearances before the Court was "first, an easy relaxed manner of presentation; second, the knack of reducing a complicated case to one or two starkly simple issues; third, illuminating those issues with homely illustrations; and fourth, never using the full time allotted to him" (1980, p. 184).

Beginning in the last half of the twentieth century, the justices began to express displeasure over the quality of advocacy. Justice Douglas, who served a record 36 years on the bench (from 1939 to 1975), claimed that 40% of oral advocates were "incompetent" and "only a few were excellent" (1980, p. 183). Lewis Powell, on the Court from 1972 to 1987 and a more gentle soul than Douglas, had nonetheless harsh words about advocates. When he joined the Court he anticipated excellence, but later revealed that the bar's performance "has not measured up to my expectations" (Roberts, 2005, p. 78). Harry Blackmun, a justice from 1970 to 1994 and meticulous to a fault, gave numerical ratings or letter grades to each advocate (Greenhouse, 2005a). For example, Ruth Bader Ginsburg's first oral argument before the Court in 1973, 20 years before she became a justice, garnered her a grade of only C+ from Justice Blackmun. He also made comments about the physical appearance of various advocates (such as "dark mustache" or "looks tired") (Mauro, 2004d).

Two consecutive chief justices publicly complained about the quality of advocacy before the highest court in the land. Warren Burger made the improvement in advocacy before the Court one of his goals as chief justice. He was particularly critical of those who represented state and local governments before the Court (Burger, 1984; Roberts, 2005). At a conference on Supreme Court advocacy, Chief Justice Burger stated:

> With some exceptions, state and local governments have not pro-
> vided experienced and qualified personnel skilled in arguing cases
> before the Supreme Court. My experience is that many who rep-
> resent the states and local communities...fail to appreciate fully
> the critical importance of well-organized and carefully researched
> briefs, especially when confronted with a thirty-minute limit on
> arguments in the Supreme Court. (1984, p. 525)

And in a speech published in 1984, Justice Rehnquist remarked on the decline in oral advocacy, noting that for many attorneys who appeared before the Court, their oral arguments seemed to be only a written brief "with gestures" (Rehnquist, 1984, p. 1024; Roberts, 2005).

But in the last couple of decades, the deteriorating quality of advocacy seems to have turned around. In an article published in 2005 and written before being named chief justice, John Roberts concluded that "[o]ver the past generation, roughly the period since 1980, there has been a discernible professionalism among the advocates before the Supreme Court, to the extent that one can speak of the emergence of a real Supreme Court bar" (2005, p. 68). He supported this claim with data, by comparing the level of experience by advocates in the October 1980 term with that of those who argued during the October 2002 term. (Attorneys for the solicitor general's office were not included in the analysis.) In the earlier term, more than 80% of the advocates were appearing before the Court for the first time! In the 2002–2003 term, that number had dropped to around 55%. Furthermore, over that time period, an increased number of attorneys had appeared more than once or twice, some having three or more oral arguments per term. During the 1980s and 1990s a number of major law firms, mostly based in Washington, D.C., developed appellate practice departments, with lawyers who came to specialize in petitions at the Supreme Court level. Roberts concluded:

> I would not go so far as to say that the re-emergence that I have
> identified of a Supreme Court bar was a response to the judicial
> criticism prevalent a generation ago. But perhaps to the extent that
> the justices at that time identified an opportunity for improved
> quality and professionalism, the bar identified the same opportunity
> and responded. The Supreme Court bar that I have been discuss-
> ing is, of course, nothing like the Supreme Court bar of the John
> Marshall era. No one today is going to argue in half of the Court's
> cases, as William Pinkney did one year. But more and more, there
> are familiar faces appearing at the lectern—not just the curiously
> attired lawyers from the Solicitor General's office, but faces from the
> private bar and from states as well. (2005, pp. 78–79)

Chief Justice Roberts' impression is seconded by Justice Alito. After a year on the Court, he told reporter Tony Mauro, "I'm very impressed with the quality of the briefing and the advocacy. I think it's considerably better than what I saw 20 years ago" (when he was an attorney in the office of the solicitor general) (Mauro, 2007a, p. 12).

The Unique Contributions of the Oral Argument to the Decision Process

A recent book by political scientist Timothy Johnson raised the question of "why the Court continues to hear oral arguments when it can readily obtain an abundance of information about the case from any number of credible sources" (2004, p. 2). Johnson answers his own question in this way:

> Almost all the information justices receive is what other actors want them to consider. In short, the Court has little control over the majority of information it obtains. Unless justices ask for re-argument...or for the parties or interest groups to file briefs that address special issues, there is only one time for them to gather information for themselves: the oral arguments. (2004, p. 2)

This endorsement of the value of oral arguments is not held by all. Chapter 2 considers the views of justices (both past and present) and other experts on the following question: do oral arguments change the position of justices? Some would argue that the process of deciding to take a case and then the consideration of briefs before the oral arguments causes justices to form irrevocable positions before the oral arguments begin. Consider the process that is initiated when a petitioner appeals to the Supreme Court. Each of the approximately 8,000 to 9,000 petitions received annually is reviewed by several law clerks. Recently Justice Stevens has had one of his clerks review each petition; the other justices participate in what is called a "cert pool," for *certiorari,* referring to the process of deciding whether to decide a case. One clerk from the pool of law clerks from these justices reviews each petition, and that clerk's comments are sent to all the justices who participate in the pool. (Before Chief Justice Roberts became a judge, he expressed some concern over the fact that only two law clerks reviewed a given petition, but at least in his early years on the Court, he joined the "cert pool," as did Justice Alito.) Most petitions are, of course, not considered worthy of review by the clerks reviewing them, but nevertheless, a report is sent to the justices. Traditionally, the chief justice chooses a certain number for discussion at the weekly cert conference, but other justices can nominate candidates. Thus, even before the conference, each justice has reports from clerks, usually about five pages in length and containing a recommendation, plus the brief from the petitioner arguing why the case should be granted *certiorari,* and an opposing brief, from the respondent, arguing why it should not. Thus any case that eventually becomes the subject of an oral argument has been considered by each justice before the cert conference.

The "discuss" list at the weekly cert conference may include around 20 petitions identified by the chief justice as possibly worthy of consideration for granting *certiorari*, plus perhaps a handful nominated by other justices. But few at each conference receive the four or more votes necessary to put them on the docket; in recent years only about 70 to 80 cases per term have passed this "rule of four." However, if the petition is granted cert, both the petitioner and the respondent prepare briefs which are allowed to be as many as 50 pages long, plus appendices. Any interest group that wishes to submit an amicus curiae brief (a "friend of the court" brief) may seek permission to do so. (While some petitions generate no amicus briefs, in a rare instance as many as 80 or 100 may be submitted in support of one side or the other in a specific case.) The justices have available not only all these briefs but also the relevant lower-court decisions, their own previous decisions, law review articles, and discussions in the media. Prior to the oral argument, justices typically discuss the case with one of their law clerks. While he was on the Court, Chief Justice Rehnquist described his procedure as follows:

> When the law clerk and I are both ready to talk about the case, we do just that—sometimes walking around the neighborhood of the Court building, sometimes sitting in my chambers. I tell my clerk some of my reactions to the arguments of the parties, and am interested in getting the clerk's reactions to these same arguments. If there is some point of law involved in the case that doesn't appear to be adequately covered by the briefs, I may ask the clerk to write me a memorandum on that particular point. (2001, p. 240)

The clerk may be asked by his or her justice to prepare a bench memo, a digest of the arguments presented in the briefs plus an analysis that identifies the strengths and weaknesses of the case for each side. In summary, the issue receives extensive and frequent review and discussion by each justice *prior to the oral argument.*

Does this mean that in the mind of the justice, it has already been determined how he or she will vote after the oral argument? That remains an open question, and one purpose of this book is to examine the place of oral arguments within the decision-making process of justices.

Overview of the Rest of the Book

Each of the following chapters contributes to an understanding of the role of the arguments within the steps of the decision-making procedure. Chapter 2 considers the ways in which justices make their decisions and the views of the justices themselves on the impact of the oral arguments. Chapter 3 describes the nature of advocacy before the Court, considers the claim by some justices that it is not up to standard, and reviews classifications of advocates. It also considers the impact of advocacy from attorneys with the office of the solicitor general of the United States. The chapter reports an empirical evaluation of the relative effectiveness of several types of advocates. Chapter 4 turns to a consideration of the behavior of the justices, the types and frequency of questions they ask, the other types of statements they offer, and the motivations for their questions and comments. Chapter 5 expands on this focus by examining the idiosyncratic quality of the questions from each of the current and recent justices—almost every justice has a "trademark" type of question or comment. The chapter classifies several justices as examples of a "Big Five" approach to the use of traits to describe human personality. Chapter 6 explores the oral arguments in a landmark case, in an effort to illustrate the possible relationship of the questions and comments during oral arguments to the eventual decision by the Court. Chapter 7 extends this inquiry, by reporting original empirical findings on the relationships between individual justices' questions and their eventual votes on the case. Chapter 8 considers contentious issues and possible changes in the oral-argument procedures, including the possibility of televising oral arguments. This concluding chapter also presents an empirical test of the observation that the change in chief justice has led to an atmosphere more receptive to advocates.

2

Justices' Views on the Significance of Oral Arguments

I don't see the need for all those questions. I think justices,
99 percent of the time, have their minds made up when they go
to the bench.

> —Justice Clarence Thomas (quoted by Rombeck,
> 2002, p. 5B)

When Do Justices Decide Cases?

If the above statement by Justice Thomas is accurate, the oral arguments play no determinative role in the Court's decision-making process. But is his assessment shared by the other justices? And if it is, why do justices make up their minds before hearing the arguments? The purpose of this chapter is to examine just what current and former justices, other judges, and researchers say about the impact of oral arguments before the Court. The chapter also examines several conceptions of how judges make their decisions and just what role the oral arguments play in each of these conceptions. It introduces the distinction between ideological and nonideological cases and proposes that oral arguments play a different role in these two different types of cases.

As described in Chapter 1, numerous opportunities exist for justices to form positions, at least tentative and perhaps unchangeable ones, before the advocates get a chance to argue their cases before the Court. The justices may review those appeals from the cert pool recommended by the law clerks, they again review the set of petitions that make it to the chief justice's "discuss" list before the cert conference, and they discuss and vote whether to grant *certiorari* at this conference. Justices claim that the decision to grant cert is based on narrow grounds, such as the conflict in rulings made by two different circuit courts, or a statute being challenged as unconstitutional. Also, disputes between two states over such matters as water rights or states' boundaries go directly to the Supreme Court for resolution. The Court, claim its justices, does not accept a petition for review simply because it was wrongly decided by a lower court; justices will tell you that the Supreme Court's purpose is not to remedy all the mistakes made in the legal system. But the justices are human, and as a Court they have unlimited discretion in deciding which petitions— even how many petitions—to resolve. This point is relevant to the claim that justices prematurely form decisions, because a justice may even seek out a particular type of case among the thousands of petitions received annually in order to bring about a desired policy change, whether that be about abortion, affirmative action, or the death penalty. Although the situation is probably not as blatant as a justice telling his or her clerk to be on the lookout for petitions dealing with a specific topic, some justices have a goal of influencing public policy, and their law clerks have a good idea of the types of cases that would interest their boss. Thus, it is possible that some justices will encourage granting cert to a petition because it provides the opportunity to reconsider an earlier decision that, in their view, needs to be changed or rectified.

Even though the nominal steps of the process up to the cert conference are done to identify petitions that fit the Court's criteria for review, it is inevitable that the justices are also contemplating what their votes would be later, after the appeal has been granted *certiorari*. The position advocated in this chapter is that the justices, like all of us, are active information processors. For example, justices are attuned to what is going on in the world; they read newspapers and watch television news programs; they receive and read mail from the public. The degree to which public opinion sways their decisions is debatable, but they inevitably relate national and world developments to their duties as judges. For example, early in 2006, the legitimacy of President George W. Bush's use of electronic surveillance became a matter of debate. Critics claimed that the National Security Agency (NSA), at the president's behest, was acting illegally by monitoring communications secretly without first getting warrants from a judge. The administration argued that it was proper for a president, in times of war, to bypass Congress's legislation of surveillance in the Foreign Intelligence Surveillance Act (FISA). Even before President Bush's action was challenged in any lower court, it was quite likely that justices on the Supreme Court began to anticipate that they might eventually need to arbitrate the controversy. And, inevitably, I would argue, most of them began to side, at least tentatively, with one position or the other, given that this issue seemed to reflect a basic question: Does the Constitution permit strong action by the executive branch in foreign affairs, or does the legislative branch provide oversight in times of war (Kmiec, 2006)? Their awareness that they might face the issue was doubtless heightened when, in August 2006, federal district judge Anna Diggs Taylor, in a broad and controversial decision, ruled that interception of such calls was not only illegal but unconstitutional.

The Briefs versus the Oral Argument

Once *certiorari* has been granted, both the petitioner and the respondent are given deadlines by which to submit their briefs and the oral argument is scheduled. (These merit briefs differ from the two parties' earlier submissions. For example, in his or her first brief the petitioner argues that the Court should resolve the issue; in the second the petitioner argues why the Court should decide in its favor.) Experts place more weight on the briefs than on the oral arguments as influences on the justices' decision making. As W. J. Bauer and W. C. Bryson wrote:

> Although judges and practitioners may disagree about the relative importance of oral argument in the appellate process, no one disagrees with the fundamental proposition that the brief is far and away the most important feature of the appeal.... Most cases are won or lost in the briefs. If you file a good brief, you will probably be okay, no matter how ineffective your oral argument. If you file an ineffective brief, however, you are almost certainly in deep trouble, regardless of your oratorical skills. (1983, p. 12)

In a textbook on appellate advocacy, Clary, Paulsen, and Vanselow concur: "Most appellate judges and attorneys would agree that the brief is the most important part of the appeal" (2004, p. 30). They offer the following reasons:

1. It is the first opportunity to create a favorable impression.
2. It can lay out an analysis in detail with supporting citations.
3. The justices may forget the oral argument, but they always have the brief available to them.

But to argue over which is *more* important, I believe, is erroneous, because the brief and the oral argument fulfill different functions. The situation for the justices is something like that of students in a college course. The textbook offers much more material in each chapter than does each 50-minute or 80-minute lecture, but a lecture that simply parrots what is in the textbook chapter is not meeting the goals of what a lecture should accomplish. An oral argument, like a lecture, seeks to make the salient points about the issue at hand, but it provokes the recipients to question, to clarify, and to identify weaknesses. Most reading of a textbook, and perhaps often the reading of a brief, is not very interactive. Readers may think of questions as they read, but their questions are often unanswered. But a good oral argument, like a good classroom lecture, is essentially interactive, even becoming a conversation. As Johnson (2004) noted in Chapter 1, the oral argument is the one opportunity for the justices to play an active role in the information-gathering part of the decision process.

How Do Justices Decide?

A discussion of *when* justices decide cases cannot be disentangled from the issue of *how* they decide cases. Legal scholars, social psychologists, and political scientists who study judicial processes have proposed four different explanations for how these decisions are made; these have been labeled the legal model, the attitudinal model, the strategic model, and the motivated reasoning model. Each will be described here in detail. Purists will argue that such determinations do not "kick in" until it is time for the justices to read the merit briefs prior to oral argument, although, as indicated above, I consider this a process that is initiated much earlier, especially if the case triggers an internalized set of values in the justice.

The Legal Model

The legal model proposes that a judge, in determining the merits of a petition, examines past resources for guidance. In the matter of electronic surveillance in which one person is in the United States and the other person is abroad and suspected of being a terrorist, the justice would examine the wording of the Foreign Intelligence Surveillance Act and try to determine the intent of Congress when it passed this legislation in 1978. In addition, the justice would examine previous Court decisions regarding the war powers of the president. Last but not least, the justice would examine the Constitution and try to fathom the intent of its framers with regard to the powers of the executive and legislative branches.

Psychologists classify mental activities as cognitive, emotional, and motivational. Clearly, among the three types of activities, the legal model assumes the predominance of a cognitive focus. The justice is assumed to operate in an almost impersonal way, matching the contrasting claims of the petitioner and the respondent with the relevant information from precedents, statutes, and the Constitution.

Many of those political scientists interested in judicial decision-making reject the validity of the legal model, claiming it is an aspiration rather than a reality. In fact, political scientists who advocate the attitudinal model devote little space to the legal model, other than to reject it as idealistic. But in some cases before the Court, I believe it does serve as an accurate blueprint of how the judges decide.

For example, in the case of *Wachovia Bank v. Schmidt* (2006), argued before the Supreme Court in November 2005, the issue was whether a national bank was a "citizen" of every state where it had a branch, or only a citizen of the state where it was chartered. This was not one of those cases that drew attention from the national media when submitted to the Court, when cert was granted, or even when oral arguments were held. It is offered here as an example of a case that is an important one, but not one that triggers deeply held values in the justices. It is, in the terminology that I will use throughout this book, a *non-ideological case*. Certainly some if not all the justices formed tentative opinions as they read the briefs, discussed the case at the cert conference, and decided to grant cert, but their focus remained on the interpretation of the law.

For the respondent, the question turned on the meaning of the wording in 28 U.S. Code 1348, which states that national banking associations "shall be deemed citizens of the States in which they are respectively located." The respondent had filed suit in a state court in his home state, and hoped to keep the jurisdiction there. But did the statute intend to permit such suits? The facts of the case are these: Wachovia Bank is a national mega-bank with its main headquarters in North Carolina but branch offices in more than 20 states. The respondent, David Schmidt, III, a resident of South Carolina, had purchased tax shelter–related investment advice offered by Wachovia Bank; its goal was to limit the capital-gains taxes he was required to pay after he had sold his businesses. But Schmidt suffered financial losses as a result of this investment, and so he filed a suit against Wachovia Bank in a South Carolina state court, claiming fraud among other charges. Wachovia Bank responded by filing a petition claiming that arbitration in a federal court, not a state court, was required under the diversity jurisdiction as specified in 28 U.S. Code 1332. The district court ruled in favor of Schmidt, so Wachovia Bank appealed to the Fourth Circuit Court of Appeals, which, in a split vote, dismissed Wachovia's suit for lack of diversity jurisdiction, concluding that the bank should be considered a citizen of every state in which it maintained a branch. That is, the circuit court interpreted United Sates Code Section 1348 to mean unambiguously that Wachovia Bank could be sued in a state court in South Carolina, because it had a branch there. This circuit court's decision differed with the interpretations of U.S.C. Section 1348 by three other circuit courts, thus the Supreme Court agreed to take the case.

What was the intent of Congress in drafting the legislation? Just what did the word "located" mean? The Supreme Court opinion, written by Justice Ginsburg, concluded that Congress meant the words "located" and "established" to have the same meaning, which would make a bank a citizen of the state where it had its main office, thus the bank was able to claim federal jurisdiction in those lawsuits against it that originated with a party in another state. The presence of a branch office in another state did not automatically create citizenship in that state. She concluded that recodifications of Section 1348 over the years reflected a "substantially similar" position to the original statute. Her opinion received unanimous support from the voting justices.

The unanimous vote in this case provides indirect support for the legal model being a legitimate conception of decision making in at least some cases. One of the major reasons for the Court granting cert to a petition is that it reflects a decision by a circuit court that is in conflict with decisions by other circuit courts on the same question. Recent research by Lindquist and Klein (2006) indicates that in such cases, the justices use legal reasoning to resolve such conflicts.

Decisions in around 40% to 50% of cases are unanimous, and in the term ending in June 2007, 47% of the decisions had no dissenting votes. This unanimity might imply several things: in those specific cases differing attitudes of the individual justices are not salient, or there is clarity about the operative rule of law. In a number of decisions both are true.

The Attitudinal Model

Many political scientists who study judicial behavior believe that there is more to decision making than the rather dispassionate application of precedents prescribed by the legal model. Using our simplified psychological classification, these scholars see the decision being based primarily on emotion; the justice's attitudes contribute to his or her decision in the sense that attitudes are defined as evaluations of objects. Underlying attitudes are tied to basic values. For example, those who support the legitimacy of domestic surveillance in wartime may value security; those opposed may support privacy and civil liberties. According to the attitudinal model, these attitudes and values serve as filters and cause the decision maker to pay more attention to those arguments supporting his or her bias, while denigrating those arguments that do not. For many of the petitions coming before the Court, but certainly not for all of them, justices may possess an ideological viewpoint that leads them to decide in a certain way. The clearest distinction in ideologies is between conservative and liberal viewpoints, with (to simplify) conservatives valuing the power of the state, traditions, security, and property rights, and liberals valuing individual freedoms, rights of minorities, and those of the underprivileged. Thus, in this book those cases dealing with these types of topics will be labeled *ideological* cases. An example follows below.

On November 7, 2005, the Court granted cert to the case of *Hamdan v. Rumsfeld*, which considered whether an enemy combatant who was detained at Guantanamo Bay is protected by the articles of the 1949 Geneva Conventions as a prisoner of war. That is, does the prisoner have the right to a trial by civilians, or does his jurisdiction fall under the Department of Defense, which, following the President Bush's directive of May 2001, established "military commissions" to try suspected terrorists. Salim Ahmed Hamdan admitted that he was Osama bin Laden's personal driver and bodyguard, but he disputed the charges that he was a party to his supervisor's conspiracy to kill civilians. He was captured by Afghan soldiers in November 2001 and eventually put in detention by the U.S. military, as the president had declared him an enemy combatant. After Hamdan's attorneys challenged the legality of his prolonged detection, claiming it violated both the Constitution and the Geneva Conventions, the U.S. District Court for the District of Columbia ruled that he was entitled to protection under the Geneva Conventions. But the U.S. Circuit Court of Appeals for the District of Columbia reversed this decision, holding that Hamdan was not protected by the Geneva Conventions because he did not fit that statute's definition of prisoner of war. When it was announced that the Supreme Court would decide Hamdan's appeal, Court observers were surprised, as the Court had considered his petition at three previous cert conferences and had taken no action, leading to speculation that Hamdan's appeal would not be granted cert (Denniston, 2005). But it was finally granted, with the oral argument scheduled for March 28, 2006. Chief Justice Roberts recused himself because he had been on the panel of the District of Columbia circuit court that had unanimously upheld the power of "military commissions" to decide the fate of detainees.

This case was among the most important during the October 2005 term, as it dealt with the sweep of presidential powers. As Stuart Taylor has questioned, does the president have "the authority to detain, indefinitely and without trial, suspected 'enemy combatants' seized around the globe; to subject them to...interrogation; and to prosecute them in Bush-created 'military commissions'—with possible penalties including death, with fewer protections than those enjoyed by defendants in ordinary military and civilian courts, and with no appeals outside the military chain of command?" (2005, p. 60).

Between the granting of cert in November 2005 and the oral arguments in late March 2006, each of the eight justices who would decide the case doubtless gave it some thought and review. But Justice Antonin Scalia did more; on March 8, he gave a speech at the University of Fribourg, in Switzerland. During the question-and-answer period, he responded to an inquiry about affording constitutional rights to Guantanamo detainees by stating, "War is war, and it has never been the case that when you captured a combatant you have to give them a jury trial in your civil courts" and "foreigners in foreign courts have no rights under the American constitution" (Isikoff, 2006, p. 6). He added, "Nobody has ever thought otherwise." He expressed incredulity at the suggestion that detainees captured "on the battlefield" should receive a trial in civil courts; that proposition, he said, was a "crazy idea." He interrupted a subsequent question on the topic by claiming, "If he was captured by my army on a battlefield that is where he belongs. I had a son on that battlefield and they were shooting at my son. And I am not about to give this man who was captured in a war a full jury trial. I mean it's crazy" (Isikoff, 2006, p. 6).

Justice Scalia's pronouncement, *prior* to the oral arguments, reflects the attitudinal model, as his statement is unequivocal and highly emotional. (The fact that his son Matthew served with the U.S. Army in Iraq seems determinative.) The justice's comments drew criticism from a variety of sources. Michael

Ratner of the Center for Constitutional Rights stated, "I can't recall an instance where I've heard a judge speak so openly about a case that's in front of him—without hearing the arguments" (Isikoff, 2006, p. 6). Stephen Gillers, a law professor at NYU who has written extensively on legal ethics, said, "As these things mount, a legitimate question can be asked about whether he is compromising the credibility of the Court" (Isikoff, 2006, p. 6). Five retired generals and admirals asked Justice Scalia to recuse himself and not participate in the oral arguments for *Hamdan v. Rumsfeld*. Their letter to the Clerk of the Supreme Court stated that his remarks "give rise to the unfortunate appearance that, even before the briefing in this case was complete, the justice had made up his mind about the merits" (Denniston, 2006).

Justice Scalia did step aside in one previous case, *Elk Grove Unified School District v. Newdow*, in 2004, because he had previously been reported as having said "Judges who ban…the words 'under God' in the Pledge of Allegiance are misinterpreting the Constitution" (Lederman, 2006). But in another case that involved the constitutionality of closed-door committee meetings of a governmental group chaired by Vice-President Cheney (*Cheney v. U.S. District Court for the District of Columbia*, 2004), Justice Scalia did not recuse himself from participating in the decision, despite the fact that he had gone on a duck-hunting trip with the vice-president. It should be noted that if the justice had recused himself in the *Hamdan* case, the decision would have been determined by only seven justices, but that is acceptable procedure.

In fairness to Justice Scalia, it is unclear whether in his remarks in Switzerland he was thinking specifically of the *Hamdan* case. He referred to detainees captured "on the battlefield" and his son fought in Iraq. Hamdan was captured in Afghanistan. The solicitor general's brief stated that "in November 2001, petitioner was captured in Afghanistan during the course of active hostilities in that country and transferred to the control of the United Stated armed forces. After an extensive screening process, petitioner was determined to be an enemy combatant and transferred to the U.S. Naval Station at Guantanamo Bay, Cuba, for detention" (Lederman, 2006). However, Hamdan's brief said that he was "captured in Afghanistan by indigenous forces while attempting to return his family to Yemen" and "turned over to American forces in exchange for a bounty" (Lederman, 2006).

Justice Scalia did not recuse himself despite the criticisms directed to him. He was present at the special 90-minute oral argument of *Hamdan v. Rumsfeld* and through his usual vigorous questioning appeared to be the justice most supportive of the government's position. For example, he was the very first justice to question the attorney representing Hamdan, he disagreed with this attorney's interpretation of the law on several occasions, and he appeared sympathetic to statements by the government's attorney. He directed 22 questions or comments to Hamdan's attorney and only 12 to the government's side. In fact, his questions to the solicitor general, Paul Clement, were briefer as well as less frequent, and when they occurred, they took the form of offering a helping hand to the solicitor general.

In contrast to Justice Scalia's comments, most of the justices seemed to question the government's claim of blanket authority by the president to determine detainees' treatment; Justices Kennedy, Souter, Breyer, and Ginsburg questioned the solicitor general. Justice Alito, by his few questions, seemed supportive of the government; Justice Thomas typically did not speak.

When the decision was announced on June 29, 2006 (the last day of the term), the Court rejected President Bush's plan to use military commissions to try the detainees. Justice Stevens' 73-page opinion garnered the support of five of the eight justices. Justice Scalia authored a dissent in which he criticized the Court's opinion as fundamentally inconsistent with common law and with the evolving nature of warfare.

The most visible proponents of the attitudinal model are political scientists Jeffrey Segal and Harold Spaeth, whose book *The Supreme Court and the Attitudinal Model* (first published in 1993 and revised in 2002) provides research support for this position. These and similarly minded political scientists would probably conclude that Justice Scalia's remarks on detainees' rights, prior to oral arguments, are only the tip of the iceberg of justices' predispositions, with "[o]ral argument frequently provid[ing] an indication of which is the most likely basis for decision. Oral argument does not, however, provide reliable clues as to how a given justice may vote" (Rohde and Spaeth, 1976, p. 153). More recently, Segal and Spaeth have suggested that "the extent to which [oral argument] affects the justices' votes is problematic. The justices aver that it is a valuable source of information about the cases they have agreed to decide, but that does not mean that oral argument regularly, or even infrequently, determines who wins and who loses" (2002, p. 280).

In Johnson's review of Supreme Court oral arguments he concludes, "The dominant view among Court scholars is that oral arguments have little influence over case outcomes because voting preferences are stable or exogenous. As such, so the argument goes, an hour of debate about the legal and policy merits of a case will not change a justice's likely vote" (2004, p. 2). And the reason that the vote is predictable, according to the attitudinal model, is that it derives directly from the justice's attitudes and values. It is certainly true that in *some* cases the votes of justices are predictable from their values; on matters of civil rights, the death penalty, abortion, and related topics, liberals often vote differently from conservatives.

For example, in the October 2001 term, nine cases dealt with defendants' rights. The three most conservative justices, Rehnquist, Scalia, and Thomas, rarely supported the defendants in these cases; out of 27 votes by these justices in these nine cases, only 3 favored the defendant's position, and 24 ruled in favor of the government. The two "swing voters," Justices O'Connor and Anthony Kennedy, supported the defendants a little more, with 5 votes out of 18 in the nine cases. In contrast, the four relative liberals voted for the defendant and against the government the majority of the time, with 24 of their 36 votes (Thimsen, 2003; Wrightsman, 2006). In eight cases involving prisoners who challenged their treatment, the voting patterns were even more disparate.

Only 2 of the 24 votes by the three most conservative justices supported the prisoners; the four relative liberals supported the prisoners with 28 out of 32 possible votes (Thimsen, 2003; Wrightsman, 2006). But not in every case do ideological values contribute to the decision. As demonstrated in the *Wachovia* case, sometimes they are not salient.

The Strategic Model

Partly in response to the claims of some political scientists that the attitudes of justices determine their votes, other political scientists have argued that the determination of decisions and votes in the Court is more complex (Epstein & Knight, 1998; Maltzman, Spriggs, & Wahlbeck, 2000). First, they emphasize that the Court is an institution and, like all institutions, it has constraints that it places on behavior. Justices, in their actions and decisions, must take into account that they are operating within a system that assumes a collegial way of behaving. Thus justices may sometimes go along with other justices to maintain civility or win allegiance from the others in subsequent cases. The strategic model (sometimes called the rational-choice model) proposes that many decisions and votes are hence made on grounds extending beyond the issues in the specific case. A justice may agree with the thrust of a majority opinion but not with the arguments supporting it; rather than writing a concurrence (which may blunt the impact of the majority opinion), the justice simply goes along. Or a justice who is a solitary dissenter in a relatively unimportant case may conform to the overwhelming majority in order not to alienate the justices whose votes he or she may need later. For example, a highly developed statistical model (based on prior voting by each justice) predicted that in the October 2002 term, only 7 of 72 cases would result in a unanimous decision, while 20 of the 72 would lead to an 8 to 1 decision. In actuality, 31 of 72 decisions were unanimous while only 4 were 8 to 1 (Wrightsman, 2006).

It should be noted that the proponents of this view of voting as strategic emphasize that its application by justices is selective. Proponents are not saying that justices would disavow their positions when it really mattered, but in some cases, justices act like members of Congress—in the words of former Speaker of the House Sam Rayburn, "they go along in order to get along."

The strategic model has a second component: that justices' decisions reflect their preferences for public policy. Rather than deciding on the basis of precedents or their own attitudes, they are assumed in this model to make decisions on the basis of what they consider to be best for the country. Although their attitudes and values certainly contribute to what they believe to be in the national interest, their actual votes are a reflection of other considerations, such as institutional norms, the wishes of Congress, and the nature of public opinion.

For example, when Earl Warren became chief justice of the United States in the fall of 1953, the Court was considering the *Brown v. Board of Educa-*

tion appeal. (This case is the topic of Chapter 6.) Warren was opposed to the segregation of schools on the grounds of fairness, and he knew that he wanted to overturn those state laws that required separate schools for blacks and whites. But he was also aware that in the term previous to his appointment, the Court had considered this petition but was unable to reach a decision. Some justices sought the same outcome as Warren, but some were Southerners who were accustomed to segregation, and two (Justices Felix Frankfurter and Robert Jackson) were opposed to segregation but supported judicial restraint and hence were reluctant to overturn those precedents that had supported a "separate but equal" procedure. While Warren was eventually able to obtain a unanimous decision outlawing school segregation in a decision announced on May 17, 1954, he had to tread carefully and make concessions. For example, the original *Brown* decision did not specify any timetable for the achievement of desegregation, and even the second *Brown* decision, announced a year later in 1955, told school districts with segregated schools that they should desist "with all deliberate speed," an unfortunate term because of its ambiguity. Not only did Warren have to deal with the preferences of some of his colleagues, but he also had to respond to the fact that the desegregation decision would be quite unpopular in parts of the country. Thus, the actual opinion that Warren wrote was short in length and written in a straightforward way, free of jargon, and accessible to the public. Furthermore, not only did Warren persuade those who were recalcitrant that it was essential that such a controversial decision be a unanimous one, but those initial holdouts realized that it was in the best interest of the country that the nine justices band together.

Similarly, when the Supreme Court dealt with challenges to the affirmative action procedure used in determining admissions to the University of Michigan School of Law in *Grutter v. Bollinger* (2003), Justice O'Connor's decision for the Court reflected a strong policy thrust. She accepted the procedure because of the benefits to society in general from having a diversified population of professional persons, even as she hoped that such affirmative-action programs would not be necessary 20 years in the future.

The view that justices act strategically implies that they use oral arguments to further their goals. For example, they may ask questions of the advocates to bolster positions they support. They may seek information that is not in the briefs, but that will be useful in the conferences and in the opinion-drafting stage. On the matter of secret governmental surveillance of communications between suspected terrorists abroad and persons living in the United States, a justice might approve of the procedure because of his or her view that it is vital to the national defense, even while holding concerns about invasions of privacy. For example, Judge Richard Posner of the Seventh Circuit Court, anticipating a challenge before the Court, has provided a nuanced recommendation reflecting policy preferences. He wrote, "Permit surveillance intended to detect and prevent terrorist activity but flatly forbid the use of information gleaned by such surveillance for any purpose other than to protect national security" (2006, p. 16).

A Social-Psychological Viewpoint: Motivated Reasoning

The three positions described here have been related to differing mental processes. Social psychologist Ziva Kunda has offered a position that capitalizes on both cognition and motivation, called "motivated reasoning." Thus she implicitly rejects the attitudinal model, stating that "people do not seem to be at liberty to conclude whatever they want to conclude merely because they want to" (1990, p. 482). While this motivation may be the source, people also operate from a desire to be rational; thus they develop a justification for the outcome they desire that "would persuade a dispassionate observer" (1990, p. 482). However, they maintain the desired conclusion only if they can generate the evidence to support it. That is, they maintain an "illusion of objectivity" (1990, p. 483).

This view is supported by Judge Jerome Frank, who wrote extensively about the courts for the layperson many years ago:

> Since the judge is a human being and since no human being in
> his [sic] normal thinking processes arrives at a decision (except
> in dealing with a limited number of simple solutions) by the
> route of any such syllogistic reasoning, it is fair to assume that the
> judge, merely by putting on the judicial ermine, will not acquire
> so artificial a method of reasoning. Judicial judgments, like other
> judgments, doubtless, in most cases, are worked out backward from
> conclusions tentatively formulated. (1930, p. 101)

The *Bush v. Gore* (2000) decision, arguably the most controversial decision ever made by the Court, has been subjected to a variety of explanations; motivated reasoning provides one explanation. It has been suggested that both the conservative justices, who voted to support Governor Bush's appeal, and the liberal justices, who did not, were sensitive to different features of the case: "the conservative justices may have been more sensitive to arguments based on Article II and the Equal Protection Clause than they otherwise would have been, and the liberal justices more sensitive to the weaknesses of those arguments than they otherwise would have been" (Posner, 2001, p. 180).

Complicating Matters Further

No one model fits every justice in every case. The legal model appears to assume that the process of deciding how to vote is a straightforward one, and that it matters not at all whether the issue at hand is the water rights of competing states or the privacy rights of homosexual persons convicted of sodomy. The attitudinal model does not distinguish between unimportant and important cases, although one could assume that in some cases a justice would simply not have an attitude on the issue beforehand and be completely open-minded. Similarly, motivated reasoning would "kick in" only when the justice held a desired position on a case. The strategic model would, I believe, make a distinction between cases if indeed "what is good for the country" is a motivating determinant of a vote.

Ideologically Related Cases versus Nonideological Cases

As suggested earlier, I propose that, with regard to the determinants of a justice's opinion on a case, not all cases are the same. First of all, justices may have much more information about some petitions than about others. Some cases deal with issues, even specific issues, on which the Court has ruled before. For example, in the term ending in June 2007, the Court responded to an appeal on the legality of partial-birth or late-term abortion (a matter it had dealt with in 2000), two on racial diversity in the schools (also considered in 2004), and several on search-and-seizure and prisoners' rights (issues that emerge each term.) Other cases lack a track record. For example, cases in which a state is the petitioner and another state or the federal government is the respondent, such as *Alaska v. United States* (2005), are "original jurisdiction" cases that go directly to the Supreme Court without any district-court or circuit-court review. These are infrequent, but there are other cases, mostly civil suits, that have not garnered much attention in the media and do not relate to highly visible issues.

I divide cases before the Court into *ideological* and *nonideological* categories, this distinction being central to understanding the impact of oral arguments; it will come up again in subsequent chapters. Ideological cases are those that elicit predispositions to favor a particular side from at least some of the justices, because they are related to basic values such as individuals' rights, states' rights, property rights, privacy, executive power, or other equally salient concerns. As noted before, some of these values can be associated with conservative political positions, some with liberal positions. Of the 69 signed opinions by the Court during the 2006–2007 term, more than 37 or 53% were ideological in nature. These included cases on defendants' rights, prisoners' rights, abortion, school desegregation, the death penalty, sex discrimination, and the insanity defense. The vast majority were criminal cases rather than civil. As noted earlier, there is systematic evidence that for ideological cases conservative justices and liberal justices vote differently (Segal & Cover, 1989; Thimsen, 2003). For such cases, I propose that a rudimentary reading of the issue at hand will trigger a predisposition to vote in a predictable way for most justices. For nonideological cases, it takes longer for the justice to form a tentative opinion; a value-related reaction is not triggered by a one-sentence description of the issue.

One may say that there are two dimensions here and that I am confounding them. The distinction between an ideological and a nonideological issue can be differentiated from the amount of prior knowledge a justice has about an issue. But I believe these two dimensions are related; justices know more about abortion, free speech, or the death penalty as an issue than they do about the federal Longshore and Harbor Workers' Compensation Act (the interpretation of which was at issue in the 2005 *Stewart v. Dutra Construction* case) or the federal Truth in Lending Act (as in *Koons Buick Pontiac v. Nigh,* another 2005 case).

It follows that for some types of cases, justices feel better informed going into the oral arguments than they do in others. I will return to this important point after reviewing what the justices themselves say about the importance of oral arguments.

The Justices' Position on Oral Arguments

This section approaches the position of justices' views of oral arguments in two ways. First, the behavior of certain justices on the bench is described; second, written comments by the justices are reported. The conclusion from each of these approaches is the same: justices differ with regard to their positions on the value of oral arguments.

Behaviors on the Bench

Justice Thomas's position was quoted at the beginning of the chapter. Furthermore, he has told his law clerks that "he relies on the briefs and sees no need to quiz the lawyers, and that he thinks oral arguments are overrated. They may make for a good show, but they are not altogether significant in the outcome" (Savage, 1997, pp. 55–56). He very rarely participates, and his nonverbal behavior on the bench (leaning back, looking at the ceiling, whispering to the adjacent justice) communicates to observers someone who is not involved in the give-and-take of the oral argument. Reasons for his behavior will be described later in this chapter as well as in Chapters 4 and 5. But even more extreme in their behavior on the bench were Justice Oliver Wendell Holmes, Jr., who often took catnaps there, and Justice Douglas, who answered his mail or drafted sections of his books while listening to the dialogue.

In contrast was Justice Blackmun; his note taking and rating of advocates was described in Chapter 1. He strived to pay attention and he "became annoyed when other justices chatted with one another...as Brennan and White frequently did" (Biskupic, 2005, p. 106). Justice Blackmun once passed a note to Chief Justice Burger threatening to walk out in the middle of the session if "the din at the bench" did not stop (Biskupic, 2005, p. 106).

Viewpoints

Some justices who served on the bench earlier than Justice Thomas have also felt that the oral arguments are not useful. Chief Justice Warren concluded that they were "not highly persuasive" (O'Brien, 2000, p. 260). And it follows from the criticisms of the quality of advocacy that were rampant 20 years ago, described in Chapter 1, that concern has been expressed regarding their usefulness.

But far more justices have been more supportive of oral arguments than critical of them. Among the most developed views was that of Justice John Marshall Harlan II, who served on the Court from 1955 to 1971 and was highly respected by his colleagues. He wrote, "The view is widespread that when the Court comes to the hard business of decision, it is the briefs, and not the oral argument, which count. I think that view is a greatly mistaken one" (1955, p. 6). He gave several reasons for his position, among them that judges differ in their work habits; some listen better than they read. But his most important reason was the interactive nature of the arguments:

> The job of courts is not merely one of an umpire in disputes be-
> tween litigants. Their job is to search out the truth both as to the
> facts and the law, and that is ultimately the job of the lawyers, too.
> And in that joint effort, the oral argument gives the opportunity
> for interchange between court and counsel which the briefs do not
> give. For my part, there is no substitute, even within the time limits
> afforded by the busy calendars of modern appellate courts, for the
> Socratic method of procedure in getting at the real heart of an issue
> and in finding where the truth lies. (Harlan, 1955, p. 7)

Several chief justices have supported the impact of oral arguments. Charles Evans Hughes, chief justice from 1930 to 1941, commented that oral argument helps the Court "separate the wheat from the chaff" (1928, p. 61). Chief Justice Rehnquist endorsed this position:

> Lawyers often ask me whether oral argument "really makes a differ-
> ence." Often the question is asked with an undertone of skepticism,
> if not cynicism, intimating that the judges really have made up their
> minds before they ever come to the bench and oral argument is
> pretty much a formality. Speaking for myself, I think it does make a
> difference; in a significant minority of cases in which I have heard
> oral argument, I have left the bench feeling differently about a case
> than I did when I came to the bench. The change is seldom a full
> one-hundred-and-eighty-degree swing, and I find it is most likely to
> occur in cases involving areas of law with which I am least familiar.
> (2001, pp. 243–244)

On this matter, Justice Brennan agreed with his frequent adversary, stating, "often my idea of how a case shapes up is changed by oral argument. I have had too many occasions when my judgment on a decision has turned on what happened in oral argument" (O'Brien, 2000, p. 254).

Among current justices, Ruth Bader Ginsburg gives an interesting perspective, having written that during her years as a circuit-court judge and

Supreme Court justice, "I have seen few victories snatched at oral argument from a total defeat the judges had anticipated on the basis of the briefs. But I have seen several potential winners become losers in whole or in part because of the clarification elicited at oral argument" (1999, p. 570). Also, with respect to current justices, Antonin Scalia has come to change his opinion on the utility of oral arguments. Before joining the bench he considered them "a dog and pony show" but has since come to the position that "things can be put in perspective during oral arguments in a way that they can't in a written brief" (O'Brien, 2000, p. 260).

In a dissenting opinion in *Pennsylvania v. Mimms* (1977), Justice Stevens wrote in support of oral arguments: "My limited experience has convinced me that one's initial impression of a novel issue is frequently different from his final evaluation" (1977, p. 123, note 13). Justice Kennedy has emphasized the oral argument as a way of justices communicating with each other: "When the people come...to see our arguments, they often see a dialogue between the justices asking a question and the attorney answering it. And they think of the argument as a series of those dialogues. It isn't that. As John [Stevens] points out, what is happening is the Court is having a conversation with itself through the intermediary of the attorneys" (O'Brien, 2000, p. 260).

Views of Other Appellate Judges

Appellate judges at other levels have also reflected a range of opinions. Judge Paul Michel of the United States Court of Appeals for the Federal Circuit has written that "in perhaps half of the cases, it is clear from the briefs that the lower court must be affirmed. The other half are closer cases where oral argument could influence my vote, and it does so far more than 20 percent of the time" (1998, p. 21). A survey done by the Federal Judicial Center in 1975 found, however, that all of those federal appellate judges and trial judges who responded to a questionnaire agreed with a statement advocating the restriction of an oral argument to 15 or 20 minutes; 90 percent of these judges believed that in cases in which issues and precedents were clear, the oral argument could be eliminated entirely (Goldman, 1975). Of course, circuit courts do not have the luxury of the Supreme Court to decline to take cases, and thus many of their cases can be decided on the basis of the briefs.

A survey of 15 of the 18 judges then on the Ninth Circuit Court of Appeals, done by Wasby (1981, 1982), led to different conclusions. These judges found that the argument process helped them clarify matters and focus on important issues. They noted that a "public relations" reason also exists for oral arguments; attorneys and their clients want their cases to be heard. The oral argument proves that the judges have focused on the case (otherwise litigants have no indication that they have read the briefs). These judges also noted that occasionally a lawyer is "a better talker than a writer"

(Wasby, 1982) and, as Justice Harlan opined, some justices listen better than they read.

Conclusion: How Often Have Justices Made up Their Minds before Oral Arguments?

Recall Justice Thomas' introductory claim that "99 per cent of the time justices have made their minds up" before hearing the oral arguments. Is this true? I think the comment (perhaps made without enough thought, since it was given on the spur of the moment) is too simplified and too extreme. Some justices, in some types of cases, have formed an unchangeable position after learning only the basic issue in the appeal. Justices Brennan, Marshall, and Blackmun were so opposed to the death penalty when they were on the Court that their votes were completely predictable. But on other types of cases they were not. It is likely that some justices, because of their personalities, may generally be more persuaded by oral arguments than are some of their colleagues. The questions of Justices Kennedy and Breyer during oral arguments frequently reflect that they are uncertain of their positions and that they seek clarification from the advocates. Their behavior can be contrasted with that of Justice Thomas, who remains silent on the bench except for one or two comments during an entire term. Although a number of explanations can be given for his silence (considered in Chapter 5), perhaps he has, like his attribution of "most justices," already determined his vote.

Just as there are differences in justices, there are differences in cases. Some cases reflect issues that the Court has considered before; justices are quite familiar with *Miranda* rights and the rules about search and seizure. They are already up to speed on these cases, so they do not need to ask so many questions that clarify procedures. A particular case may cover the same issue as one considered by the Court a few years earlier. But some cases involve obscure laws or issues the Court has not confronted before. Here, the questioning can be especially valuable.

Thus, the answer to the question, do oral arguments change justices' positions is, it depends. Any change reflects an interaction between the specific judge, the nature of the case, and the quality of the oral arguments. The following are factors:

1. The topics in some cases elicit strong attitudes and values. For these ideologically related cases, oral arguments are less likely to have an influence.
2. Some justices are more open-minded than others (a topic described in Chapter 5), regardless of the issue. They acknowledge that their initial reaction is provisional and subject to change.
3. Some advocates do a better job in the oral arguments than others. As Justice Ginsburg remarked, a poor oral argument can more likely lose a

case than a good one can win it, but the bottom-line conclusion is that in *some* cases, the quality of the oral argument makes a difference.

I subscribe to the position of the late Chief Justice Rehnquist, quoted earlier, that an oral argument can *sometimes* shift a justice's position to *some* degree. While it is difficult to prove this position empirically, several analyses described in subsequent chapters provide support. For example, the impact of the position offered by the office of the solicitor general is strong, as described in Chapter 3. The background of the advocates contributes to the impact of oral arguments, also described in Chapter 3. Questions asked by the justices reflect the direction of their votes, at least for some justices, as described in Chapter 7.

3

The Behavior of Advocates
before the Supreme Court

> Not many cases, it is true, are won on the oral argument alone,
> but a case can be lost if a lawyer is unable or unwilling to answer
> a justice's question honestly and persuasively.
>
> —Justice Ruth Bader Ginsburg (2003, p. x)

The Frequency May Vary, but the Reactions are the Same

For most attorneys who argue a case before the Supreme Court, the experience is one that they never forget. For some, it is literally a "once-in-a-lifetime" opportunity, but even for those who are veteran appellate advocates, the experience continues to be indelible. John Roberts, before he became a federal judge, argued 38 cases before the Court, and he recalled that every time he approached the Court he had a lump in his throat. Justice Ginsburg also has described the impact of arguing before the Court:

> Still vibrant in my mind is the first of my six 1970s arguments
> before the Supreme Court. In those years, the Court regularly heard
> four arguments in a sitting day. I was scheduled to appear in the
> afternoon. Anxiety mounted as I observed the morning's arguments. I skipped lunch to guard against the butterflies fluttering
> inside. Then, after delivering a well-rehearsed opening sentence, I
> looked up at the bench and experienced a feeling of extraordinary

power. There sat the nine top judges in the land. They had no place
to go. They were my captive audience for the next several moments.
Then a teacher by trade, I relished the opportunity to persuade
them that my cause was just, my legal argument sound. (2003, p. ix)

Experienced appellate advocates recall their first arguments as gener-
ating fear, exhilaration, and more significant physical symptoms. Talbot
D'Alemberte lost 10 pounds before his first argument in 1993; Ian McPherson
lost his lunch before his first argument in 1980 (Mauro, 2003d). If fear and
physical sickness are frequent reactions before the argument, the experience
of being at the podium may be stupefying. "The justices are less than 10 feet
away, and their near-semicircular bench is low to the ground, so that they
are looking you right in the eye. You have to crane your neck to address the
least senior members sitting at the ends of the row—no small matter in such
a formal setting" (Cullinan, 2004, p. 30). Sometimes the reactions afterward
are more complex—perhaps satisfaction but also frustration and disappoint-
ment. Even Justice Robert H. Jackson, commenting on his time in the solicitor
general's office as an advocate, wrote that he gave three arguments in each
Supreme Court case: "First came the one that I planned—as I thought, logical,
coherent, complete. Second was the one actually presented—interrupted, in-
coherent, disjointed, and disappointing. The third was the utterly devastating
argument that I thought of after going to bed that night" (1951, p. 803).

Pitfalls and Pratfalls

The ideal oral argument has often been characterized as a conversation. But
as described by appellate advocate Philip Lacovara, it is just not any conversation. The advocate is a walk-in guest at a party at someone's house. He or
she does not know the host very well. The host and all his other guests seem
to be well acquainted, as there is banter between them recalling exchanges
with former guests over other matters. The advocate needs to be aware of this
undercurrent but not intrude upon the relationship between the host and the
other people at the party. The moral is that even extensive preparation may
not ready one for the subtleties and nuances of the Court's procedure.

Some Monumental Errors

Despite the importance of the occasion and the grandeur of the courtroom—
or perhaps *because* of these—some advocates commit egregious blunders
when they appear before the justices. Among these are, more frequently than
one would expect, confusion over justices' names. On at least six occasions
Justice Ginsburg has been addressed by an advocate as "Justice O'Connor."
Even such distinguished and experienced attorneys as Carter Phillips, Lau-
rence Tribe, and former Acting Solicitor General Walter Dellinger have done

that, as well as at least two of Justice O'Connor's former law clerks (Mauro, 2003e). Some would say that these particular confusions occurred with the advent of two women on the Court, but these two justices certainly did not look alike nor sound alike, nor did they sit side by side.

Perhaps the most notorious of such mix-ups, because it occurred during the oral arguments for the *Bush v. Gore* case, came from the mouth of Joe Klock, an attorney representing the Florida secretary of state, who had been given 10 minutes' time to justify the state's position supporting Governor Bush, as he sought to terminate the re-counting of ballots. After responding to several questions, Klock received one from Justice Stevens. His response began, "Well, Justice Brennan, the difficulty is that…," only to be interrupted with courtroom-wide laughter. At that point, Justice Souter made a comment, only to have Klock address him as "Justice Breyer." Once again the audience roared. It would take a superhuman effort for an advocate to regain his or her concentration after such a string of gaffes.

A more egregious error, perhaps also explained by nervousness and the demand characteristics of the situation, occurs when the advocate seemingly ignores the rules of decorum. In the oral argument for the case of *Bradshaw v. Stumpf*, argued on April 19, 2005, Alan M. Freedman, the attorney for the respondent, forgot the salutation, and began as follows: "In light of the questioning, I'd like to indicate what actually was argued below and what was the ruling. In the first Stumpf trial, they—they argued that there was, quote/unquote, ample evidence to point…" He was summarily interrupted by Chief Justice Rehnquist: "Who is 'they'?" At that point Freedman answered, "The prosecutors," and, recognizing his oversight, then said, "I'm sorry. Mr. Chief Justice, and may it please the Court" (*Bradshaw v. Stumpf*, 2005, transcript of oral argument, p. 27). Mistakes like these can be attributed to a kind of performance anxiety; perhaps even the most extensive rehearsal cannot completely prevent them. For example, Neal Katyal, a Georgetown University law professor, practiced his argument for *Hamdan v. Rumsfeld* before an audience 15 times, and still, at the actual oral argument, responded to a series of questions from Justice Alito by first saying, "Justice Scalia" before quickly correcting himself (Bashman, 2006; Goldman, 2006). A more serious pratfall is illustrated when the attorney cannot answer a relevant question—even a factual question—about the case. The following exchange illustrates how even a seasoned advocate might falter when he or she does not foresee a question (Frederick, 2003a, p. 37). The case was *Lee v. Weisman* (1992), which dealt with the constitutionality of clergy giving a prayer at public-school graduation ceremonies. The attorney for the school district had barely begun when Justice Blackmun interrupted him.

> Mr. Cooper: Mr. Chief Justice, and may it please the Court.
> At the 1989 graduation ceremony of the Nathan
> Bishop Middle School in Providence, Rhode Island,
> Rabbi Leslie Gutterman opened the exercise with an

	invocation—one characterized by the district court as an example of elegant simplicity, thoughtful content, and sincere citizenship.
Justice Blackmun:	How old were these youngsters, Mr. Cooper?
Mr. Cooper:	I beg your pardon, Justice—
Justice Blackmun:	How old were these youngsters graduating?
Mr. Cooper:	Your Honor, the graduates themselves were graduating from middle school and into high school. So they were just completing their eighth grade.
Justice Blackmun:	Well, how old were they is my question. You haven't answered me.
Mr. Cooper:	Your Honor, I think–
Justice Blackmun:	About 13 or 14, aren't they?
Mr. Cooper:	Yes, Your Honor.
Justice Blackmun:	Are we getting so–
Mr. Cooper:	I'm sorry, I could not hear you.
Justice Blackmun:	Never mind, go ahead. (*Lee v. Weisman,* 1992, transcript of oral argument, pp. 3–4).

As Frederick has observed:

It was an inauspicious start to Cooper's argument. Justice Blackmun's aim obviously was to show that middle school students, in particular, were young and impressionable, so young that they would be heavily influenced by the state's decision to include clergy of a particular faith and denomination in the commencement exercises. It is difficult to say for certain whether Cooper's stumbling at the beginning of the argument contributed to the Supreme Court's 5–4 ruling that the inclusion of such clergy is unconstitutional, but the opening paragraphs of Justice Anthony M. Kennedy's opinion for the Court noted that Deborah Weisman "was about 14 years old" when she graduated from Nathan Bishop Middle School. (2003a, p. 38)

The most serious kind of misjudgment occurs when, in the view of the Court, an advocate is completely unprepared. Two examples are illustrative.

In the case of *Shalala v. Whitecotton*, argued in February 1995, Robert Moxley responded unsatisfactorily to questions from several justices. Chief Justice Rehnquist then intervened: "How can you stand up there at the rostrum and give those totally inconsistent answers?" When Moxley tried to say he was sorry, the Chief Justice retorted, "Well, you should be." Moxley only dug himself in deeper by saying, "I don't mean to confuse the Court," at which point Rehnquist replied, "Well, you…haven't confused us so much as just made us gravely wonder…how well-prepared you are for this argument." As Moxley tried to pick up the pieces, the chief justice abruptly told him, "Your time has expired." Moxley lost the case by a 9 to 0 vote (Perry, 1999a).

More recently, in December 2005, in an oral argument in a death-penalty case (*Oregon v. Guzek*), several justices, including Rehnquist, Scalia, and Stevens, continually questioned the rationale for the argument posed by Randy Lee Guzek's attorney. Guzek had been convicted of aggravated murder and sentenced to death. In the brief and oral argument, the attorney, Richard L. Wolf, did not respond to the petitioner's brief but instead audaciously proposed that the Supreme Court lacked jurisdiction and that the Court should, in effect, change its collective mind about whether it was proper to grant cert to the appeal. He also argued that the Oregon Supreme Court's reasoning, in overturning Guzek's death sentence, was improper when it relied on the Eighth Amendment. All the issues could be resolved, he claimed, through the application of Oregon state law. The justices especially questioned the advocate about his position on the relevance of the Eighth Amendment. Justice Breyer repeatedly asked him to answer a question posed to him, and an exasperated Justice O'Connor told Wolf that "perhaps we should appoint some amicus here, Counsel, to argue in support of the merits" (*Oregon v. Guzek,* transcript of oral argument, p. 53). Not surprisingly, the Court ruled unanimously the next February against Wolf's client, specifically that the Eighth Amendment does not guarantee a defendant the right at his sentencing hearing to recall a trial witness to present new evidence about his innocence.

Similarly, an advocate may have thought that he or she did an adequate amount of preparation, only to find out the hard way that it wasn't enough. An example comes from the oral argument of *DaimlerChrysler v. Cuno*, argued before the Court in March 2006. During the proceeding Justice Ginsburg asked the attorney for Cuno, Peter Enrich, to name the very best precedent for the point he was making in his argument. "*Craig v. Boren,*" he replied, referring to a case going back to 1976. As Tony Mauro recounts the exchange, it was not the best answer: "Bad choice. Turns out, Ginsburg wrote a brief on the case as a lawyer for the American Civil Liberties Union. Armed with a strong memory of the case's holding, Ginsburg was all over Enrich, asserting that the case stood for a different proposition" (2006a, p. 10).

Classifications of Mistakes

In *The Art of Oral Advocacy*, David Frederick (2003a) has provided a taxonomy of common mistakes made by lawyers at the oral arguments:

1. Speaking style errors, including reading to the Court, speaking with too much rhetoric or passion, or speaking too loudly
2. Substantive errors, including avoiding direct answers to questions, using ill-considered metaphors, and arguing about issues beyond those of the questions presented
3. Errors in citing materials, including citing an authority or the record incorrectly, relying on citations of material not found in the brief, and citing cases without explaining them

4. Errors in interacting with the justices, including interrupting one of them, misaddressing one of them, and asking a question beyond that needed for clarification
5. Decorum errors, including using sarcasm, intemperate language, or inappropriate humor; showing anger or frustration with the Court; attacking opposing counsel (2003a, p. 130)

A Content Analysis of Oral Arguments

In my analysis of desirable and undesirable actions by advocates in oral arguments I came up with several examples of each type. An effective oral argument, for example, may begin by stating a few basic points. The attorney arguing in behalf of the United States (which supported the petitioner) in *Merck KGaA v. Integra Lifesciences* (2005) used this tactic to his advantage to keep the justices focused on his argument. Daryl Joseffer began, "I believe the question before the Court is the proper construction of the statute, and we believe the lower courts committed three important legal errors that should be corrected" (transcript of the oral argument, p. 17). Subsequently, both Justice O'Connor and Justice Souter returned to his main points. Justice O'Connor asked, "Would you state again what you say the second error was?" (p. 18) and later Justice Souter questioned, "Is that going to be your third point, the third error that the court supposedly committed?" (p. 22). The advocate's side did win this case.

In contrast, the advocate makes a mistake when he or she starts too broadly. Consider this opening by the petitioner's attorney in the case of *Wilkinson v. Austin* (2005): "The purpose of any hearing process is to get a better answer. If the question is what happened in the past, an adversarial fact-finding can help provide the answers. If, however, the question seeks to look forward and predict future behavior, then a slightly more limited procedure will serve to expedite and arrive at the best possible answer to this predictive question" (*Wilkinson v. Austin*, transcript of oral argument, p. 3.)

The reader's reaction may be "Huh, what did he say, what does this mean?" In any event, this was enough for Justice Scalia to interrupt with the first question and forever derail whatever the attorney had planned to say. His first three sentences had given no direction nor made any critical points. The result was 25 minutes of free-for-all questioning. (However, the attorney did save time for a rebuttal, in which he made a convincing statement, and he won the case.)

A second important aspect of oral arguments that emerges from this analysis of transcripts is an awareness of the need to relate the advocate's position to decisions of previous cases. In *Small v. United States* (2005), Justice Scalia did the honors of asking, during the time that Justice Rehnquist was ill, "Let me...ask you the question the Chief Justice would ask, were he here, because he always asks this kind of question....If you had to pick your best case of ours which interpreted the word 'any' in the way you would like us to interpret it here, what's the best case you have" (*Small v. United States*, 2005, transcript of oral argument, p. 22). The ability to relate past cases to the current one is critical because, as noted in Chapter 2, some justices rely on *stare decisis* and precedents in making decisions. (And, as we saw earlier in this chapter with respect to the advocate's answer to this question by Justice Ginsburg in the case of *DaimlerChrysler v. Cuno*, the attorney needs to know details about the previous cases.)

The advocate errs if he or she assumes that one previous case "fits all." In *Grable v. Darue* (2005) the petitioner tried to argue that the ruling in a previous case involving Merrill Dow extended to the actions of concern in the present case. Justice O'Connor quickly informed him that several relevant actions were not encompassed by the Merrill Dow decision, but he persisted in his efforts to make it fit. Finally, Justice Scalia, seething with discontent with the petitioner's obtuseness, asked the advocate, "And you think that explains all of these cases?" (transcript of oral argument, p. 11). The petitioner lost unanimously.

Some justices may, of course, differ with the advocate as to which previous case is most applicable. In *Johnson v. California* (2005), Justice Stevens believed that the correct case to apply was what he called "the Turner case," but this case did not fit exactly with what the petitioner was arguing:

> Justice Stevens: Mr. Deixler, do you think you lose if we apply Turner?
> Mr. Deixler: No, Your Honor. We believe that even under Turner....
> Justice Stevens: Well, why isn't that the right approach to the case then if that's the—we don't have to meddle with the rules governing—the conduct of prisons, if you can prevail under that theory. (*Johnson v. California*, 2005, transcript of oral argument, p. 11)

Mr. Deixler had another case that he felt was more appropriate, and thus lost Justice Stevens' vote because he could not convince him that the Turner standard paralleled his argument.

A variety of experts tell advocates not to quote from their briefs, but I found in the transcript of the case of *Merck KGaA v. Integra* (2005) another reason beyond the obvious ones not to do so. In this case the counsel for the respondent attempted to quote from his brief and got questions from several justices as to the specific location, thus wasting time and losing momentum for his argument. Justice Ginsburg asked, "Where is this? Where are you quoting from?" and Justice Kennedy asked, "Is this just before the letter 'b' on 14a?" (transcript of oral argument, p. 28).

Opportunities for Preparation

Although some advocates do not perform well before the Court, it is not because they lack opportunities and materials to assist them in preparation.

Throughout the history of the Republic, suggestions have been made about how to act before the Court. Chapter 1 presented some advice from Justice Story, in verse form, almost 200 years ago. He also suggested, "Be brief, lucid in style and order. Condense. Strike but a few blows, strike them to the heart. And leave off when done" (Ginsburg, 1999, pp. 670–671). Contemporary advice comes in a variety of formats; the last 5 years have seen an increasing number of law schools providing Supreme Court litigation clinics. There is even a mock Supreme Court courtroom at the Georgetown University Law Center, complete with the bench, the carpet, and the space separating the advocate from the justices (Cullinan, 2004). The Supreme Court Institute at Georgetown offers any advocate scheduled to appear before the Court a chance to practice in its facility before a panel of mock judges. In practicing, advocates may discover major problems, such as weak points in their case, as well as procedural remedies, for example, that the height of the lectern can be manually adjusted by turning the handle in a counterclockwise direction to raise the lectern. But if the advocates do not know that in advance, they may betray their inexperience while fumbling with the lectern as the justices sit, watch, and fume (Frederick, 2003b).

Books

Several books deal specifically with appellate advocacy. Some like the one by Clary, Paulsen, and Vanselow (2004) cover the preparation of briefs as well as the oral arguments. David C. Frederick, a former staff member of the office of the solicitor general and now an appellate attorney with the Washington, D.C. law firm of Kellogg, Huber, Hansen, Todd & Evans, has authored two books, one specific to Supreme Court advocacy (Frederick, 2003b), and a second that is an abridged and revised edition of the first book, encompassing advocacy at all appellate levels (Frederick, 2003a). These books contain much practical advice, some obvious ("Stand up straight"), some less so ("End, if possible, before the time expires").

Journal Articles

From the beginning of the federal courts, experienced advocates have passed their knowledge on to neophytes by word of mouth, if not in writing. In the twentieth century, such advice took a written form. For example, in 1958, Frederick Wiener, an appellate advocate, wrote a 20-page article in the *Harvard Law Review* that was full of practical suggestions. Noteworthy during this time period was a brief article in the *American Bar Association Journal*; it was distributed to every member of the American bar Association, and its author was John W. Davis. As noted in Chapter 1, in the first part of the twentieth century Davis was the leading advocate in the country. He argued more than 100 cases before the Supreme Court, placing him in the pantheon alongside such legendary advocates as Daniel Webster and William Pinkney. Davis' article offered 10 instructions for novice Supreme Court advocates:

1. Change places (in your imagination) with the justices.
2. State the nature of the case and briefly its prior history.
3. State the facts.
4. State next the applicable rules of law on which you rely.
5. Concentrate on the most important point, "the hub of the case."
6. Rejoice when the Court asks questions. (Questions permit you to understand the thinking of the justices.)
7. Read sparingly and only from necessity.
8. Avoid *ad hominem* comments.
9. Know your record from cover to cover.
10. Sit down.

Of course, when John W. Davis argued before the Court, the pace was more leisurely. Justices did not pepper the lawyers with questions as they are prone to do today. Each side typically was allowed at least 1 hour for its oral argument, and sometimes more. Currently, with argument time limited to 30 minutes per side, and as many as 100 quick comments or questions fired at each advocate during that time, flexibility has emerged as a key skill. Before John Roberts was a judge, he annually spoke to a group of high-school teachers attending a summer workshop on the Court. One teacher asked him how long a speech he prepared for each appearance. "One minute," he responded. Given the inevitability of interruptions, the advocate must be skilled in weaving his or her points into the discourse, despite the barrage of interruptions.

Continuing Education, Workshops, and Panel Discussions

During a 1997 panel discussion, "Arguing a case before the Supreme Court," chaired by Robert Bennett, four distinguished appellate advocates responded candidly to questions related to their presentations. The discussion was interesting in that they did not always agree. Selections from their responses are given below.

1. "How do you prepare?"

E. Barrett Prettyman, Jr.: "I write myself questions—as many as 300 questions—for which I then develop answers." He also presents before two moot courts, the first a structured presentation without questions but with a critique from an audience of attorneys, and then later, a presentation with questions, again followed by a critique. In an article directed to prospective Supreme Court advocates, Prettyman wrote:

> I agree with those who advocate that you practice before a "moot
> court" of your partners or associates before the actual presentation
> to the Court. You should first give the argument you intend to

make—not from a written speech but from key words or phrases that remind you of what you want to say. This should be done without interruption so that you can be judged on the quality and persuasiveness of your basic approach. Next, you should go through the exercise again, this time allowing your compatriots to interrupt you at will with pertinent, tough questions and well as impertinent, wide-of-the-mark ones. The point is not only to prepare you but to dislodge you, upset you, throw you off balance, because this is precisely what may happen when you get to your feet in the real world of the courthouse. (1978, p. 17)

Philip Lacovara: "I am one of the few who does not use moot courts, although I think they have a great utility. It undercuts my desire to have spontaneity and flow. I do discuss the case with colleagues."

Maureen Mahoney: "I always do a formal moot court, but only questions and answers. I don't write a 30-minute argument."

John Roberts: "I do a minimum of three moot courts, the first one very early on, a month or so before, and a second a couple of weeks later, and a final dress rehearsal a week before the oral argument."

2. "What do you take to the podium?"

Prettyman: "I take a notebook, with key words and phrases."

Roberts: "I take one piece of paper on which I've written some key phrases. I have never once had an occasion to actually look at that piece of paper. But I'm just afraid that if I went up there with nothing, I'd forget which case it was.…I think you should bring to the podium what you feel you are comfortable with and then never look at it. As soon as you pause, especially in the Supreme Court these days, one of the nine justices will view that as a signal to pounce and in that slight pause they will ask you a question and odds are it will not be what you are looking at the piece of paper for."

Lacovara: "I take nothing to the podium itself; I'm atypical and perhaps relentlessly so. I don't want anything viewed by me as a crutch. I realize that's highly unusual and perhaps irresponsible. Don't take a prepared text; it's supposed to be a conversation, not a lecture. I've seen experienced lawyers, as they flip through pages, knock over the water glass. I discourage the use of charts and exhibits…My view is less is more at the podium."

3. "How important is your opening statement?"

Roberts: "If you look at a lot of textbooks or articles about preparing for an argument, they'll state a little bit about the background of the case, where it's from. I never do any of that. If you have only a minute, try to give one sentence that gives the essence of your argument, and make it a sentence that is not going to trigger a question.…You may not get another uninterrupted minute the rest of the half hour."

Mahoney: "Pick two basic arguments. Tell them you have two arguments. After you've spoken for a while about the first argument, they may ask you what is the second argument. Speak with conviction but don't make it too dramatic or theatrical."

Lacovara: "If you read some of the expert commentary on how to present an argument...you get the idea that when you get up there you should introduce yourself, you should say how the case arrived at the Court, etc. That in my view gets in the way of making an effective opening and [besides] all those things are obvious anyway."

   4. "Should you pitch your argument to one or two justices?"

(The relevance of this question became especially salient in the spring of 2006, when the Court announced it would hold re-arguments in three cases for which arguments had been held the previous fall. Although the Court did not say why, it seemed obvious that in each of these cases the vote was 4 to 4, and the re-argument was necessary so that newly appointed Justice Alito could participate. Assuming the other eight justices did not change their votes in the brief interim, Justice Alito's vote would be decisive. Should the advocates on re-argument direct their appeals specifically to him?)

Roberts: "It would alienate eight of them and would probably lose 8 to 1."

Prettyman: "You may be wrong in where you think the [problem] justices are."

   Equally self-defeating may be a decision to avoid one justice because he or she is considered a cinch vote for the other side. Frank Dunham, Jr., a federal public defender, was preparing the oral argument for the important case of *Hamdi v. Rumsfeld*, argued in April 2004 and dealing with the rights of captured enemy combatants. He told a reporter, "the mooters all told me that Scalia was the devil" and no energy should be expended in trying to win his vote (Mauro, 2004a). After Dunham had won the case—the Court agreed that his client deserved due process—he learned that while Justice Scalia was in the minority, it was because he felt the Court had not gone far enough in rejecting the administration's position. It is possible that if Dunham had changed his strategy, he might have captured Scalia's vote (Mauro, 2004a).

   5. "If you are arguing for the petitioner, should you save time for rebuttal?"

Prettyman: "Always save time for rebuttal but don't always use it." In an article, Prettyman explicated his position: "If you are the petitioner, prepare two arguments. The first should be about ten minutes, and the second about twenty, in length" (1978, p. 16). He noted that "you should know within a few minutes after you have risen whether you will be forced to give your ten-minute argument or whether you will be graced with the chance to give the longer version" (1978, p. 17).

Lacovara: "Take the time to use the rebuttal. You may think you've already won, but you can't be too sure."

Roberts: "You always find one little point, cover that, and get out quickly."

   In an analysis of oral arguments over the last four terms, I found that in every case except one, the petitioner's attorney asked the presiding justice to reserve the rest of his or her time for rebuttal; usually this was between 2 and 4 minutes, but in one case the attorney did so with 17 of his 30 minutes left!

Justices' Views of the Advocates

It is inevitable that the justices form opinions about the quality of advocacy in general and the performance of specific advocates before them. Chapter 1 described how Justice Blackmun rated each presentation and made descriptive comments about the advocate and the argument. William Rehnquist was on the Court for more than 30 years and sat through more than 3,000 oral arguments. In his book on the Court, he offered a classification of types of advocates:

- The lector, who reads his or her argument. "Questions from the judges, instead of being used as an opportunity to advance one's own arguments by response, are looked upon as an interruption in the advocate's delivery of his 'speech,' and the lawyer after answering the question returns to the printed page at exactly where he left off" (2001, p. 245).
- The debating champion, who is "so full of his subject, and so desirous of demonstrating this to others, that he doesn't listen carefully to questions" (2001, p. 246). His or her responses to questions reflect stock answers, usually not helpful to the justice who has asked the question.
- The type of advocate who is called by Justice Rehnquist simply "Casey Jones" because "he is like an engineer on a nonstop train—he will not stop to pick up passengers along the way" (2001, p. 247). "He speaks very rapidly, without realizing that when he is arguing before a bench of nine people, each of them will require a little time to assimilate what he is saying" (p. 247).
- The spellbinder: the opposite of "Casey Jones" in that the advocate has a good voice and a "presence" that permits him or her to converse with the justices. But the advocate tries to substitute these qualities for any careful analysis of the legal issues.

Backgrounds of Advocates

Advocates can come from a variety of positions. When a state is a party, that state's attorney general or a deputy attorney general usually argues the case. As noted, the federal government is usually represented by an attorney from the office of the solicitor general but it is somewhat of a tradition that the attorney general of the United States will argue at least one case during his or her tenure. Usually it is a case dealing with a familiar issue, because those who are chosen to be attorney general are not chosen on the basis of their appellate-advocacy skills. In December 1996, Attorney General Janet Reno chose to do so; the case *Maryland v. Wilson* (1997) addressed the question of how much discretion the police have in dealing with passengers in cars that are stopped for speeding or other violations. The specific case involved a man named Jerry Lee Wilson, from Florence, South Carolina, who was arrested in Baltimore County, Maryland, after the car in which he was riding was stopped on an interstate highway. He was a passenger, not the driver, but the police asked him to step out of the car. When he did, a packet of crack cocaine fell out. Back in 1977, in *Pennsylvania v. Mimms*, the Supreme Court permitted police to order a driver out of the car. The question before the Court was, does this procedure extend to passengers?

Ms. Reno spoke as a friend of the court and was given 10 minutes to present, but in the words of an experienced observer, "by the time the Attorney General got up to take her turn before the justices, 20 minutes into the hour-long argument, the case was a shambles" (Greenhouse, 1996c, p. A20). The attorney general of Maryland, who preceded Ms. Reno, "had managed to confound the justices with an extravagant argument that went far beyond the case the Court had agreed to decide" (Greenhouse, 1996c, p. A20). He argued that the police had the right to not only order passengers out of the car but also prevent passengers from leaving the scene. Even conservative justices on the Court, including Chief Justice Rehnquist and Justice Scalia, objected; "What is the reason for detaining the passenger? What is the Fourth Amendment rationale?" asked Chief Justice Rehnquist. Linda Greenhouse described the Court's reaction when it was the U.S. attorney general's turn:

> It fell to Attorney General Reno to try to calm the matters in the ten minutes of argument time assigned to her. She was only partly successful. Speaking softly and deliberately, Ms. Reno neither embraced nor disavowed [Maryland's] broader argument, focusing instead on the rationale for giving the police the discretion to order passengers out of the car. The justices treated her with marginally greater respect than they did Mr. Curran, but they interrupted her repeatedly. (1996c, p. A20)

Despite the penetrating questions directed to the Maryland attorney general and Ms. Reno, the Court ruled, 7 to 2, in their favor, stating that police may order passengers, as well as drivers, to get out of vehicles stopped for routine traffic violations. The Court's opinion, written by Chief Justice Rehnquist, stated that the concern for the safety of police officers justified the "minimal" intrusion on a passenger's Fourth Amendment right to be free from unreasonable seizures. Justice Stevens wrote a dissenting opinion, joined by Justice Kennedy.

Some attorneys who appear before the Court are doing so for the first time. In fact, for some it will be the only time, as it is their only case that has had the importance to survive the scrutiny of the cert process. One of the most important cases of the 2006–2007 term, *Meredith v. Jefferson County Board of Education*, dealing with racial diversity in the public schools, had a Louisville sole practitioner representing the plaintiff. Teddy Gordon had never been inside the Supreme Court building. Despite offers from such experts as former Solicitor General Theodore Olson to take over his case, he refused to give up a case he had been working on for 7 years. And he won (Mauro, 2006f). Should a lawyer from a small town or a novice attorney, who has been with the case since its inception, argue the case before the Supreme Court, or should he or she defer to more experienced advocates? More and more frequently, the attorneys who argue before the highest court are "repeat players" and among the legal elite who specialize in appellate advocacy (McGuire, 1993). In a book on the reemerging Supreme Court bar, Kevin McGuire (1993) makes the distinction between an "elite community" or "inner circle" of experienced appellate lawyers and an "outer circle" of practitioners who rarely appear before the Court. Increasingly, those who appear before the Court are among the elite. The supposition is that inexperienced lawyers, based far away from Washington, often don't do well before the Court, but they persist in wanting to appear. An experienced advocate told McGuire:

> A lot of that work is pretty bad. I think a couple of things happen, one of which is that it's such an exciting experience to have a case in the Supreme Court, people tend not to let loose of it. They don't want to say to the client, "I'm not competent to take your case." Indeed, I suppose in the worst-case scenario, they don't know they're not competent because they don't really understand what it would mean to be competent. I think you get a lot of people who should have let someone else take the case over, either because of their own ego or just a naive failure to understand what's involved in the case. (McGuire, 1993, p. 74)

But occasionally a relatively new associate in a law firm gets the opportunity and has a positive outcome. That was what happened to William Colby, an associate in a Kansas City, Missouri, law firm, who argued the case of Nancy Cruzan before the Supreme Court in 1989. Ms. Cruzan had been seriously injured in an automobile accident and had been in a persistent vegetative state for 6 years. Her parents wanted permission for her to be allowed to die (Colby, 2002). William Colby had represented the family through a long, drawn-out set of trials and appeals, and when the Supreme Court agreed to decide the case, he rejected advice to turn the case over to an experienced appellate attorney. "I was young and headstrong enough to think I could do the argument," he concluded (Mauro, 2003d, p. 10). Colby lost the appeal in *Cruzan v. Director, Missouri Department of Health*) by a vote of 5 to 4. But the Court's opinion did permit a right to die if new evidence surfaced about the person's earlier intent, and thus another trial a year later permitted Nancy Cruzan to die with dignity.

Even rarer is the instance of petitioners or respondents representing themselves, *pro se*, but this happened during the October 2003 term, in the case of *Elk Grove Unified School District v. Newdow*. Michael Newdow, a lawyer, argued that the "under God" portion of the Pledge of Allegiance violated the First Amendment. While arguing *pro se* is certainly not recommended by the Court, Newdow did have the good judgment to do a moot court, using the Stanford Law School's Supreme Court Litigation Clinic (Mauro, 2004a). However, he still lost his case before the Court.

Sole practitioners and lawyers who practice far from the shadows of the Supreme Court building are increasingly being asked to turn their cases over to specialized law firms. Schwartz and Mauro have described one example:

> The state of Montana's cert petition had not even been filed when Michael Sherwood received a call from a big-firm attorney (he won't disclose which one) hoping to take over the case. Sherwood, a Missoula, Montana, sole practitioner, is representing Omer, the defendant in a bank fraud case being appealed. Three more calls followed. "They were saying, 'Look, you should hand the case over to our firm.' I just think there are people who would prefer to see their names on Supreme Court briefs," he says....."Certainly no one knows the factual and legal background in the case better than I, and my client is comfortable with that." (2006, p. 1)

Should the novice relinquish the case? I present empirical evidence on this question at the end of this chapter.

The Reemergence of a Supreme Court Bar

Increasingly, when seeking to get a favorable judgment from the Supreme Court, major corporations are forsaking their own legal staffs or their usual law firms and instead hiring advocates who specialize in appearances before the Supreme Court. As one lawyer from the office of the solicitor general put it, "It's gotten to the point now where, at least the major corporations that want somebody in the Supreme Court probably have a list of ten people to go to. I think the average lawyer is not going to be called" (McGuire, 1993, p. 61).

The matter of *eBay v. MercExchange* (a one-time on-line auction site) was considered so important by eBay that it hired Carter Phillips, an attorney with Sidley Austin Brown & Wood in Washington, D.C., to argue its case on March 29, 2006. It was Phillips' 49th appearance before the Court (he argued his 50th case the next month, for a total of six in one term). A recent article described Phillips as the quintessential Supreme Court advocate: "if you were to poll the justices about the model Supreme Court advocate, the winner would be Carter Phillips" (Scheiber, 2006, p. 15). Phillips has all the credentials: a law degree from Northwestern University, a clerkship with Chief Justice Warren Burger, and a job for several years in the office of the solicitor general. He now heads the Washington headquarters of the 1,600-lawyer Sidley Austin firm, where he charges his clients more than $700 an hour for his expertise (Biskupic, 2003). A longtime friend of John Roberts, he argued the very first case over which Roberts presided after he was installed as chief justice.

What makes Phillips in such demand? According to one Supreme Court observer, he possess two traits to an extraordinary degree: "He has a very strong virtue of humility in the finest sense of the word....It allows him to stand in others' shoes, the shoes of his opponent and the justices who ask the questions....He also has the fastest analytical mind I've ever had the privilege to deal with. It's quite scary" (Coyle, 2006, p. 18).

Not to be outdone, the other party in the eBay suit, MercExchange, discarded its law firm and substituted it with Seth Waxman, who was solicitor general of the United States in the Clinton administration and since then has specialized in Supreme Court advocacy at the law firm of Wilmer Cutler Pickering Hale and Dorr. The lead partner of MercExchange's law firm said, "When you get to the Supreme Court, it's a very small club, and you want people who are polished practitioners" (Schwartz & Mauro, 2006, p. 22). In February 2007, Phillips and Waxman again opposed each other, when Microsoft and AT&T were in conflict over a patent issue.

A distinguishable Supreme Court bar has reemerged in the last two decades, as described by John Roberts in Chapter 1. Large law firms across the country are beginning appellate advocacy departments. Fulbright & Jaworski's nationwide firm now has an appellate practice with 35 attorneys. Such departments do not always generate huge profits for the firm, but they offer a great deal of prestige, and they attract former Supreme Court law clerks to the firm, always a plus. Schwartz and Mauro describe the evolution:

> Firms began forming discrete Supreme Court practices about 25 years ago. Among the first to make the move was Mayer, Brown, Rowe, & Maw, which began plucking attorneys from the solicitor general's office in the early 1980s, including Robert Stern, a one-time acting solicitor general, and Stephen Shapiro, a former deputy solicitor general. Such luminaries came with a ready-made reputation, and clients soon followed. (2006, p. 22)

Other firms emulated them, including such major firms as Jenner & Block, Jones Day, and Sidley Austin. These and other firms have strengthened their appellate departments by hiring a number of former staff attorneys from the office of solicitor general, including Drew Days and Walter Dellinger, both of whom headed the office, and Maureen Mahoney, a deputy, plus Richard Taranto, Kent Jones, and Beth Brinkmann, each a former assistant to the solicitor general. The move has paid off in greater involvement; for example, during a 2-week period in February and March 2005, lawyers with the Jones Day firm argued 3 of the 10 cases before the Court. That same firm argued 6 of the 70 cases that term, the record for one law firm (Mauro, 2005a).

Some attorneys have taken a different track and formed their own firms that concentrate on Supreme Court advocacy (Mauro, 2006b). The most innovative and successful of these is Thomas Goldstein, who, at the age of 29 and using his laundry room as an office, began cold-calling lawyers in 1999 to offer them assistance in getting their cases through the Supreme Court; in fact, the firm he helped found, Goldstein & Howe, devoted itself almost entirely to Supreme Court litigation. His zealous pursuit of clients—some would call it a form of "ambulance-chasing"—violated the traditions of the Supreme Court bar. Furthermore, Goldstein had none of the accouterments of the typical member of the Supreme Court bar—he had not graduated from a prominent law school, he had not clerked at the Supreme Court (though he had clerked with a circuit-court judge), and he had never worked in the office of the solicitor general. His success is attributed as follows:

> The way Goldstein's cold calls work will be familiar to anyone who has ever tried to sell something by phone. Goldstein calls up a lawyer, says he thinks their case might be Supreme Court material, and then commences making small talk and, eventually, his pitch. The process involves the stick-to-it-iveness of a used-car salesman and frequent rejection. But it also succeeds at a surprising rate. The reason is that Goldstein was among the first to identify a vast, unexplored market. What's been happening for decades, he says, is that sophisticated clients like wealthy corporations have been filing lots of cert petitions.... But people without money and knowledge of how the Supreme Court operates almost never file cert petitions, even when the Supreme Court is certain to take their case. These are the clients Goldstein pursues. (Scheiber, 2006, p. 16)

Goldstein also established a Supreme Court blog (titled SCOTUSblog), which provides links to commentary by other bloggers, summarizes cases coming before the Court, lists coverage of the Court in major newspapers, and generally provides detailed information about Court happenings. Goldstein and his wife and law partner, Amy Howe, were able to build a multi-million-dollar practice; for example, he served as co-counsel for E. Pierce Marshall in the *Marshall v. Marshall* case described in Chapter 1 and he represented Scott Randolph in the case of *Georgia v. Randolph*, to be described in Chapter 7. In the 2004–2005 term, he set what has to be a modern record for an uninterrupted opening statement when he represented the respondent–862 words, or a full 4 minutes before he was questioned by Justice Breyer (*National Cable & Telecommunications Assn. v. Brand X Internet Service*. 2005, transcript of oral argument, pp. 29–33). In the 2005–2006 term he was either counsel or co-counsel in more than 10% of the Court's entire case load, including, in addition to the above two cases, the noteworthy cases of *Hamdan v. Rumsfeld* and *Randall v. Sorrell* (Scheiber, 2006). By design, half of Goldstein's cases are done on a *pro bono* basis (Mauro, 2004a).

In the words of Noam Scheiber, Goldstein's brashness "has not endeared him to the inhabitants of the world's last great bastion of elitism" (2006, p. 14). Goldstein does not have the patrician image of Carter Phillips (nor does he have Phillips' fee structure, although his fee for paying clients is $450 per hour). Rather than graduating from a top-tier law school, he went to American University, where he barely was admitted (only the intervention of a distant friend got him in). Scheiber, who interviewed both Phillips and Goldstein for his article in the *New Republic*, reported that Phillips "couldn't say for sure how many other firms aggressively solicit business. But he did know one thing: 'Obviously Tommy Goldstein has. He doesn't blink an eye about it'" (2006, p. 15). Scheiber noted that

> [Chief Justice] Roberts, a former Supreme Court advocate himself, is on the record deriding the practice of Supreme Court cold calling. If you need a heart surgeon, Roberts once mused to a reporter, you wouldn't hire the one who called you out of the blue. According to former clerks, other justices have shared Roberts' reservations about Goldstein's entrepreneurial style. Former Justices William H. Rehnquist and Sandra Day O'Connor were known to look pained when presiding over Goldstein cases. Many of the clerks themselves—some of the top legal minds in the country, who exert enormous influence behind the scenes—apparently feel the same. Each year, they perform an annual review, in which they impersonate the justices and a small number of unofficial fixtures at the Court. It is a sign of both his status and the scorn he evokes that Goldstein has merited his own personal roasting. And yet it is Goldstein, and not his detractors, who will surely win out in the end. In fact, he already has. These days, almost all but the whitest of white-shoe Supreme Court advocates do business the Goldstein way. (2006, pp. 14–15)

After several years of rejecting offers to become a part of a larger firm, Goldstein & Howe joined the large Akin Gump firm in May of 2006, because it gave them "access to more clients...and a bigger team who can do Supreme Court work" (Schwartz & Mauro, 2006, p. 22). Additionally, Goldstein now holds adjunct positions at the Harvard and Stanford law schools, where he prepares law students for appellate advocacy.

Another route was developed by Jeffrey Fisher, who clerked for Justice Stevens and watched almost every oral argument the year he was at the Court. Later, as an associate at a large firm in Seattle, he developed two appeals on a *pro bono* basis that were granted cert by the Supreme Court in 2004. He argued both, and won both, against the odds, as he was representing criminal defendants. In April of 2006 he again appeared before the Court—once more representing a criminal defendant—in *United States v. Gonzalez-Lopez,* and again he won, even persuading Justice Scalia, who wrote the opinion for the

Court. As is Goldman, Fisher is now on the faculty of Stanford University, which has a litigation clinic useful in preparing novices of advocacy.

The Role of the Office of the Solicitor General

Some appeals granted cert involve the federal government as a party. In the October 2005 term, 14 of the 72 oral arguments had as either the petitioner or the respondent the United States government or one of its departments or one of its officials (including Vice President Cheney and Attorney General Ashcroft). If the federal government has an interest in the outcome of other appeals, it will submit a brief and ask for time during the oral arguments. (Usually, when the government is an interested third party, it will be allocated 10 minutes of the 30 minutes' time for the side it supports.) In that term, the solicitor general's office participated in that role in an additional 42 cases. So for some cases, 1 of the 20 attorneys from the solicitor general's office may be the sole attorney for one side, and in others he or she may be one of the two advocates representing one side. Attorneys for the solicitor general's office are well trained and experienced in appellate advocacy; for example, when Deputy Solicitor General Lawrence Wallace retired in May 2003, he had argued 157 cases before the Supreme Court (Mauro, 2003a). The solicitor general is frequently called "the 10th justice"; it is even the title of a book (Caplan, 1987). But as former Solicitor General Seth Waxman notes, none of the nine justices refer to the solicitor general that way (Mauro, 2003b).

Regardless, the attorneys from the office of the solicitor general are effective. To determine just how successful these attorneys are, we first examined 12 cases during the 2004–2005 term in which the government prepared an amicus brief and hence the office of solicitor general participated in the oral arguments. In nine of these, the federal government sided with the petitioner, in three, it sided with the respondent. Of the 12 cases, the office of the solicitor general was on the winning side in 11 cases, or 92% (Austin, 2006). In the term completed in June 2006, attorneys from the solicitor general's office were on the winning side in 38 of their 56 cases, or 68%. In the next term, these attorneys participated in 51 cases, winning 42, or an even more impressive 86%. These findings confirm previous research concluding that the federal government does well, compared with other litigants, when it seeks redress in the Supreme Court. For example, in the 1995–1996 term, cert was granted to appeals by the federal government in an amazing 77% of times it requested it (Baum, 1997).

Our findings for the last two terms confirm earlier research that found that historically the side supported by the solicitor general's office has won between 75% and 80% of the time, although there is some variation between presidential administrations (Deen, Ignagni, & Meernik, 2003). One reason the solicitor general's office does so well is that it decides when to take a case.

Just because the federal government has lost at a lower-court level is no guarantee that the solicitor general's office will appeal. As Seth Waxman has explained, he would often tell a cabinet secretary, "I know you feel really strongly about this and are upset that your agency lost. But I just don't think it's really in the interest of the United States for us to take this any further" (Mauro, 2003b, p. 26). Advocates who represent private clients, whether they're financially flush corporations or impecunious criminal defendants, usually don't have this freedom.

Does the Quality of Performance Make Any Difference in the Outcome?

Interestingly, success as a trial attorney may not mean success as an appellate lawyer. "Supreme Court work just calls for different skills than trial work," one Washington attorney told McGuire (1993, p. 71). What are these skills? One attorney at the office of the solicitor general has suggested the following:

> Lawyers have to learn to get away from the facts a little bit, because the Supreme Court is interested in the implications of its decisions, not just the facts of particular cases. You see a lot of advocates who have worked on cases at the trial level where the main idea was to hammer the facts at the court, and they have a hard time in the Supreme Court deviating from their own factual pattern. (McGuire, 1993, p. 71)

Also, the transition from arguing before a state supreme court or a federal circuit court to arguing before the Supreme Court is not always an easy one. Advocates often make the mistake of relying on precedent, which worked at lower-court levels. But, as McGuire has observed, the problem of determining the value that the Court attaches to precedent as well as the substantive meaning of that precedent further distinguishes Supreme Court cases from other appellate litigation. One lawyer told McGuire:

> It's hard to tell the Supreme Court what it meant last term in the XYZ case, when they're all sitting there, and they all participated and wrote it.... You've got to tell them what they *should* have meant or they should do now that they didn't clarify.... They're not bound by precedent in the same way that lower courts are, and they don't give a damn if the circuits have gone one way. If they think that's wrong, they'll just do it—end of discussion. (McGuire, 1993, p. 55)

Advocates whose main appellate experience has been in front of lower courts fail to recognize that the Supreme Court justices are very able; an experienced member of the Supreme Court bar told McGuire: "The quality of work [from the Supreme Court] is exquisitely good, whereas the quality of work that comes out from...the circuits is really an uneven mix. I mean, some of the judges are excellent...but for the most part, they're hacks, really disappointing, some of the garbage they put out" (McGuire, 1993, p. 56).

It is hard to define what makes a good advocate, even though a mass of books, articles, and workshops provide advice. However, one prerequisite for effective practice before the Supreme Court is versatility. As a former staff member of the office of the solicitor general has said, "You cannot hold yourself out as a [Supreme Court] practitioner without the ability to kind of dance through a diverse set of legal issues. And that's not a talent that everybody has. A lot of people get good because they focus on one thing, learn it very well, and stick with it. But that's not a luxury Supreme Court lawyers can afford" (McGuire, 1993, p. 76).

No single pathway to success exists, although in reading a set of oral argument transcripts certain arguments stand out, because of either their effectiveness or their inadequacy. Nevertheless, the goal should be to determine whether effective oral advocacy makes a difference in outcome and, if so, how often it does. Do attorneys who are experienced advocates before the Supreme Court do better than novices who appear for one time only?

I carried out a study to answer these questions. Granted, it is an indirect test, which examines the success rate for advocates with different types of backgrounds. Specifically, it was hypothesized that those advocates who appear before the Court frequently are on the winning side more often, while the "one-and-done" advocates lose more often. In one empirical study seeking to determine if experience as an appellate advocate pays off, McGuire examined the cases decided by the Court from 1977 to 1982 and divided them into three categories: those in which the counsel for the petitioner had more experience, those in which the counsel for the respondent had more experience, and those cases in which neither counsel had more experience. He then determined, for each category, the success rate for the petitioner. When the petitioner's attorney had more experience, this side won 75.3% of the time; when the other side had more experience, the petitioner won only 55.2% of the time. When the two were equal, the petitioner's side won 57.5% of the time. Interestingly, advocates for the petitioner had more experience in more of the cases—369 over this 5-year span, compared to 261 times when the respondent's attorney had more experience. McGuire's conclusion was that experience does make a difference.

An empirical study like McGuire's needs replication, especially since it dealt with the Court more than 20 years ago and it really did not go into detail about the type of experience. I extended the work and differentiated types of experience. The names and titles of the advocates were obtained from the transcripts of the oral arguments on the Supreme Court Web site. Advocates were classified into four types:

1. Attorneys employed by the office of solicitor general
2. Attorneys from state attorney generals' offices

3. Those advocates who have appeared before the Supreme Court several times, i.e., those who have come to be recognized as members of the loosely defined "Supreme Court bar"
4. Those who are arguing before the Supreme Court for the first time; ordinarily, these are attorneys from the home town of one of the parties—those who have been with the case from its origins.

For each case, the decision of the Court and the votes of each justice were determined. For each advocate, a win or loss was recorded, and these were tabulated by category and averaged. Each oral argument in two terms (October 2005 term and October 2006 term) was included.

I described this as an "indirect test" because even if experienced advocates win more often than less-experienced advocates, one cannot conclude that the determinant was solely the quality of their oral advocacy. Too many other variables are uncontrolled—for example, the quality of the written briefs (it is likely that experienced attorneys from larger firms prepare better briefs). It may even be the case that experienced attorneys take on more "winnable" cases, cases that are likely to draw a responsive chord from the justices. The first-time Supreme Court advocate cannot pick and choose cases. And it may be that the justices treat experienced advocates differently, as recognition of their familiarity with the attorney and his or her reputation. Certain advocates may have an established reputation (and an "Establishment" reputation) such that traditionalists on the Court may give them the benefit of a doubt. When their names are on the petition for *certiorari*, it's a signal to the justices that "this guy knows what he's talking about" (Coyle, 1997, p. A12). Others may have an image not in keeping with what the justices think an advocate should be, such as Thomas Goldstein, whose cold-calling of possible clients was viewed unfavorably by Chief Justice Roberts. Does this carry over to a justice's treatment of the advocate during the arguments? Consider the oral arguments for *Georgia v. Randolph*. Representing Scott Randolph, Goldstein was able to utter only one sentence—28 words—before Chief Justice Roberts interrupted him. Later Justice Roberts asked a hypothetical question of Goldstein, and then interrupted him during Goldstein's response answer to insist, "What is your answer to that case?" (*Georgia v. Randolph,* transcript of the oral argument, p. 54). Chief Justice Roberts eventually voted against Goldstein's client, although there are numerous reasons (beyond any possible animosity) for his doing so, stemming from his ideology, his take on previous cases, and his interpretation of the Fourth Amendment.

For the 2005–2006 term the results are as follows. As noted earlier, attorneys from the office of solicitor general argued before the Court in 56 cases; their side won 38 cases, or 68% of the time. Attorneys who were members of the Supreme Court bar won less often; in fact, their winning percentage was barely more than half of the cases—18 of 35 appearances, or 51%. (Of course, it should be noted that in some of these cases, each side had as its advocate a member of the Supreme Court bar, so both could not win.) Surprisingly, attorneys from state attorney generals' offices were quite effective, winning 19 times and losing only 8 times, for a success rate of 70%. The least successful group was the one-time attorneys, with 28 wins and 45 losses, or 38% successes.

For the term ending in June 2007, results were generally consistent with those of the previous term. The success rate of 86% for attorneys from the office of the solicitor general was even higher than the term before. Once again, the first-time advocates were the least successful group; appearing 62 times, only 20, or 32%, were on the winning side. (It should be noted that in seven cases, the two attorneys opposing each other were both first-timers, however.) Attorneys from state attorney generals' offices again won more than they lost, with 12 cases versus 9, but their success rate of 57% was below that of the term before. Members of the Supreme Court bar were successful more often than they lost—27 times versus 16 times, or 63%—but again perhaps not as high as one would expect.

Conclusion

Successful advocacy at the Supreme Court level is a learned skill and a highly specialized one. Just because an attorney has been an eminent trial lawyer is no guarantee of success at the appellate level. Opportunities for errors are rampant, and the best guarantee to avoid them is to practice and observe others at the task. Some evidence exists that those attorneys whose specialty is appellate practice win a higher percentage of their cases before the Supreme Court.

4

Justices' Questions and Statements

I think the simplest way to put it is, in the courts of appeals
you're basically talking about what the law is. In the Supreme
Court, you're talking about what the law ought to be. It's
more policy-oriented, much more inclined to go beyond the
narrow confines of a particular case to talk about how this
decision would impact on the development of the law generally.
—An experienced advocate quoted by McGuire (1993, p. 53)

What the Oral Argument Is and Isn't

An oral argument is not like an interview that one reads in a newspaper or
magazine, which presents questions and answers distinctly separated. Nor is
it like an interview that one watches on television, in which the interviewee
may occasionally interrupt the questioner, but still maintain the format of
question–answer–question–answer, etc.

The analogy of the advocate being a guest at a party, presented in Chapter 3, gets closer, but still lacks some essential ingredients. A psychological
analysis of Supreme Court oral arguments emphasizes the following points:

1. The justices are in control and hold the power. If the analogy of a "conversation" is maintained, it is more like that between a superior and a
   subordinate.

2. The standard operating procedure permits the justices to interrupt counsel at any time. They may make statements as well as questions, they may make comments back and forth to each other, they may change the topic at will without apology, and they may focus on rather trivial aspects of the case. The ground rules of ordinary conversation are routinely violated.

3. Because advocates are in the position of supplicants, they must tolerate abuses of the traditional social exchange out of the fear of gaining the ire, or the further ire, of a justice or justices.

4. The give-and-take during an oral argument is like no other phenomenon in regard to the number of exchanges per minute, the number of interruptions, and the shifts from one questioner to another.

5. An oral argument is an atypical conversation, not one between two friends who see each other at a cocktail party and catch up on recent developments in their lives. The justices know quite a bit about the advocate's position; it is not a conversation that begins at the beginning but rather reflects a great deal of shared knowledge between the two participants.

6. To continue the analogy of a cocktail party, the Court values some guests more than others. As discussed in Chapter 3, there may be some tension between Chief Justice Roberts and frequent advocate Thomas Goldstein. Likewise, some advocates, because of their reputation or their entrenched position in the Supreme Court bar, get cut some slack:

> An attorney who routinely crafts excellent opening statements is Deputy Solicitor General Michael R. Dreeben. He is one of the few advocates in recent years that Supreme Court justices have permitted to give his complete opening with any regularity, and he gets to deliver it about half the time. The Supreme Court gives Dreeben that leeway out of respect for his ability to answer their difficult questions and because the Court knows that its patience will be rewarded with a succinct expression of the points the government wants to make. (Frederick, 2003b, p. 22)

Consider each 1-hour session. Our analysis of 24 oral arguments during the 2004–2005 term found that petitioners were the recipients of an average of almost 50 questions or statements from the justices during their 30 minutes, and respondents were the recipients of more than 40 during an equivalent time. This means an exchange between the advocate and a justice took, on average, only about 30 seconds, an amazing figure, especially given that advocates more generally permitted some extended time at the beginning of their presentations to introduce their main point or points.

We also analyzed the length of time, measured in words spoken, before advocates were interrupted when they began their presentations. For example, in the 2005–2006 term, on average, petitioners spoke 169 words before being interrupted; respondents spoke 125 words before a justice intervened. That may seem like a long time—169 words constitute about eight sentences, enough to get a basic point introduced. But there was tremendous variation in length of utterances by petitioners before an interruption, from 38 words in *House v. Bell* to 518 words in *Merrill Lynch, Pierce, Fenner, & Smith Inc. v. Dabit*. The petitioner in the latter case got more than 5 minutes of uninterrupted time at the beginning of his presentation.

As noted previously, respondents generally received less uninterrupted start-up time, but again there were huge variations between cases. Chief Justice Roberts interrupted the respondent, Solicitor General Clement, in *Wisconsin Right to Life, Inc. v. Federal Election Commission* after 24 words (one sentence). In contrast, in *Laboratory Corp. of America Holdings v. Metabolite Laboratories, Inc.*, the respondent, Miguel Estrada, was allowed to utter 536 words without interruption. (Estrada, a former Supreme Court law clerk and now with the law firm of Gibson, Dunn, & Crutcher, had been nominated by President George W. Bush to a position on the D.C. Circuit court but the nomination was withdrawn after it generated a filibuster by Senate Democrats.) Perhaps the Court let Estrada speak so long because his introductory statement was so well organized and expressed in plain language:

> This was a hard fought jury trial in which the jury rejected everything LabCorp had to sell. That judgment should be affirmed for three reasons. The first is LabCorp never asked the trial judge or the Federal Circuit to declare the patent invalid under Section 101, which is an affirmative defense they had to plead in the answer and prove by clear and convincing evidence. Second, they're simply wrong on the merits of the 101 case under this Court's cases. And third, you can search their brief in vain for a workable test for patentable subject matter that would invalidate this patent and not wreak complete havoc to the patent world by calling into question numerous diagnostic tests in medicine and otherwise, pharmaceuticals and other inventions (transcript of oral argument, pp. 29–30).

Classification of Questions

Several observers of the Court have offered systems to classify questions and statements by the justices during oral arguments. In a study described in detail in Chapter 7, Sarah Shullman (2004) classified each on one dimension, as sympathetic or hostile, on a five-point scale. Aaron Hull (1997) suggested they could be put into one of three major categories:

1. Affirming questions: those that are asked to aid an attorney in answering a question, or to provide a new direction of thought. "They are generally signaled by a calm voice tone of the justice, and an enthusiastic affirmative response by the attorney" (p. 28).

2. Inquisitive questions: those dealing with case facts alone, as in case-framing at the beginning of the oral argument. An example would be, "Mr. Tribe, isn't this case about...?"
3. Challenges, or abrupt interruptions of attorneys in a harsh tone of voice. The net result of these is often to corner attorneys into saying things that are potentially damaging to their case.

The most comprehensive classification of questions is found in Frederick's *The Art of Oral Advocacy* (2003b). He proposed four major types of questions, with specific subtypes within each one:

1. Background questions, including questions about the parties involved, the opinion under review, the record, and the positions of different courts on the issue
2. Questions about the scope of the rule being advocated, including questions about the party's position about precedents, about case law, about statutory text and legislative history, and questions seeking concessions from the counsel
3. Questions about the implications of the rule being advocated, including hypothetical questions and questions about analogous legal contexts
4. Questions reflecting judicial idiosyncrasies, including those from the prior experience or personal knowledge of the justice, and questions based on the justice's philosophy or constitutional approach

An elaboration of each type follows.

Background Questions

As Frederick (2003b) has observed, the variety of background questions can be quite broad, and so an advocate needs to spend a great deal of time preparing for them. Chief Justice Rehnquist was well-known for his tendency to check on the citations whenever an advocate referred to a precedent, and his seemingly infinite knowledge of past cases meant that advocates had to be on their toes when citing past rulings.

Justices may inquire about the specific meaning of a sentence in the district court's or circuit court's opinion. In *Toyota Motor Manufacturing v. Williams* (2002) such an interaction occurred between the justices and John Roberts, who at the time was an attorney with the Hogan & Hartson law firm, specializing in appellate advocacy, and representing Toyota. The specific issue concerned a claim that Toyota had violated the 1990 Americans with Disabilities Act (ADA) by not accommodating a worker's claim of inability to perform certain manual tasks on the assembly line. Mr. Roberts needed to be alert to questions about the circuit court's opinion so that he could point out what was, in Toyota's view, the error in that court's ruling.

Question: Mr. Roberts, may I just stop you on something you just said? I thought the Sixth Circuit said in its opinion that it had considered recreation, household choices, living generally, as well as the work-related impairments.

Mr. Roberts: A very important sentence that I think has to be read carefully. In the first place, it doesn't say that we've looked at the record and considered those. It was a generic assumption: The assumption is, well, if she can't do this assembly line work, that must affect other areas, recreation and household chores. A generic assumption like that is wrong, first, because the ADA specifies you have to look at the individual impacts; second, because the impairments we're talking about, myotendinitis and that sort of thing, affect different people in widely different ways. You can't assume, just because someone cannot do the repetitive work for an extended period of time, that's going to have an effect. (*Toyota v. Williams*, 2002, transcript of oral argument, pp. 9–10).

(Prior to the October 2004 term, the transcripts of oral arguments did not identify which justice was speaking. From the way the question was introduced, it probably was Justice Stevens.)

Questions about the Scope of the Rule Being Advocated

Frederick (2003b) noted that the basic focus of the oral-argument proceedings is the rule of law at issue. Thus, the Court will want to know how the advocates and their clients see the contours of the rule, its legal basis and origins, as identified through precedents, text of statutes, or legislative history.

It has been said that the Supreme Court feels less requirement to follow precedents than do the lower courts. As Frederick notes, "precedent becomes less important as the case moves from the court of appeals to the Supreme Court, where the advocate is less likely to face questions raising distinctions or nuances of doctrine. In the Supreme Court, for example, oral arguments rarely turn on debates or colloquies involving precedent. The justices will have read the key cases and decided for themselves how applicable they find those precedents to the case" (2003b, pp. 51–52).

But still, counsel can be asked about precedents. In 1998 the Court dealt with the conflict between New Jersey and New York over which state held jurisdiction of Ellis Island. This was a case decided under the Court's "original jurisdiction," that is, disputes between two states avoid the lower federal courts and go directly to the Supreme Court for resolution. One of the justices asked one of the advocates about the applicability of a case between Washington and Oregon, extending back to 1908, a case that might have reflected the same principle.

Similarly, advocates have been accustomed to invoking the legislative history of a statute to support their position. But Justice Scalia has expressed his hostility to the use of legislative history "for the purposes of giving authoritative context to the meaning of a statutory text" (*Wisconsin Public Intervenor v. Mortier*, 1991, dissent, p. 2490). His view was grounded in the position that "the entire Congress has not passed or offered support to a House or Senate committee report" (Frederick, 2003b, p. 55). So such questions are predictable.

Questions about Implications of the Rule Being Advocated

What are the consequences that will occur if the Court rules in a certain way? It is inevitable that justices will want to know how each advocate would answer this question. Two types of questions deal with implications: hypothetical questions and questions dealing with analogies.

Hypothetical Questions

Even 20 years ago, hypothetical questions were recognized as "a way of life in today's Court" (Prettyman, 1984, p. 556), queries that every conscientious advocate must expect. Justices relish hypotheticals. Frederick noted that "In court an observer can see the way members of the Court lean forward in anticipation of getting the answer to a hypothetical and then lean back when the advocate answers, 'Yes, because————.' Alternatively, when an advocate begins with the explanation rather than a simple answer, members of the Court tend to become frustrated. They lean forward even more and become more prone to interrupt" (2003b, pp. 60–61).

Why are there so many hypotheticals? Prettyman has suggested several reasons:

> One may be that prolonged periods of listening to argument, good and bad, the justices are simply reaching for anything that varies the routine, dispels the gloom, enlightens the proceedings, or adds luster to an otherwise unvarying occasion. A more generous view is that the Court is testing the outer reaches both of what the advocate is asking it to declare and of what the Court may, in fact, have to decide. "If we take this tack," the justices are asking, "how will it affect a different set of facts?" "What happens if we add this or that variant?" "What are the outer limits of what you are proposing?" "What will the next case look like?" "And the next?" "How narrowly must we construct our decision in order to avoid all kinds of problems?" "Or how broadly must we fashion it in order to cover the essential points that may be troubling the lower courts?" It is a testing, a probing, an evolving process that hopefully will illuminate the whole. (1984, p. 556)

The use of hypothetical questions sometimes suffers from the temptation to escalate beyond all reasonable grounds. The oral argument in the case of

Maryland v. Pringle, held on November 3, 2003, is an example. The facts of the case are as follows. Joseph Pringle was a passenger in a car that was stopped on a routine matter in Baltimore, Maryland. When the police officer asked for identification and the car's registration, the driver reached over and opened the glove compartment. The police officer spotted a large wad of money (later determined to be $763, it belonged to Pringle). On that basis, he searched the car and found five baggies of crack cocaine jammed behind an arm rest in the back seat. The officer took the three occupants of the car—the driver, Mr. Pringle (who was seated in the front seat), and a passenger seated in the back seat—into the police station for questioning. Pringle confessed that the drugs belonged to him, upon which the other two occupants were released. After he had been convicted, Pringle appealed, claiming a violation of his Fourth Amendment rights to be free of searches and seizures, because the police did not have probable cause to suspect him of drug possession. The Maryland Court of Appeals agreed with him, noting that since Pringle was in the front seat and the drugs were in the back, there was no probable cause to arrest him.

Gary E. Bair, assistant Maryland attorney general, represented the state of Maryland, and he found himself confronted with an escalating list of hypothetical questions, as follows:

Question: In your view, is this very fact-specific so it might come out differently if the money and the drugs had been located in some little pocket next to the driver as opposed to some rear-seat passenger or other passenger?

Mr. Bair: I think one factor that would significantly change the totality of circumstances here would be, for instance, if the drugs had been found on the person of one of the passengers.

Question: No, that wasn't my question. What if—

Mr. Bair: If it had been

Question: —they were found very close to the driver, you know, sometimes there's a little pocket right next to—

Mr. Bair: In the door?

Question: —on the door, on the driver's side. Suppose it were there but you had a passenger in the front and in the rear. Any different result?

Mr. Bair: Not in this case, no. I think—I think if—if the drugs are found in a common area of the passenger compartment of the car—

Question: How about the trunk?

Mr. Bair: I think the trunk changes things a little bit, but of course you have to look at the totality of circumstances, Justice Ginsburg.

Question: Why a little bit? I thought this whole case was predicated— your whole case was predicated on those drugs between the

Mr. Bair: That's—

Question: Now, if you have something in a locked trunk, it truly is not accessible to the passengers.

Mr. Bair: It certainly is not as accessible, but, for instance, if there had been a large quantity of drugs in the trunk or if there had been a dead body in the trunk, I think then there is a—the calculus changes in terms of the totality of circumstances, and I think if it were that situation, even though the particular evidence was in the trunk, I think there's still a—a strong inference that could be drawn that everyone in the car knew about it, because who would take the chance in terms of taking along innocent passengers—

Question: Well, let's stick to the five—these five bags that were stuck in a Ziploc bag. The Ziploc bag is in the trunk, not a dead body.

Mr. Bair: I understand. I think in that case there would be a much closer case. It would be a much more difficult case vis-a-vis all three occupants of the car.

Question: But under—

Question: Okay, what about the—

Question: —under—under your view, if—if the car is in a high-crime area and some mother gets a ride from her son who she perhaps doesn't know has been involved in drugs, then if drugs are found anywhere in that car, she's subject to arrest and—sufficient for charge?

Mr. Bair: Not—not—

Question: I mean, suppose it's at—in the middle of the day and she's going to the grocery store, we don't have it at 3:00 A.M. in an area where drugs are frequently sold. Does that enter into the calculus?

Mr. Bair: I think it does, Your Honor. I think, obviously with—with—with the totality of the circumstances anytime you change—and, of course, some of these are going to have more minor impact, some are going to have more major impact. But in this case you had, of course, 3:16 in the morning, three men who were roughly of the same age who appeared to be intimately connected with one another, you had the drugs and the money. I think here's a very strong case, but I agree, Justice O'Connor—

Question: What if there had been four people in the car?

Mr. Bair: I don't know that four people would change things.

Question: How about six?

Mr. Bair: I think within the—

Question: Or what if it was a minivan and there were eight in the minivan?

(Laughter.)

Mr. Bair: I'm not sure it changes it significantly, Your Honor. I think that the most significant—

Question: You think that with eight people in the minivan you could arrest all eight and hold them over for trial?

Mr. Bair: I think if you have the identical circumstances to these in terms of the time, how well-acquainted they all appeared, the fact there was money, the fact that there were drugs packaged for distribution. It appeared to the officer, a reasonable inference, that there was a drug-distribution common enterprise.

Question: But the distribution, as I understand it, was just enough to take care of a big party. There was no evidence that they were for sale, was there?

Mr. Bair: Well, the evidence, at the time the officer made the arrest, I think he could draw an inference that there was cash proceeds perhaps of former drug sales, prior drug sales, and there were five individually packaged crack—hits of crack cocaine.

Question: And the charge was possession with intent to distribute, wasn't it?

Mr. Bair: Yes, it was both simple possession and possession with intent to distribute, and he was convicted.

Question: How about if it had been a bus? Now, we've gone from the sedan to the minivan, how about the bus?

Mr. Bair: I think a bus is different, Your Honor. I think a bus changes things significantly in the—in the context of, of course, the numbers of people are much greater, and then there's—

Question: Are you talking about a public bus or you're talking about a chartered bus?

(Laughter.)

Mr. Bair: I think that would affect obviously the totality of circumstances as well. (*Maryland v. Pringle,* 2004, transcript of oral arguments, pp. 7–12.)

And this was not all. Justices O'Connor, Ginsburg, Stevens, and Souter, at different times, offered a variety of "for instances": "What if it were undisputed that one of the three men were a hitchhiker?" (Souter). "What if it was the driver and two hitchhikers?" (Stevens). "What is there's a young child in the car, and it's the middle of the day, and he's dropping the child off at school?" (O'Connor). It was left to Justice Kennedy to broaden the fact situation; he asked whether the police, upon finding a dead body and two possible killers, each claiming the other did it, could arrest them both. (Bair answered that both potential killers could be subject to arrest.)

This torrent of hypothetical questions consumed about one fifth of the time allotted to Mr. Bair. But despite the apparent leaning of the justices from their questions, the Court ruled unanimously that the police officer's actions did not violate Fourth Amendment protections. One possible contributing reason for the outcome was that Pringle's attorney, Nancy Forster, Maryland's deputy public defender, did not fare any better in her oral argument. In response to a question from Justice O'Connor, she corrected the justice: "It was 3:16 A.M." (never a good idea!) And then added, "Anyone with children that age knows that on Saturday night the evening doesn't even begin until; 10 or 11" (p. 32), causing Chief Justice Rehnquist to respond, "Well, a lot of people wouldn't refer to children as being in their 20s, I think" (p. 32). She disputed that the amount of cash in the glove compartment was really an issue, leading Justice Souter to inquire, "Do *you* have a roll of bills exposed in your glove compartment?" "At times I do," she responded.

The fact that hypothetical questions can be quite lengthy poses a challenge to counsel. One hypothetical question in the case of *Board of Education v. Pico* (1982) was 142 words long. Furthermore, these questions may stretch the limits of credulity such that if the advocate were in a situation where his or her answer was not so important; the response might be hearty laughter or a heavy expletive.

For the unrehearsed advocate, hypothetical questions present a challenge. One experienced member of the Supreme Court bar told McGuire:

> I'm astonished how many people argue before the Court who have not prepared to answer even the simplest hypothetical....A good example is the argument [in a case] where they stopped people to test for alcohol, and O'Connor, for example, was asking, "Well, if you had a section of Detroit that was extremely drug-ridden and dangerous, could you stop people to check, you know, identification and so forth?" And I was surprised to read that [the lawyer] seemed not to have anticipated that question. (McGuire, 1993, p. 54)

Even in the courtroom, inexperienced advocates sometimes respond to hypotheticals by saying, "That's not my case." Frederick concluded that "this has to rank among the most insulting answers possible to a question from the bench" (2003b, p. 60).

Use of Analogies

Sometimes a hypothetical question can take the form of an analogy that seems to deal with a situation far afield from the facts at hand, and hence belittle the significance of the issue presented (Frederick, 2003b). An example of this scenario is described below.

In 1865 a ship sank off the coast of California with a shipment alleged to contain $2 million in gold and an army payroll of $250,000. Many such wrecks lay undiscovered for years, but new technology has led to finding many of them. Under the Abandoned Shipwreck Act of 1987, Congress provided that going back in history, each of those abandoned shipwrecks in the coastal waters of the United States belongs to the state to which it is adjacent. But Congress did not specify the definition of "abandoned," and if the property was abandoned, whoever found it got to keep it. But if the vessel was not considered abandoned, the owner retained ownership rights and the treasure finder was only entitled to an award for salvage costs and time. Thus the issue in a case that came before the Court in 1998, titled *California v. Deep Sea Research,* was to determine the legal standard for abandonment. The United States argued that under maritime law, an object is considered "'abandoned' if a long period of time has elapsed and the owner has not taken steps to recover the property" (Frederick, 2003b).

In an attempt to raise an analogy, Justice Scalia posed the following hypothetical question to the government lawyer during the oral argument in this case:

> Suppose I drop a silver dollar down a grate, and I try to bring it up with a piece of gum on a stick, and I can't do it, and I shrug my shoulders and walk off because I have not gotten it, and then somebody comes up and lifts up the grate and gets my silver dollar. Is that his silver dollar? Have I abandoned it just because I could not get it? I still think it's my silver dollar, I haven't said, you know, I don't want it any more. (*California v. Deep Sea Research,* 1998, transcript of oral argument, pp. 30–31)

But the lawyer's response adroitly put his answer back in the context of his theory of the case: "Justice Scalia, if you waited 130 years without attempting…to get your silver dollar, it might be appropriate to infer that you have abandoned it" (p. 32).

Questions about Judicial Idiosyncrasies

The fourth type of question in Frederick's taxonomy reflects the fact that "each judge will bring a distinctive style to the bench at oral argument" (2003b, p. 67). The styles of current and recent members of the Court will be explored in Chapter 5.

Motives of the Justices' Questions

Why does a justice ask a question during the oral argument? Several possible reasons exist:

A. To learn information perceived to be missing from the record

Justices may believe that they lack some essential information that they must have before deciding a case. An analysis of transcripts finds that such questions may occur, especially at the beginning of the oral argument. The advocate probably reacts to such questions with mixed feelings—both relief ("Here's a beginning question that I can clearly answer!") and chagrin ("Did I really fail to cover that in the brief?")

B. To clarify what the advocate's position is

Justices inform the advocate just what question they want them to consider, both in their briefs and oral arguments. (Sometimes appeals will raise a multitude of issues, but the Court narrows the focus.) This occurred in the case *Regents of the University of California v. Bakke.*

Allan Bakke was denied admission to the medical school of the University of California at Davis in 1973, even though his grade point average was higher than those of minority students who were granted entrance through a separate admissions process. He filed a lawsuit claiming that preferential treatment of minorities was a form of racial discrimination against whites and that the university's procedure of reserving some of its admissions for minorities denied him equal protection of the law under the Fourteenth Amendment. He received support from the state trial court and the California Supreme Court, so the university regents appealed to the U.S. Supreme Court (in *Regents of the University of California v. Bakke,* 1978). Bakke's lawyer, Reynold Colvin, had never before argued a case before the Supreme Court. He used his precious oral-argument time to introduce his client and himself, to give a background to the case, and to detail his efforts to get relief in the past. The justices grew increasingly frustrated:

> Finally, Justice Lewis F. Powell, Jr., broke in impatiently. "The University doesn't deny or dispute the basic facts. They are perfectly clear. We are here—at least I am here—primarily to hear a constitutional argument. You have devoted 20 minutes to laboring a fact, if I may say so. I would like help, I really would, on the constitutional issues. Would you address that, please?" (McGuire, 1993, p. 3).

C. To point out problems in the advocate's argument

This certainly is the most important type of question. It may be motivated by a justice who has already made up his or her mind, or it may reflect a justice who is sympathetic but uncertain. Sometimes the justice expresses his or her concern quite explicitly. In the case of *Dodd v. United States*, Chief Justice Rehnquist told the petitioner's attorney:

> The problem with your argument, Mr. Bergmann, seems to be addressed to the idea that Congress intended to sweep quite broadly here. But I don't think that the necessary inference at all. We're dealing with a situation, as Justice O'Connor points out, where we have very rarely held that a decision is retroactive. So it's already a very small class of cases, and the Government's view makes it an even smaller class of cases. But that doesn't mean the statute

doesn't work. It just means it doesn't work for a lot of people who are excluded from it. (*Dodd v. United States*, 2005, transcript of oral argument, p. 18)

D. To present a viewpoint contradictory to that of the advocate

The case of *Carey v. Musladin*, heard by the Supreme Court in October 2006, was generated by a murder trial in which members of the victim's family sat on the front row wearing buttons with a photograph of the victim. The defendant, Matthew Musladin, was found guilty. He appealed his conviction, claiming that the spectators wearing buttons had prevented his receiving a fair trial. The 9th Circuit Court of Appeals agreed with him; hence the state of California appealed to the Supreme Court.

After Gregory Ott, the Deputy Attorney General of California, said a couple of sentences, Justice Souter interrupted to challenge his interpretation that the closest cases to this one were not relevant. Justice Souter had a different take on these: "It went a little beyond that. [In those cases] Justice Marshall announced not only the possibility of inherent prejudice, but he spoke of practices which raised a risk that improper factors would come into play.... It seems to me that if you're going to talk about a criterion of a test or a standard...you have to [discuss] the acceptable risk of improper factors" (*Carey v. Musladin*, 2007, transcript of oral arguments, pp. 3–4).

E. To determine the implications or limits of the advocate's position

The use of hypotheticals may be motivated to test the limits of an advocate's position. In his assault on the petitioner's argument in the *Carey v. Musladin* case, Justice Souter later asked him, "Instead of putting a picture of the victim, [suppose the button has] a statement 'Hang Musladin,' which is worn everyday by three members of his family who sit behind the prosecution table within sight of the jury. Assume these facts. Would habeas relief be required?" (transcript of oral arguments, p. 21).

F. To provide support for the advocate's position

In the oral arguments during the *Musladin* case, Justice Scalia supported the argument that the defendant had received a fair trial. He showed his support for the California state attorney who had been challenged by Justice Souter by offering a benign motive for the family's wearing buttons. He told the attorney, "It [the buttons] just conveys at most to the jury...we have been deprived of someone we love, you should take this matter very seriously and consider the case carefully. It is an important matter to us. And therefore, you should deliberate carefully. I don't know it means anything more than that" (*Carey v. Musladin*, 2007, transcript of oral argument, p. 22).

G. To provide tension reduction, or at least humor

Among current justices, it is Antonin Scalia who most often asks the impish question or interjects the off-the-wall comment; some of his classic moments are described in Chapter 5. But in the case of *eBay v. MercExchange*, a patent-infringement case, argued before the Court on March 29, 2006, it was Justice Kennedy who provided some humorous relief. "Patent troll" has emerged as a pejorative phrase for companies or individuals that have dormant patents and use them to challenge the validity of patents held by large corporations. Justice Kennedy asked Carter Phillips whether "troll" meant the ogre under the bridge or fishing for something (p. 26).

H. To communicate with another justice rather than the advocate

In a broad sense, all communication at the oral argument is a dialogue between justices; the advocate may become "a mere conduit for the members of the bench to speak to one another" (Frederick, 2003b, p. 5). Certainly some questions addressed to counsel are really messages to other justices (Prettyman, 1984). They may in reality be saying, "Look, if you start down that road, this is where it will lead you." Or: "Do you really want to go as far as I think you are heading, even if you have the votes" (Prettyman, 1984, p. 556).

The present composition of the Court exudes collegiality and only a few comments or questions during oral arguments appear to be veiled attacks on colleagues. Early in Justice Ginsburg's tenure on the bench there was some rumbling in reaction to her tendency to interrupt the questions by other justices. And for all his boisterousness, Justice Scalia mostly saves his criticisms of his colleagues for his memorable "Ninograms" and written dissents.

But 40 years ago the tendency of Justice Felix Frankfurter to consume so much time during the oral arguments created tension and conflict (Cooper, 1995). During one oral argument, Frankfurter repeatedly insisted that the advocate provide one case that supported the proposition he had advanced. Justice Douglas looked at the advocate and said, "Don't bother to send Justice Frankfurter the list he wants: I'd be happy to do it myself" (Douglas, 1980, p. 181). Even Chief Justice Warren was frustrated by Frankfurter's behavior during oral arguments. During one session, "Frankfurter interrupted Warren and reworded a question which the Chief Justice was putting to counsel. Warren angrily said: 'Let him answer *my* question. He is confused enough as it is.' Frankfurter bitterly retorted, 'Confused by Justice Frankfurter, I assume.'" (Cooper, 1995, p. 73).

On rare occasions two justices may forego the dialogue with an advocate and start addressing each other directly. This occurred in the re-argument of the case of *Kansas v. Marsh*, on April 24, 2006. The case dealt with the instructions in death-penalty cases, and Justices Scalia and Souter engaged in a dialogue as follows, as the attorney general of Kansas stood and listened:

Justice Scalia: It seems to me it sounds different if you put it differently. Surely, it's a reasoned moral response to say, "We have found these horrible aggravating factors in this murder. It's not even your usual murder. There are these terrible aggravating factors. Three of them, we found.

	And we further find that there is no mitigating evidence to outweigh those aggravating factors." That seems to me a perfectly valid moral response.
Mr. Kline:	That is correct, Justice Scalia.
Justice Souter:	But that is not our case, is it? Because our case is not, "We don't find that the mitigators outweigh." Our case is, "We find the mitigators are of equal weight." That's why you get to equipoise. It's not a question of the failure of mitigators to predominate.
Justice Scalia:	No.
Justice Souter:	It is the sufficiency of mitigators to equal in weight. And that's what poses the problem, it seems to me.
Justice Scalia:	But it seems to me that to be equal in weight is not to predominate. And that's all the jury is saying—
Mr. Kline:	I would agree, Justice Scalia—
Justice Scalia:	—if there's nothing to outweigh the aggravating factors.
Justice Souter:	Of course it is not to predominate, but it is something more precise than merely not predominating. It is a fact, in effect, that you really don't know, if all you know is that they don't predominate. (*Kansas v. Marsh*, 2006, transcript of oral argument, pp. 10–12)

A Case as an Example

In order to classify motive-based questions, I have selected a sample case, *Beard v. Banks*, argued before the Court on March 27, 2006. (The Supreme Court had decided another case titled *Beard v. Banks* 2 years earlier, but that one dealt with another prisoner, George Banks.) The issue in this case was whether a maximum-security prison's policy of denying nonreligious newspapers, magazines, and photographs is related to its goals of protecting prison security and promoting prisoner rehabilitation. The Long Term Segregation Unit of Pennsylvania's Department of Corrections, at Pittsburgh, confines those prisoners considered to be violent or disruptive and denies them access to nonreligious periodicals, but they can earn access if they display good behavior. Ronald Banks sued the Secretary of Pennsylvania's Department of Corrections, Jeffrey A. Beard. Beard moved for a summary judgment, which the district court granted, concluding that the prison's policy was rationally related to its goals of security and rehabilitation. In doing so, it relied on a four-part analysis spelled out in an earlier decision, *Turner v. Safely* (1984). The U.S. Court of Appeals for the Third Circuit overturned the decision, concluding that the Department of Corrections failed to present evidence that this action could accomplish its goal of rehabilitation. By a 2-to-1 vote the circuit court ruled that the policy violated the First Amendment. Interestingly, the dissenting judge in the Third Circuit was Samuel Alito. His appointment as a Supreme Court justice was confirmed before the oral arguments for this case in March 2006, so he did not participate in them or vote on the case.

The justices asked the attorney for the petitioner; Louisa Rovelli, Executive Deputy Attorney General of Pennsylvania, and the attorney from the office of the solicitor general, Jonathan Marcus (the federal government was an amicus curiae), a total of 56 questions during their allotted time. The attorney for the prisoner, the respondent, was asked 49 questions. An analysis of the types of questions led to the following observations:

1. The first questions to the petitioner were of a predictable type. In fact, each of the first five was a fact-seeking one (and each was by Justice Stevens). These were easily classifiable; they asked about the number of prisoners involved, how long they had been on the Long Term Segregation Unit, and how frequently their status had been reviewed.
2. Later in the oral argument, the frequency of fact-seeking questions to the petitioner diminished, although Justice Stevens did direct a few to the solicitor general's office attorney, when he took over. In contrast, of the 49 questions to the respondent, only 3 were classified as fact seeking.
3. As the frequency of fact-seeking questions diminished, those questions seeking clarification and those expressing problems with the advocate's position became more frequent. The difference in these is not always clear, but here is an example of a clarification question:

> Justice Souter: Now, on your theory of behavior modification, would it, nonetheless, be open to the State to say, no, you may not receive any more legal materials and you may not go to the library to look at them? Because that's something you very much want to do. And in order to do that, you've got to shape up—and get moved down to a lesser level of security. Would that—I'm not saying that the State is—is about to do that, but on your theory, could the State do that? (p. 11).

In contrast, questions and comments that point out a perceived problem in the advocate's position have a different focus:

> Justice Ginsburg: But I thought that there was a genuine security concern, which I think you pretty much said doesn't exist here when you consider what they can have in the cell (p. 16).
>
> Justice Kennedy (to the respondent's attorney): But—but—the whole rationale of your case—if I were you writing your brief, I

would have this problem. This really matters to the inmates, but that's exactly the State's point. That's the reason it's taken away. It really means something. And I—I just—I just don't know what to do with that conundrum (p. 30).

4. Not surprisingly, Justice Scalia was the justice who most often provided humor or tension reduction. Only 10 of the 105 questions and statements by the justices were made by him—much below his typical rate of comment—and three of these were humorous. For example, discussion had focused on the presence of newspapers in cells as a security threat, because inmates could set them on fire, and Justice Scalia interjected: "Do you know what kind of fire you can make with the Sunday *New York Times?*" (p. 41).

5. Sarcasm and ridicule were quite infrequent. In fact, only two questions were so classified, and to do so was a stretch.

Justice Ginsburg (to the petitioner's attorney):   Apart from these two, access to the courts and cruel and unusual punishment, then anything goes for this set of incorrigible prisoners? They can take away—the First Amendment in other words is out the window. They have no First Amendment rights that the State needs to respect. (p. 22).

Justice Breyer (to the respondent's attorney):   But is there other—are there other bases? Because so far your argument is they're [the prisoner] so bad that you might as well give them whatever they want because it won't matter. (p. 38)

6. Questions made to persuade another justice are very hard to detect, and none was so coded. Doubtless, this could have been the intent of several questions to one advocate or another, but it seemingly requires the other justice to be addressed in order for the question to be so coded.

7. Similarly, concession-seeking statements and questions were rare. The only one that was so coded revealed itself in its wording:

Justice Scalia: Do—do you concede that just because a right is enumerated, it means it cannot be entirely taken away in prison? (p. 21).

(The attorney answered, "No.")

8. Hypothetical questions could fit into several motive categories, most typically in the "limits-testing" category. But they were almost nonexistent. By far the most frequent goals of questions were to gain more information and facts, to clarify what the attorneys are claiming, and to present the justices' problems with these claims.

5

The Idiosyncratic Nature of Justices' Behavior during Oral Arguments

He [Justice Scalia] asks far too many questions and he takes over the whole argument of counsel.

—Justice Harry Blackmun (O'Brien, 2000, p. 261)

An Example—Idiosyncratic, But Was It Unanticipated?

The case was presumed to become a landmark case, because it was expected to define the limits of First Amendment rights to free speech. More specifically, it dealt with the legality of a St. Paul, Minnesota, ordinance that prohibited cross-burning on public or private property. And it attracted attention because a known racist, albeit an adolescent, had sought to intimidate an African-American family only several months after they had moved into a mostly white working-class neighborhood.

But when the oral arguments for *R.A.V. v. City of St. Paul* were held on December 4, 1991, few could have foretold what would be the initial set of questions directed to Thomas Foley, representing the respondent. Even before Foley could say, "May it please the Court," Justice Blackmun took over:

Question: Mr. Foley, before you get started, let me ask a couple of questions. You are the county attorney, aren't you?

Mr. Foley: Yes, I am, Justice Blackmun.

Question: And yet the city is the respondent here.

Mr. Foley: Yes, under Minnesota law, Justice Blackmun, the county attorney handles all matters involving juveniles and this matter was a prosecution of a juvenile, so we represent any activity, whether the matter is under a city ordinance or State ordinance or a Federal crime.

Question: And this is why the city is a party to one of the amicus briefs as well as being the respondent in the case?

Mr. Foley: That's correct, Justice Blackmun.

Question: A little unusual, I suppose.

Mr. Foley: It is an unusual—

Question: Let me ask you one other trivial question. The cross burning took place on Earl Street, didn't it?

Mr. Foley: Yes, it did.

Question: Whereabouts on Earl Street? That is a long street, it runs from Mounds Park to Finland Park.

(Laughter.)

Mr. Foley: 290 Earl Street.

Question: Hm?

Mr. Foley: 290 Earl Street.

Question: I know that, but where is 290? What is the cross street?

Mr. Foley: I don't have the cross street, Justice Blackmun.

Question: You don't know—

(Laughter.)

Question: Is it near Mounds Park or is it near Finland Park?

Mr. Foley: It's near Mounds Park.

Question: I was up there last June with some U.S. Marshals who had never been there. And I think it's one of the most beautiful views in the City of St. Paul. But the grass is so high you couldn't see the view. Have your maintenance man cut the grass.

(Laughter.)

Mr. Foley: Justice, under our Constitution everyone is presumed innocent until they've had a trial.

(Laughter.)

Question: Mr. Foley, if you're going to make all these concessions you might as well sit down right now.

(Laughter.) (*R.A.V. v. City of St. Paul*, 1992, transcript of oral arguments, pp. 24–26.)

(The last comment was made by Justice Scalia, not Justice Blackmun.)

On June 22, 1992 the Court unanimously struck down the St. Paul ordinance, and it is certainly only a coincidence that Foley was ignorant about street locations and that he ended up on the losing side. But could he have anticipated Justice Blackmun's seemingly off-the-wall questions? Edward J. Cleary (1994), who represented the criminal defendant—identified by the

Court only by his initials, R.A.V.—recounts that as he prepared for the oral argument, a former Supreme Court law clerk warned him that Justice Blackmun, who grew up in St. Paul, would often inquire about the specific geographical location in a case originating in that city. So Cleary had familiarized himself about the location of the house with the cross-burning. But Justice Blackmun instead chose to ask the other advocate, the unfortunate Thomas Foley.

Thus the moral for advocates is know your justices' personal interests, and try to be prepared for obscure questions reflecting them. For example, Chief Justice Rehnquist was a student of history. In the case of *Clinton v. Goldsmith* (1999), when a question arose about the role of the Board of Correction of Military Records, the organization that processes appeals by those in the military protesting personnel decisions, Rehnquist interrupted to ask if this was the same organization that was currently ruling on the appeal by the descendants of Dr. Samuel Mudd, who had been convicted by a military tribunal of a conspiracy to assassinate President Lincoln (Frederick, 2003a).

Justices as Individuals

Each justice is different. Even their behavior on the bench is distinguishable. When asking a question, Justice Scalia is crouched forward, his head "sunk so low that only the top half of his face is visible to the gallery" (Henninger, 2006, p. A19). Justice Souter looks directly at the attorneys with a stiff stare. Chief Justice Roberts peers over his glasses. Justice Breyer and Justice Thomas, who sit next to each other, may chat with each other about some point. Justice Stevens, wearing his ever-present bow tie, is alert despite being in his late 80s. Justice Ginsburg appears dwarfed by her large chair. Their uniqueness has implications for not only the decisions the justices make but also the questions they ask in oral arguments. In a television interview, Justice Breyer (1997) once said: "I'm a human being.... Because I'm a human being, my own background...my own views, will of course shape me. They make a difference. Somebody with different life experiences has different views to a degree; that will influence the way they look at things."

For more than a century, psychologists have sought to determine a comprehensive but manageable way to describe our individuality and still offer comparisons between human beings. As recently as 25 years ago no consensus existed, even though the need was recognized. In 1986, Myron Zuckerman wrote:

> If we are ever to agree on a paradigm for a science of personal-
> ity we must begin with agreement on what constitutes the basic
> dimensions of personality. It is difficult to imagine a physics which
> studies matter without some classification of particles; a science
> of astronomy that studies "heavenly bodies" without distinction
> between moons, planets, stars, and galaxies; or a science of biology

without a taxonomy of living creatures. Yet much of personality today [in 1986] consists of studies of ad hoc traits applicable to limited areas of situation-person interaction. (1986, p. 1)

For many years traits were proposed by some personality theorists as the building blocks in a description of the psychological nature of persons. *Traits are generally defined as broad and enduring human characteristics that affect behavior across a variety of situations.* For example, if a man is suspicious, he is likely to question the word of his boss, distrust his wife, and be cautious in his dealings with strangers. In the opinion of many psychologists who study human individuality, traits are important indicators of occupational success, the quality of social relationships, and psychological well-being (McAdams & Pals, 2006).

But what traits are crucial? After all, more than 18,000 words in the English language refer to what we call traits (Allport & Odbert, 1936), albeit some are obscure or infrequent and many pairs are redundant. Starting about two decades ago, psychologists found that five factors consistently emerged in comprehensive studies of personality traits (McAdams & Pals, 2006). These came to be called the "Big Five"; although various researchers gave them different names, they are generally referred to as the following:

1. Extraversion
2. Agreeableness
3. Conscientiousness
4. Openness to experience
5. Negative affectivity, or anxiety, or neuroticism

Each of these traits can be thought of as a continuum; thus one person may be quite extraverted, another somewhat extraverted, and yet another quite introverted. Two individuals may both be quite conscientious but one may be much more introverted than the other. While most of the Big Five traits have positive labels, each represents a basic component of personality for which a given individual can be at either end of the continuum, or toward the middle. Extensive factor analyses have led to a conclusion that the five factors are not related to each other, that all five are needed to attempt to describe one's psychological essence, and that a given person might possess an extreme amount of one of these traits but not of others (Pervin & John, 2001).

So the Big Five serve as the salient qualities in describing a human's psychological individuality, just as height, weight, gender, race, eye color, and other features are central to describing the person's physical individuality. Each person possesses a measurable amount of each trait, thus just as for any other individual, we can assign a Supreme Court justice positions on each trait. But how do we do that? We cannot ask each justice to complete a personality inventory. We cannot ask the justice's friends and family to rate the justice on each of the qualities that contribute to these traits. We must rely on public information, and, despite the justices' desire for anonymity, there is much of that. Judging one's personality traits from one's public behavior has been done with other types of individuals (U.S. presidents, for example), but it remains a challenging enterprise. What I have chosen to do here is less extreme but still speculative: to identify a justice who seems to exemplify the extreme of each one of the Big Five, based on the justice's behavior during oral arguments, plus other information gleaned from the justice's public appearances, speeches, and interviews.

Our focus is on what the justices' responses to oral arguments tell us about them. Justices do not leave their personalities behind them when they pass through the curtains to enter that impressive courtroom. Their questions and comments—the content of these, the frequency, and, in the case of one justice, their infrequency—are manifestations of each justice's uniqueness. Most of them have distinctive ways of questioning, such that an experienced Court watcher can determine the identity of a questioner most of the time when reading a transcript of the oral arguments that does not give the questioner's identity. For example, Justice Ginsburg typically asks "very precisely worded questions that rarely leave any doubt or ambiguity as to her meaning, but that require special attentiveness" from the advocate (Frederick, 2003a, p. 71). Justice Ginsburg is quite soft-spoken, and would even be recognizable on an audiotape if she were not the only woman currently on the Court. Similarly, Justice Souter's strong New England accent is distinctive; it can even cause confusion in advocates. In an affirmative-action case, Souter asked, "Did your complaint specify the presumption [that racial minorities are economically disadvantaged] as being the flaw in the statutory scheme?"

Counsel:	Excuse me, Your Honor, the floor?
Souter:	No, flaw.
Counsel:	Oh, flaw.
Souter:	The constitutional infirmity. I'm sorry.
Counsel:	Excuse me, Your Honor.
Souter:	It's my regional accent.
(Laughter.)	
Counsel:	It's my hearing. (Biskupic, 1995, p. 34)

Sometimes, the identifiability of the questioner may be signaled by the style of the question rather than by its content. For example, Justice Stevens usually initiates his comments with a gracious preface: "May I interrupt…" or "May I ask…" No other justice does that. Sandra Day O'Connor, while she was on the bench, would occasionally exclaim, "My goodness!" or "Goodness sakes," followed by a question that communicated her displeasure or disagreement with the position being expressed by the advocate. In her next-to-last term on the bench, during the oral argument in the case of *Wilkinson v. Austin* (2005), Justice O'Connor told the respondent's attorney, "This is a prison classification, for goodness sakes" (p. 32) and then asked, "What in the world is the matter with that?" (p. 40). She later voted against the respondent.

Perhaps the most important of such utterances by Justice O'Connor came during the oral arguments for the *Bush v. Gore* (2000) appeal. O'Connor asked David Boies, Vice President Gore's attorney, "Well, why isn't the standard the one that voters are instructed to follow, for goodness sakes? I mean, it couldn't be clearer. I mean, why don't we go to that standard?" (Biskupic, 2005, pp. 307–308).

The frustration that Justice O'Connor sometimes reflected on the bench was manifested in sharp and demanding questions, often coming immediately after the advocate had approached the podium. For example, in the case of *Bradshaw v. Stumpf* (2005), the advocate for Bradshaw had spoken only four sentences before Justice O'Connor began a rapid-fire set of questions and comments that took almost 4 minutes of the advocate's 30 minutes of allotted time. In that term (2004–2005), in 29 oral arguments she was the first justice to question the petitioner, and on several of these occasions as few as 25 words had been uttered when she intervened. For example, in *Muehler v. Mena*, Carter Phillips had offered a mere one sentence when Justice O'Connor asked what she called "one preliminary question." Similarly, in *Tenet v. Doe*, Solicitor General Paul Clement got a chance to make only one statement when Justice O'Connor began a series of four questions. She also aggressively questioned respondents' attorneys; the ultimate occurred in the case of *Dodd v. United States* (2005), when she began questioning James Feldman, assistant to the solicitor general, before he even got to say, "Mr. Chief Justice, and may it please the Court."

Justice Scalia, an Example of Extraversion

Justice Scalia often is a dominant presence at the oral argument. The excerpt from the oral argument for *R.A.V. v. City of St. Paul* earlier in this chapter illustrates one of his typical contributions: a comment that has the effect of producing some comic relief to the tension of the occasion. His behavior on the Court epitomizes the Big Five factor of Extraversion; the descriptive adjectives that load on this factor include talkative, assertive, active, energetic, outgoing, outspoken, dominant, forceful, enthusiastic, show-off, sociable, spunky, adventurous, noisy, and bossy (John, 1990). (Each of these descriptors has a loading of .58 or more on the Extraversion factor.) Each is an apt label for Justice Scalia: over a set of oral arguments he asks more questions and makes more comments than any other justice, he communicates a sense of urgency on the bench, and his style is forever forceful (many advocates see him as overbearing). His adventurousness is indexed by his frequent travels abroad and his extensive travel within the United States (during the year 2005 he took 24 trips, to such places as Australia, Ireland, Turkey, and Italy). "Show off" is not too extreme; for example, he delighted in playing a bit part (donning a powdered wig and knee breeches) in a professional opera production in Washington, DC.

Oral arguments are, of course, serious business, and first-time observers at the Court may be surprised to find how frequently Scalia quips are interjected into the flow of questions. The official transcripts of the oral arguments indicate audience reactions with the notation "(Laughter.)," although this term may seem an exaggeration to some. The response of the audience to a question or comment does not often approach that of a laugh track from a television sit com, but for our purposes these interruptions are of interest because a recent tabulation has verified the impression that the most frequent initiator of them is Justice Scalia.

As has been mentioned, it was not until October of 2004 that the official transcripts of the arguments identified the justices by name. Prior to that they were in the form illustrated in the excerpt from *R.A.V. v. City of St. Paul* at the beginning of this chapter. Jay D. Wexler, a law professor at Boston University, was quick to capitalize on this innovation: he took all of the notations of "(Laughter.)" during the oral arguments of the October 2004 term and determined how frequently they were instigated by each justice (Liptak, 2005). Justice Scalia instigated 77 "laughing episodes," an average of once every oral argument. Justice Breyer was second, with 45, and Chief Justice Rehnquist third, with 12, even though he missed 44 oral arguments because of the thyroid cancer that led to his death. The other justices only had a few or none.

I did the same tabulation for the October 2005 term, Chief Justice Roberts' first at the helm. Justice Scalia generated 64 indications of "laughter" in the 78 oral arguments; Justice Breyer was the only justice who approached that total, with 49. Interestingly, Chief Justice Roberts was the cause of 20, indicating his contribution to a more relaxed atmosphere at the Court.

Why does Justice Scalia provoke so much audience reaction? "He plays to the crowd," is the opinion of Pamela S. Karlan, a Stanford law professor who has argued a number of appeals before the Supreme Court (Liptak, 2005). For example, in the case of *Johnson v. California* (2005), dealing with jury selection, the deputy attorney general of California was trying to explain a court procedure and maintained that the burden-of-proof rules were located in "the footnote on page 94." Justice Scalia interrupted: "A lot of people don't read footnotes" (p. 44). (The next term, in the oral argument for *DaimlerChrysler v. Cuno*, he told the respondent's lawyer, "I don't read footnotes anymore.")

Not just at the Court but also in his speeches, Justice Scalia is not afraid to vex and exasperate his audience. At a speech at the University of London he acknowledged that "I hate to be the skunk at the garden party" as he, with relish, attacked the values of many in the audience (Starr, 2002, p. 22).

A second characteristic of Justice Scalia's behavior at oral arguments also demonstrates his personification of Extraversion: he adopts a debater's style and reflects his own opinion in his questions. For example, in the case of *Illinois v. Caballes* (2005), the issue before the Court was whether a routine traffic stop in which a drug-sniffing dog discovered drugs in the car's trunk violated the driver's Fourth Amendment protection against an illegal search. Justice Scalia asked Lisa Madigan, attorney general of Illinois: "Surely you'd concede that the search is unreasonable if, for every one time…you make somebody open his bag because the dog actually smells narcotics, 99 times you make somebody open his bag because he has apples in it" (p. 12). These concession-eliciting questions, detectable by the "Surely you'd agree…" or "Surely you'd concede…" introduction, are more characteristic of Justice Scalia than any other current justice.

In a case involving tax exemption for a charitable summer camp *(Camps Newfound/Owatonna v. Town of Harrison*, 1997), Justice Scalia initiated the questioning aggressively by asking the camp's attorney, "Why should the taxpayers of Maine subsidize people from outside Maine? I don't know why they should be required to do that" (Greenhouse, 1996b, p. A12). In another oral argument he told the distinguished advocate Theodore Olson, "You don't have a single case" supporting your position (Coyle, 1996, p. A12). And in a case from a recent term *(Brigham City v. Stuart*, 2006), Justice Scalia confronted the respondent's advocate by saying, "Of course he [the police officer] had to raise his voice. I mean, there was a lot of noise going on. It just seems to me so unreasonable, when a policeman comes to tell people they're making too much noise and the neighbors have complained, that he can't do the minimum that's necessary to get their attention so he can tell them that. He has to get a warrant to tell them that the neighbors are complaining about too much noise? That just seems absurd!" (transcript of oral arguments, p. 32).

Justice Scalia is well-known among Court watchers for the enthusiasm and energy he pours into oral arguments. Following is an observer's description:

> If mind were muscle and the Court sessions were televised, Scalia
> would be the Arnold Schwarzenegger of American jurisprudence.
> When he listens to hapless litigants, he tilts his head at a show-me
> angle or taps his fingers on the desk in front of him as if he were
> playing the piano, which he enjoys doing while off the bench. When
> he speaks, he lunges forward with a jabbing forefinger to emphasize
> key words. Justice Scalia is the Court's self-appointed prosecutor,
> interrogator, elucidator or inquisitor—depending on who's catching
> his flak. (Biskupic, 2005, p. 279)

On occasion, he has been known to answer another justice's question before the advocate had a chance to do so. "Maybe we should go through counsel," Chief Justice Rehnquist tactfully interjected on one of these occasions (Tushnet, 2005, p. 170). Conceding that he can be overbearing, Scalia explained, "It is the academic in me. I fight against it. The devil makes me do it" (O'Brien, 2000, p. 261). He told an audience in 1993, "Where we see an idea that deserves clunking over the head, we clunk it over the head. Bad ideas should be shown for what they are" (Biskupic, 2005, p. 279). His aggressiveness is widely recognized, as illustrated by this apparently true anecdote:

> Once, while he was greeting Louisiana State University law students after a speech in the early 1990s, a student approached Scalia

and said, "I've named my pet fish after you." "Oh, you've named him 'Nino,' the justice said. "No," the student said, "I've named him 'Justice Scalia.'" A professor who overheard the conversation later asked the student whether he had other fish named after other justices. "No," he replied, "Justice Scalia ate all the others." (Biskupic, 2005, p. 281)

Justice Breyer, an Example of Agreeableness

Even though Antonin Scalia and Stephen Breyer were both law professors (at the University of Virginia and Harvard University, respectively) before they became circuit court judges and later Supreme Court justices, their behavior on the Court is quite different. Justice Breyer acts and speaks more like the stereotype of an academic, typically uttering complex ideas, often questioning his own viewpoints as well as those of the advocates. While Scalia is direct, Breyer is rambling; while Scalia has his mind made up, Breyer is trying to look at both sides; while Scalia is combative, Breyer is congenial.

The descriptors that index the factor labeled Agreeableness are the following: sympathetic, kind, appreciative, affectionate, soft-hearted, warm, generous, trusting, helpful, forgiving, pleasant, good-natured, friendly, and cooperative (John, 1990). Justice Breyer is often supportive and inquisitive when questioning the attorneys. For example, in a recent case (*Dixon v. United States,* 2006) he said, "But if we're thinking of things logically, logically you're right. I can see that this is in the hands of the defendant. But I've wondered why this hasn't turned into evidence of a problem in the 29 states. And the following occurred to me, which I'll put to you to see what your reaction is" (transcript of oral arguments, p. 38).

However, although Breyer often shows his support during oral arguments, he is not an easy-questioning justice. As noted in Chapter 4, he poses questions that challenge the attorney to a deeper level by often using page-long hypothetical examples that lead to further points of analysis. For example, in *Davis v. Washington* (2006), he asked the petitioner, "How would you do that? I'm interested in that because I thought it sounded good. Then I thought about it. I thought to have forfeiture, you'd have to show that this defendant, in fact, forced the wife not to testify. It's a crime to do that. So you'd have to prove another crime against the defendant in order to prove the first crime. And I thought perhaps that doctrine is not very practical. You tell me why it is" (transcript of oral arguments, p. 23).

Although he occasionally can be demanding or critical in his questions to advocates, what basically emerges from Justice Breyer's courtroom behavior is a self-deprecatory style, in which he acknowledges that he may be mistaken or that he is confused about an issue. For example, in the case of *ExxonMobil v. Saudi Basic* (2005), which concerned the circumstances under which federal courts could review state-court decisions, Justice Breyer made the following statement:

> Well, can you—can you expand on this a little? I'm not taking a view on it, I'm trying to clear up a confusion in my mind. I see how you would do this on the parallel business with—with delaying it on the docket and using the doctrine of preclusion. I understand that. But we've still got this doctrine called Rooker-Feldman out there, and as long as you have that doctrine, it strikes me as odd, if—say, it weren't a plaintiff. Say it was a losing party, you know, that was asking the federal judge, "Judge, you have this case on your docket. Let's move it up. Let's decide it now." He doesn't use the word "review" but everything else is the same. He wants a decision out of that court that is opposite of what the state court did. And what's concerning me—maybe I shouldn't be concerned, but what's concerning me is whether he can get it or not seems to turn completely on whether he uses the word "review" in the petition. (pp. 12–13)

Kenneth Starr has described Justice Breyer this way: "He avoids being argumentative.... He does his work with enormous collegiality" (2002, pp. 37–38). A telling example of Justice Breyer's modesty occurred during the Court's month-long recess in January 2005. He was called for jury duty in his hometown of Cambridge, Massachusetts, and he not only showed up, but he inauspiciously took his seat in the audience with the other prospective jurors. He did not seek a waiver, or approach the judge, or otherwise capitalize on his eminence to escape jury service. In fact, he was not even recognized by anyone in the room (including the judge) until his name was called. (He was then excused from jury duty.)

Justice Souter, an Example of Conscientiousness

As one of the Big Five traits, Conscientiousness is indexed by the following descriptors: organized, thorough, planful, efficient, responsible, reliable, dependable, precise, practical, deliberate, painstaking, hardworking, and cautious (John, 1990; Pervin & John, 2001). It can be argued, with justification, that most of these descriptors fit each justice. The present composition of the Court is impressive; everyone is well prepared for oral arguments and well versed in the law. (For the first time in history, every justice currently on the Court has served as a circuit-court judge.) Each has many responsibilities, including the writing of opinions, which they generally get done efficiently.

But it also can be argued that David Souter stands out among his peers for his extreme degree of conscientiousness. For example, his questions during the oral arguments are lengthy, detailed, and full of dependent clauses, but they tend to crystallize the essence of the case. He asks questions not to show off or to embarrass advocates but to reflect his struggling over the issue. With regard to his work habits, he spends long hours in his office (including working through his lunch hour and into the late evenings, and spending most of his weekends at the Court), he restricts his social life (he has never married), and he does not travel during the term (and only leaves Washington in the summer to return to his childhood home in New Hampshire). In contrast to several of the other justices, he avoids giving speeches; he told a colleague in 1990, "In a perfect world, I would never give another speech, address, talk, lecture or whatever as long as I live" (Baum, 2007, p. 15). In 2002, for example, he took only one trip, for a memorial service for a law professor. Despite having a net worth of at least $5.6 million, he leads an ascetic life (old car, no cell phone, no color television set). Peter J. Rubin, a law clerk of Justice Souter's in the early 1990s, recalls one late evening toward the end of the term, when he and another clerk were in their second-floor office trying to finish some opinion drafts. At 2 A.M. Justice Souter, who had been working continuously in his first-floor office, came all across the building and upstairs to deliver a draft he had just completed.

He may even be conscientious to a fault. When Professor Tinsley Yarbrough was preparing a biography of him, Justice Souter declined to be interviewed; so did his law clerks (perhaps at his instruction). The justice did tell one of his friends that "cooperation in such a project…might offend certain of his colleagues on the Court" (Yarbrough, 2005, p. 261). Likewise, Joan Biskupic, who published a biography of Justice O'Connor, mentioned that all but one of the other justices was willing to be interviewed for it. Although she did not identify Justice Souter, it is clear from the comments by each of the others in the book that he was the one holdout. Justice Souter characteristically refuses requests for interviews, even on innocuous matters unrelated to the Court. A lifelong Red Sox fan, he declined to be questioned by a reporter about his reactions when Boston won the World Series in 2004.

Justice Kennedy, an Example of Openness to Experience

Openness to Experience, as one of the Big Five personality traits, is described by such adjectives as imaginative, intelligent, original, insightful, curious, wise, and ingenious (John, 1990). Justice Kennedy is an exemplar of this trait because he is the swing voter on the Court at present and cannot be easily pigeonholed as someone with either a consistent conservative or a consistent liberal voting record. At the end of the October 2005 term he provided the determining fifth vote in two very important cases, but one was in the opposite direction from the other. In *Hamdan v. Rumsfeld* he sided with Justice Stevens' opinion curtailing the President's war powers, but in *League of United Latin American Citizens v. Perry*, a challenge to redistricting in Texas, he sided with the conservatives in allowing the procedure with only a minor modification. In the term ending in June 2007 the Court split 5 to 4 in 24 of 72 decisions, the highest percentage in a decade. Amazingly, Justice Kennedy was on the winning side in every one of these cases. Nineteen of the 24 decisions had a classic liberal-versus-conservative split; in those Kennedy sided with the conservatives 13 times and the liberals 6 times.

Kennedy's lack of conformity to one ideology is also reflected in the data on voting alignments in the Court. During the October 2004 term he agreed most often with a liberal, Justice Breyer (81% of the time), but agreed least often with Justice Stevens, another liberal (64% of the time). On civil cases, he most often agreed with two liberals, Souter and Breyer, but on criminal cases he most often agreed with the conservative, Chief Justice Rehnquist, an impressive 86% of the time, and he agreed with Justice Souter in only 40% of the criminal cases. (In the October 2005 term, he agreed most often with Justice O'Connor, the other swing voter, while she was on the bench before retiring as of late January 2006.)

In his questions during oral arguments, Justice Kennedy certainly does not show the identifiable idiosyncrasies of Justice Scalia or of Justice Breyer. Often his questions are of the information-seeking type, without any revelation of the way he is leaning. Thus his questions may be directed toward each side, but he only rarely leads off the questioning of the petitioner, as did Justice O'Connor and as do Justices Scalia, Souter, and Ginsburg. (He did so only eight times in the 78 oral arguments during the October 2005 term.) Justice Kennedy was, however, the source of one of the better laughter-inducing lines during the 2004–2005 term. In a January case, he commented on one facet of the absurdity of modern life: "Recently, I lost my luggage. I had to go to the lost-and-found at the airline, and the lady said, has my plane landed yet" (Liptak, 2005).

To say someone is open-minded can be seen either as a compliment or a criticism; someone with an open mind runs the risk of being seen as promiscuously persuadable, a dithering Hamlet on the bench (Lithwick, 2004). As Barbara Perry has commented, "To some observers, Kennedy evinces an infuriating inconsistency. They say he twists in the wind until he fastens onto an idiosyncratic reason for deciding a case. To others, he is a thoughtful jurist who steadfastly refuses to embrace a results-oriented ideology; he simply analyzes each case on its own merits" (1999b, p. 83). Journalist David Savage adds to this picture of open-mindedness: "Kennedy never gives the impression that the right answer is obvious from the start....He has no simple formula for deciding cases, and he is not determined to come out on the same side all the time" (2004, p. 40). A profile in the *New Yorker* magazine titled him "The Agonizer" (Rosen, 1996).

Justice Thomas, an example of Negative Affectivity

Only one of the Big Five personality traits has a decidedly negative connotation; this trait, sometimes titled Chronic Anxiety or Neuroticism, is indexed by adjectives such as tense, moody, overly sensitive, prone to worrying, and self-pitying (John, 1990; Pervin & John, 2001). Is this a fair characterization of Justice Thomas? His friends describe him as easy to talk to, with an uproarious laugh. Yet in his speeches he often comes across as quite tense and serious, and in those he gave for several years after his confirmation he continued to express hostility and resentment about the charges of sexual harassment made against him in 1991 by Anita Hill. A recent biography was subtitled "*The Divided Soul of Clarence Thomas*" (Merida & Fletcher, 2007).

Justice Thomas has been criticized for his decisions and dissents that seem to reflect an absence of humanitarianism and especially a lack of sympathy for those who have been injured. The case of *Hudson v. McMillian* (1992) came before the Court because Keith Hudson, an inmate in a Louisiana prison, claimed that he had been beaten by prison guards as they moved him from one cell to another; a medical examination found that several of his teeth had been loosened, his dental plate was partially cracked, his face and mouth were swollen, and he had several bruises. Were these "significant injuries" to justify a claim of cruel and unusual punishment? The Court ruled 7 to 2 that they were, but Justice Thomas dissented. To be fair, his dissent was based on his reading of precedents that narrowed the application of the Eighth Amendment, but observers pictured him as insensitive to the abuses of prisoners. Years later, he still complained about the media's treatment of him and especially of his dissent in this case.

And in more recent dissents in cases involving prisoners' rights, Justice Thomas's image has remained one lacking sympathy for prisoners. The first of these, *Hope v. Pelzer* (2002), dealt with the liability of Alabama prison guards who chained disruptive inmates to "hitching posts" and left them outdoors without food and water. In his dissent from a ruling that this reflected cruel and unusual punishment, Justice Thomas wrote that the inmates were chained for a legitimate penological purpose, to encourage compliance with prison rules while on work duty. The more recent case, *Deck v. Missouri* (2005), considered a procedure in which a defendant who had been convicted was brought into the courtroom in shackles and chains as the jury heard testimony about what sentence to give him. While the Court ruled that this procedure should not be used except in "special circumstances," in a dissent Justice Thomas wrote, "My legal obligation is not to determine the wisdom or desirability of shackling defendants, but to decide a purely legal question" (*Deck v. Missouri,* 2005, p. 2023).

His apparent lack of sympathy extends to other types of injured parties as well. In the case of *Dolan v. United States Postal Service* (2006), Barbara Dolan filed a suit against the Postal Service for injuries she suffered when she tripped and fell over mail left on her porch by the mail deliverer. The Postal Service claimed that it could not be sued in such cases because of an exception granted under the federal Tort Claims Act. The Court held, with only one dissenting vote, that her suit could go forward. Justice Thomas was the lone dissenter.

His dissent focused on the exception to the act; he acknowledged that the exception was ambiguous; he concentrated on the terms "negligent transmission" and his conclusion was that the majority failed to apply to the word "transmission" its "plain meaning." His ruling reflected his commitment to the legal model as it concentrated on precedents and the wording of the law, but at a human level it lacked any sympathy for the injured plaintiff. Recall that the issue before the Court was not whether she was entitled to an award, but rather, whether or not she would even be allowed to sue the Postal Service.

Justice Thomas differs in some respects from the other justices beyond the fact that he is the only African American on the Court and the only justice who was born in poverty. While in college he was a supporter of Malcolm X and briefly wore an Afro. He has acknowledged in speeches that there was a period in his life in which he was very bitter and angry. He is the only current justice who has been divorced; in fact, one has to go back to William O. Douglas, appointed by President Franklin Roosevelt, for the next most recently divorced justice.

Some of his present idiosyncrasies are perhaps motivated by a desire to not be pigeon-holed into a particular mold. In a city populated with zealous Washington Redskins football fans, he roots for the Dallas Cowboys, the Redskins' favorite adversary. He is a stock-car racing fan. But it is his behavior at oral arguments that particularly make him unique.

Justice Thomas rarely speaks during oral arguments. In a sample of one-third of the cases during the October 2004 term, Austin (2006) found not a single utterance by Justice Thomas. Likewise, in the term ending in June 2007 he spoke nary a word. Why? In a talk before high-school students the day after the *Bush v. Gore* decision was announced, he offered several reasons—for example, "there's no reason to add to the volume." He went on to say, "I also believe, strongly, unless I want an answer I don't ask things. I don't ask for entertainment [a comment on Justice Scalia?]. I don't ask to give people a hard time. I have some very active colleagues who like to ask questions. Usually, if you wait long enough, someone will ask your question. The other thing, I was on the other side of the podium before, in my earlier life, and its hard to stand up by yourself and to have judges who are going to rule on your case ask you tough questions. I don't want to give them a hard time" (Kane, 2000, p. 7B).

When Justice Thomas does speak at an oral argument, his pronouncements have diagnostic value in understanding his personality. He had only been on the Court for 2 months when oral arguments were held for the cross-burning case described at the beginning of this chapter, and he asked no questions of either advocate. But when another cross-burning case came before the Court 12 years later, involving acts by the Ku Klux Klan, Justice Thomas did intervene and had a dramatic impact on the courtroom.

The case was *Virginia v. Black* (2003), and the central issue was whether what the Klan had done was legal. Justice Thomas interrupted the petitioner and with great emotion described the impact of the KKK on a black man in America. A burning cross is "unlike any symbol in our society; there's no other purpose to the cross, no communication, no particular message.... It was intended to cause fear and terrorize a population." For him the cross burned by the KKK was a symbol of a reign of terror, signifying "one hundred years of lynching" (transcript of oral arguments, p. 24).

Rod Smolla, the advocate for the respondent, described the reaction in the courtroom:

> In all my life as an advocate and observer of legal proceedings, I
> have never seen the mood in a courtroom change so suddenly and
> dramatically. The impact of Justice Thomas's remarks was palpable
> and physical. Justice Breyer, who sat next to Thomas on the bench,
> drew closer to him, putting an arm on his back in a gesture of col-
> legial respect and good will. Justice Scalia, who sat on the opposite
> side of Thomas but nearly facing him (because of the curvature
> of the bench), seemed to viscerally connect with his fellow justice,
> nodding in agreement as he spoke. (2004, p. 164)

Justice Thomas has been disparaged and even ridiculed for his frequent silence on the bench. Yet he appears sincere when he said that usually the other justices' questions generated answers to the questions he had. On one occasion he not only asked a question of counsel but engaged in an uninterrupted colloquy with the advocate for nearly 10 minutes (*National Aeronautics and Space Administration v. Federal Labor Relations Authority*, 1999), and, as Frederick has suggested, it "may well have been occasioned by the lack of experience of any other justices as the head of an executive-branch agency that had dealt with an Inspector General…as had Justice Thomas when he chaired the U.S. Equal Employment Opportunity Commission" (2003a, p. 68).

The Chief Justice—Idiosyncratic, Too?

The task of the chief justice during oral arguments is a more complex one than that of the associate justices. The chief justice initiates the session, calls time at the end, and must monitor any deviations from the expected procedure. It is quite plausible that the chief justice will participate less frequently in the questioning. While William Rehnquist was chief justice he asked some questions, but not as many as any other judge except the silent Justice Thomas. In contrast, Chief Justice Roberts has taken a more active role in the questioning. In the 24 oral arguments during the October 2006 term that led to 5-to-4 splits, he asked more questions than any other justice except Scalia. In these 24 oral arguments, the chief justice made 478 questions and comments, almost 20 per case. Justice Scalia questioned or commented 606 times, for an average of 25 per oral argument. Third most frequent was Justice Breyer with 403. Justices Souter, Ginsburg, and Stevens were similar to each other, with 366, 332, and 330 questions and comments, respectively. Less frequent were Justices Kennedy (276), Alito (117), and, of course, Thomas.

Chief Justice Roberts, who began his service as chief justice in October 2005, also had other effects on the oral arguments. In a discussion of the oral arguments for the first 30 cases of that term, the *New York Times* concluded that the mood of the Court had "brightened," as reflected in an increased number of laughter-inducing comments. As noted earlier, Justices Breyer and Scalia had their usual number of laughter-generating comments, but Chief Justice Roberts was third (Liptak, 2005). For example, on October 31, 2005, during an oral argument, a light bulb suddenly and noisily exploded in the courtroom. "It's a trick they play on new chiefs all the time," commented Chief Justice Roberts. "Happy Halloween," replied Justice Scalia, only to have Chief Justice Roberts retort, "We're even more in the dark now than before" (Liptak, 2005).

As the period for oral arguments in the chief justice's first term wound down toward the end of April 2006, Linda Greenhouse, reporter for *The New York Times*, polled a number of advocates to determine if the atmosphere in the courtroom had changed with the change in chief justices. The reaction was unanimous that it had. Professor Richard Lazarus of the Georgetown University Law Center said, "They're not stepping on each other; they take longer before someone asks the first question. They give the lawyers more time to answer" (Greenhouse, 2006c, p. A1). Carter Phillips, earlier described as one of the most prominent members of the Supreme Court bar, was quoted as saying that the change had been so abrupt that it could be a trap for unwary advocates. "You have to be ready now to make some kind of affirmative presentation" at the beginning of an oral argument (Greenhouse, 2006c, p. A1). Why the change from the previous term? Two reasons seem paramount. Sandra Day O'Connor retired from the Court. As noted earlier, she often asked the first question and frequently it came only after the advocate had uttered a few sentences. But Greenhouse gives much of the credit to the new chief justice: "with justices sitting back and allowing colleagues to ask follow-up questions, and with lawyers given an actual chance to answer, there is a new coherence and civility to the sessions" (2006c, p. A17). We will evaluate these conclusions empirically in Chapter 8, when we consider whether the Court's procedures effectively achieve the goals of advocates who appear before it.

The conference that the justices hold a few days after the oral arguments, where they take a provisional vote, is, of course, secret, and it is speculation to say that the new atmosphere is a result of the chief justice running the conference differently from the way Chief Justice Rehnquist ran it. Greenhouse has reported that "Roberts is reliably said to be presiding over the justices' private after-argument conferences with a lighter hand, not watching the clock as closely and permitting more conversation" (2006c, p. A17). She quotes Beth Brinkmann, a frequent advocate, "If you know you'll be able to make your point in conference, you don't have to make it on the bench" (Greenhouse, 2006c, p. A17).

The Frequency of Questions

During the oral argument, each attorney may be the recipient of somewhere between 30 and 100 questions and comments from the justices. Some justices ask more questions than others; it has already been noted that Justice Thomas ordinarily asks none. Are the differences in frequency large enough to designate certain justices as dominating oral arguments?

Two surveys of the questioning are reviewed here. Sarah Shullman (2004) observed 10 oral arguments during the October 2002 term and classified the frequency and types of questions from each justice. The second survey was done by Jacqueline Austin (2006), who tabulated questions and comments in 24 of the 74 oral arguments during the October 2004 term. (Both of these studies are described in more detail in Chapter 7, as they are concerned with the relationship of justices' questions to their eventual votes.)

Shullman was present during the oral arguments; Austin used transcripts. Each of these methods has its unique limitations. On-site observation, at least in Shullman's study, lacks reliability, as she was the only observer who classified each comment. Furthermore, her task was not an easy one. As noted earlier, the oral arguments take the form of a conversation, with interruptions, uncompleted statements, and even two people trying to speak at once. Shullman had to record each statement separately, indicate the justice, and rate—on a scale of 1 to 5—the statement as helpful or hostile. She commented, "While my methods were not scientifically exact, they were consistently applied to each argument. If there was any uncertainty about the content or tone of a particular question, it was excluded from my analysis. Likewise, if there was any uncertainty about which justice was speaking, those questions were also excluded" (2004, p., 273, Footnote 7). The availability of transcripts with identification of the justice who was speaking permits certain advantages, including the establishment of an estimate of the reliability of classifications and resolution of discrepancies in ratings. However, if one works with a transcript, there is no indication of the nuances in tone of the questioner.

In the 10 argument sessions observed by Shullman, Justice Ginsburg asked the most questions, and Justices Thomas and O'Connor the fewest. Justice O'Connor asked only about a third as many questions as Justice Ginsburg did. Justice Thomas did not ask a single question at any of the 10 sessions attended by Shullman. Austin analyzed 24 of the 74 cases in the October 2004 term for which there were signed opinions (32%). She did not randomly select cases; instead, she chose 12 cases that clearly could be seen as ideology related and 12 cases that were not related to the justices' ideologies. She found that, on the average, 47.5 questions were directed to the petitioner's attorney or attorneys, and 48.1 questions were directed to the respondents' attorney or attorneys. For the cases she surveyed, the justices differed in their frequency of questions from what Shullman found. Justice Scalia was the most active justice, with an average of 19.5 questions per case, followed by Justice Breyer (14.1), Justice Souter (14.0), and Justice Ginsburg (12.1). Justices Kennedy, Stevens, and O'Connor each asked an average of 10 or 11 questions per oral argument. Chief Justice Rehnquist had significantly fewer, 6.5. Only the results for Justice Thomas were consistent with Shullman's; once again, he did not ask any questions during the 24 oral arguments we studied.

Shullman reported that Justice Breyer asked the most hostile questions of all the justices, although he was equally hostile to both parties. This, too, is inconsistent with my reading of his questions in many oral arguments spanning several terms; it is my impression (illustrated in Chapter 4) that he bends over backward to be fair. In fact, he often will express his misgivings about his own viewpoint and give the advocate every opportunity to persuade him how he is wrong. Shullman's take on the nature of Justice O'Connor's questions also differed from Austin's and mine:

> Justice O'Connor falls somewhere in the middle when her questions are evaluated on the basis of content. She ranks fifth overall in hostility or argumentativeness, third in asking helpful questions of the party she supports, and sixth in asking hostile questions of the party she opposes.... In other words, her questions are neither very hostile nor very helpful. (2004, p. 283)

As indicated at several points, my position on Justice O'Connor's behavior at oral arguments was that she asked very penetrating questions that clearly conveyed her sense of error in the advocate's position. She was quite impatient with positions that she saw as patently ridiculous, and she had no reluctance in saying so.

There was some predictability in certain aspects of the questioning. For example, when the petitioner's attorney was initially interrupted during his or her opening statement, it was most often by Justice O'Connor, Justice Scalia, or Justice Souter. Justices Ginsburg, Stevens, or Kennedy occasionally asked the first question. Justice Breyer never did, in any of the 24 cases Austin sampled. More than any other justice, Justice Kennedy was more likely to ask each side an equal number of questions. Shullman also found this to be the case, and more of his questions were information seeking. Justice Breyer's questions, which usually came later rather than earlier, seemed to seek a dialogue with the advocate. The general pattern of results confirmed a conclusion that each justice truly does differ in his or her style of questioning.

How Well Should the Advocate Be Able to Anticipate Questions?

This chapter began with an example of an idiosyncratic set of questions by Justice Blackmun and a demonstration of how one advocate stumbled over an answer while another advocate anticipated his question. The chapter ends with another example illustrating how justices can come up with questions stemming from their own experience and background, and how advocates sometimes can be blindsided by them.

In the oral argument for the case of *Florida v. Nixon* (2005), argued in November 2004, Edward H. Tillinghast, II, an attorney from New York City, was representing the respondent, Joe Elton Nixon, a prisoner in Florida. Nixon had been sentenced to death after his trial lawyer (not Tillinghast) had pleaded him guilty without his consent. Prior to trial, Nixon had been uncooperative and had refused to give his attorney an answer as to how he wanted to plead. After several questions to Tillinghast from Justices Scalia and Souter, the following exchange occurred:

Justice Stevens: Mr. Tillinghast, can I ask if you are familiar with the Loeb/Leopold trial many many years ago that was conducted by Clarence Darrow? If you're not, I won't push you on it.

Mr. Tillinghast: Unfortunately, I'm not, Your Honor.

Justice Stevens: Because he—he applied exactly this strategy and it was one of his great victories. In—in fact, it's a long, long time ago. But that was the way Clarence Darrow sized up this problem, and the—and I think in that case they were very young clients that he had. They didn't—they were not—they did not expressly consent to what he did. But it saved their lives. (transcript of oral arguments, pp. 40–41).

In actuality, Nathan Leopold, Jr., was 19 and Richard Loeb was 18 and living in Chicago, when, on May 23, 1924, they brutally murdered 14-year-old Bobby Franks, a distant cousin and neighbor of Richard Loeb's. They first bludgeoned the victim with a chisel, then suffocated him, and then burned his face with acid to make his identification more difficult. Loeb and Leopold were both very bright, they came from very well-to-do families—Loeb's father was the vice-president of Sears—and they had been students at the University of Chicago and the University of Michigan. At the age of 18, Loeb had already completed his course work at the University of Chicago, the youngest person ever to do so. Similarly, Leopold had graduated from the University of Michigan at age 17. Leopold had passed the entrance examinations for the Harvard Law School, which he planned to enter in the fall. They had their own cars, charge accounts at prominent stores, and a generous monthly allowance. Their motivation was simply to try to commit the perfect crime. (For the previous 4 years they had engaged in minor crimes—petty thefts, starting fires, and breaking windshields.)

After they were captured and had confessed to the acts, their parents hired the eminent attorney, 67-year-old Clarence Darrow, to represent them in what came to rival the Lindbergh baby's murder as the "crime of the century." As Justice Stevens indicated, Darrow had them plead guilty, thus avoiding a jury trial. Instead, he was able to plead before a single judge and ask for something less than the death penalty. He told the judge, "We were afraid to submit our cause to a jury....I am aware a court has more experience, more judgment, and more kindliness than a jury" (Stone, 1958, p. 258).

Darrow was successful, as the judge sentenced each man to life in prison for the murder and 99 years for the kidnapping. In 1958, after 33 years in prison and at the age of 51, Leopold was paroled. He died in 1971 at the age of 66. Loeb was attacked by another inmate and died as a result. In 1956 Meyer Levin published a novel called *Compulsion*, a fictionalized account of the case, and 3 years later it was made into a successful movie.

As Justice Stevens said, the Loeb/Leopold case was "many, many years ago"; even Justice Stevens, age 84 at the time of the *Florida v. Nixon* oral argument, was only 4 years old in 1924 (and, incidentally, grew up in Chicago). Because of the heinousness of the crime, the nature of the perpetrators, and its frequent presentation in the media, the case has remained a part of the body of knowledge in criminal psychology. Should an advocate before the Supreme Court have known about the case? Probably. Did it make any difference in the outcome of the appeal? Definitely not—the Court ruled unanimously that Joe Elton Nixon did not deserve a new trial because of the actions of his attorney.

Conclusions

Those attorneys preparing to argue before the Supreme Court usually undergo extensive preparation, as described in Chapter 3. The message of this chapter is that part of the preparation should be to consider each justice and ask oneself, given his or her background, orientation, and biases, what questions might the justice ask. For example, the attorney might have free-associated: "Justice Stevens, he's from Chicago....that's where Loeb and Leopold came from....that reminds me of Clarence Darrow's plea in the case....how can I prepare to answer a question about that case?" As Frederick has wisely observed:

> The more familiar an advocate is with the court conducting the argument, the easier it is to anticipate the kinds of questions a particular member of the court might ask, as well as the manner in which that jurist will ask the question. Each judge will bring a distinctive style to the bench at oral argument, and the advocate's challenge is to be familiar enough with those tendencies to anticipate (where possible) how that judge will react to the case with questions. (2003a, p. 67)

6

Oral Arguments in a Landmark Case

Those...kids in Virginia and South Carolina—and I have seen them do it—they play in the streets together, they play on their farms together, they separate to go to school, they come out of school to play ball together.

—Thurgood Marshall, oral argument in *Brown v. Board of Education*, December 7, 1953

Are the Oral Arguments in Landmark Cases Exceptional?

The decisions by the Supreme Court in landmark cases change our society and the lives of individual citizens. Because of their importance, the oral arguments in these cases are especially worthy of study. Is there any evidence that in these cases the oral arguments had a special effect on the outcome? Or perhaps because the issue received so much attention prior to the argument phase, the oral arguments had an effect that was less than in a typical case.

Even among the most important cases decided by the Supreme Court in the twentieth century, the decision in *Brown v. Board of Education of Topeka* stands out. More has been written about it, several of the participants have written memoirs about the role they played in the oral arguments, and the outcome of the case was not decided until after a second set of oral arguments had been held.

Background to *Brown v. Board of Education of Topeka*

What we usually refer to as the *"Brown v. Board of Education"* case actually refers to three cases:

1. *Brown v. Board of Education of Topeka*, decided on May 17, 1954, which ruled as unconstitutional the practice of segregation in school districts in several states, henceforth referred to as *"Brown I."* This case was actually a consolidation of four different petitions, from Kansas, Delaware, South Carolina, and Virginia, each of which challenged state-sanctioned separate schools for African Americans and whites.

2. *Bolling v. Sharpe*, decided by the Court the same day as the above case, which focused on school segregation in the District of Columbia. Although this petition had temporarily been consolidated with the above four appeals, it was later separated because the Fourteenth Amendment stated that "no state" may discriminate and the District of Columbia was not a state but a federal enclave.

3. *Brown v. Board of Education of Topeka*, decided a year later, on May 31, 1955. Now the concern was on the remedy for the previously outlawed school segregation. This decision, which will be referred to as *"Brown II,"* contained the now-famous phrase "with all deliberate speed." It placed the burden on local school systems to comply and on local courts to make sure they did (Warren, 1977).

This chapter concentrates on *Brown I*. This decision was arguably the most important decision made by the Supreme Court in the twentieth century. Legal scholar Jack Balkin refers to it as "the single most honored opinion in the Supreme Court's corpus" (2001, p. 4). The distinguished historian of the Court, Bernard Schwartz (1997), listed it as the second greatest decision of all time, behind only *Marbury v. Madison* (1803), which established judicial review as fundamental to our constitutional system. *Brown I* "revolutionized the notions of what courts, lawyers, and the law might do to expand racial justice" (Greenberg, 1994, p. 116). Now, more than 50 years later, many of us may see the *Brown* decision as a foregone conclusion, but when Court first considered the appeal the decision was by no means certain. In fact, the initial appeal created a stalemate, causing the decision to hear the oral arguments again a year later. It was only through what some would call an act of God that the decision came down as it did.

To evaluate the determinants of the *Brown I* decision, including the impact of its oral arguments, it is necessary to understand its antecedents. In what is uniformly considered to be the most unfortunate decision made by the Supreme Court in its first 200 years, *Dred Scott v. Sandford,* the Court concluded in 1857 that blacks were not and could not become citizens within the meaning of the Constitution. Furthermore, Chief Justice Roger Taney wrote that "for more than a century [the black race] has been regarded as beings of inferior order, and altogether unfit to associate with the white race, either in social or political relations" (*Dred Scott v. Sandford*, 1857, p. 407). This decision, of course, ended any hope of a rational solution to the race issue, accelerated the secession of Southern states, and led inexorably to the Civil War.

Shortly after the conclusion of that war, newly freed blacks in the Southern states had wide access to public accommodations. For example, New Orleans had fully integrated public schools in the mid-1870s, and in North Carolina blacks sat on juries (Urofsky, 2004). But things changed during the 1880s. Whites with traditional values regained control of state legislatures and began to pass Jim Crow laws that once again segregated blacks from whites in all aspects of life. One of these laws, adopted in Louisiana in 1890, required separate railway carriages for blacks and whites.

One event that led to unreconstructed white Southerners regaining control of the power in the South was the contested presidential election of 1876. In this election (reminiscent of the one in 2000), the Democratic candidate, Samuel Tilden, who led in the popular vote, was one electoral vote away from a majority, but three states had contested sets of electors (one of the states was Florida). A panel composed of five Senators, five members of the U.S. House of Representatives, and five justices of the Supreme Court was designated to decide which sets of electors were legitimate. Each panelist's vote reflected his political-party allegiance, and the Republican candidate, Rutherford B. Hayes, was declared the winner. Democrats reluctantly accepted the outcome after Hayes agreed to serve only one term and to withdraw those federal troops who were still occupying the South a decade after the end of the Civil War. When the troops left, so did the carpetbaggers, and Southern whites regained control. Blacks, while no longer slaves, were victims of an almost equally disabling caste system that lasted for almost a century. The provision of separate railway cars in Louisiana, to be "divided by a partition," was "clearly intended to promote the illusion of comfort and superiority for white passengers" (Barth, 1974, p. 30), many of whom needed reassurance that, despite their desperate lives, they remained superior to blacks.

On June 7, 1892, Homer Adolph Plessy, who was only one-eighth black but considered black by Louisiana law, bought a first-class ticket and boarded the car reserved for "Whites only" in New Orleans for a trip to Covington, Louisiana. He was asked to move to the car marked "Colored" but refused to do so, at which point he was arrested. His lawyers subsequently brought suit against the railroad. (Doubtless this was an arranged test case, as Plessy, because of his racial background, appeared to be white.) After he was convicted and fined, he appealed the railroad's action, claiming it violated his rights to equal protection, as established by a clause of the Fourteenth Amendment, but Judge John Ferguson ruled against him (hence "*Plessy v. Ferguson*"), and the Supreme Court of Louisiana unanimously upheld the judge's decision.

The *Plessy* Decision

In the subsequent oral argument before the U.S. Supreme Court, Plessy's lawyer said, "Justice is pictured as blind, and her daughter, the law, ought to at least be color blind" (Barth, 1974, p. 33). But in its *Plessy v. Ferguson* decision in 1896, the Court rejected Plessy's claim and ruled that segregation, in and of itself, did not violate the Constitution, as long as the separate accommodations for the two races were equal. (Interestingly, in no place did the opinion use the term "separate but equal," the standard that came to be seen as its message.) Justice Henry Billings Brown's majority opinion concluded that "laws permitting, and even requiring, their separation in places where they are liable to be brought into contact do not necessarily imply the inferiority of one race to the other" (*Plessy v. Ferguson,* 1896, p. 551). If blacks felt that they were the objects of discrimination, opined the Court, it was "not by reason of anything found in the act, but solely because the Colored race chooses to put that construction on it" (p. 551). Only Justice John Marshall Harlan dissented, presciently concluding that the purpose of segregation was that "of humiliating citizens ... of a particular race." He further noted that "our Constitution is color-blind and neither knows nor tolerates classes among its citizens" (pp. 559–560).

The First 50 Years after *Plessy*

African Americans were not the only minority to feel the stain of government-sanctioned segregation. In 1927, in the case of *Gong Lum v. Rice*, the Court (including such liberals as Justices Holmes, Brandeis, and Stone) ruled unanimously that a child of Chinese descent could be denied admission to an "all-white" school in Mississippi and required to attend an "all-black" one instead.

With segregation given a stamp of approval by the Supreme Court, any pretense of equality of accommodations progressively diminished. In the first half of the twentieth century, the schools for African Americans (if the schools existed at all) mocked the pretense of "separate but equal"; the buildings often lacked heat, the books were hand-me-downs, and a school bus system was nonexistent. Black teachers were paid less than half of what white teachers were paid (Carter, 2005). In 1940 the average annual expenditure per child in Southern schools was $21.54 for blacks and $50.14 for whites (Greenberg, 1994).

One of the cases consolidated with *Brown I, Briggs v. Elliott*, pointed out the appalling conditions of the black schools in Clarendon County, South Carolina. While the white schools had drinking fountains, children who attended the two all-black schools encountered galvanized buckets with dippers that all students shared. Privies served as toilets in the all-black schools. The white schools had a lunchroom with paid attendants; the black schools lacked lunchrooms. While white schools were provided janitors, in the black schools teachers and students pitched in to perform these chores. One of the black schools had no desks or decent chalkboards. With no bus transportation available, some of the black children walked 10 miles to attend school each day. (And when the parents of black children in Clarendon County complained, they were fired from their jobs, had difficulty getting their cotton ginned, and received threats from the Ku Klux Klan.)

But in the 1930s and 1940s the social climate began to change. In what C. Vann Woodward (1955) called "the new Reconstruction," President Roosevelt's New Deal brought a renewed concern for the condition of black Americans. World War II accelerated the migration of blacks from the South to industrial areas, where the wartime manpower shortage gave them a shot at factory jobs. Here they worked shoulder to shoulder with whites. The Court realized it had to take another look at school segregation. It was not surprising that the first cracks in the acceptance of institutionalized segregation by the Court came at the university graduate level, rather than at the primary grades. In the 1938 case *Missouri ex rel. Gaines v. Canada*, the Court balked at the state of Missouri's procedure of denying resident blacks admission to the state's only public law school but paying their tuition to attend a law school of equivalent standing in another state. The Court ruled that Lloyd Gaines, a resident of St. Louis, had the requisite qualifications and must be admitted to the University of Missouri's law school because the state had no separate law school for blacks. (At the oral argument, Charles Hamilton Houston, perhaps the most distinguished black lawyer in the country, represented Gaines. When it came time for Houston to speak, Justice James McReynolds, an avowed racist, swiveled his chair so that his back was to Houston.)

The experience of 900,000 black soldiers in World War II intensified the push for racial equality. African Americans were placed in combat units; many lost their lives; thousands were wounded. After such sacrifices, those who survived and had "risked their lives for the Four Freedoms [now] laid a powerful claim to the right to enjoy them" (Greenberg, 1994, p. 68). One of these returning soldiers was Heman Marion Sweatt, who sought to use his G.I. Bill benefits to further his education by attending the University of Texas Law School in Austin. At that time (the mid-1940s) the university was racially segregated, and so the board of regents' response was to initiate plans to build a separate law school (in Houston) for Sweatt and other African Americans who sought to become lawyers. In the interim the state established a makeshift law school in the basement of an Austin office building and staffed it with three lawyers who were willing to teach part-time. A dissatisfied Heman Sweatt challenged the state's response in court.

The U.S. Supreme Court ruled unanimously in favor of the petitioner (in *Sweatt v. Painter*, 1950), but not on the grounds that separate but equal facilities were unconstitutional. Rather, it concluded that the newly designed facilities could not be equal to the law school at the University of Texas at Austin; any new school for blacks would not have the same facilities and intangibles, including prominent faculty, extensive law library, and national reputation. "Whether the University of Texas Law School is compared with the original or the new law school for Negroes," wrote Chief Justice Vinson, "we cannot find substantial equality in the educational opportunities offered white and Negro law students by the State" (p. 633). Heman Sweatt, the Court ordered, was to be admitted to the law school at Austin. But even though this opinion preceded the *Brown I* decision by only 4 years, the Court refused, under Chief Justice Vinson's direction, to conclude explicitly that separate facilities were inherently unequal. It merely decided about a very limited public facility.

Sweatt v. Painter was the first case involving education and race that included expert testimony from a social scientist. This testimony, presented at the lower-court level by the petitioner, focused on the absence of any racial differences in intellectual capacity or the ability to learn; the detrimental effects of segregation on the community were briefly mentioned. The expert witness was an anthropologist from the University of Chicago, Robert Redfield.

About the same time that Heman Sweatt sought admission to law school in Texas, another black man, George W. McLaurin, sought admission to the Graduate School of Education at the University of Oklahoma. That university, also segregated at the time, admitted the applicant but segregated him from the other students, claiming that it was only obeying the "separate but equal" law. His classroom desk was separated from all the others by a railing, to which a sign reading "Reserved for Colored" was attached. He was given a study area at the library far away from all the regular reading room, and he was required to eat at the cafeteria at times when no white students were there. Everything else was "equal."

In the case of *McLaurin v. Oklahoma State Regents*, decided on the same day (June 5, 1950) as Heman Sweatt's appeal, the Supreme Court once more ruled unanimously that the Oklahoma procedure denied McLaurin his right to equal protection of the law; it concluded that such restrictions "handicapped" McLaurin and that they had the effect of impairing and inhibiting his ability to study and engage in an exchange of views with other students. But again the Court carefully sidestepped the decision to strike down *Plessy v. Ferguson.* Clinging to the principle of *stare decisis*, it maintained the mantra of "separate but equal."

The Role of the NAACP

No case comes to the Supreme Court without its own history. The decision in *Brown I* was the result "of a long and carefully orchestrated legal campaign by the NAACP's Legal Defense and Educational Fund" (Balkin, 2001, p. 29). The National Association for the Advancement of Colored People (NAACP) established its legal staff in 1933 and, beginning in the mid-1930s and continuing for the next two decades, the NAACP carried out a legal assault on Jim Crow and segregation, not just in the schools but also in transportation and housing. Playing a central role for the Legal Defense and Educational Fund during this period was Thurgood Marshall, the lead counsel, who inherited the mantle from Charles Hamilton Houston, dean of the Howard University Law School.

As noted in the *Sweatt* and *McLaurin* appeals, one goal was to attack segregation in higher education, especially in graduate education. The reasoning of Houston and Marshall was that "establishing graduate facilities for Blacks that were genuinely 'separate but equal' would either be impossible or prohibitively expensive" (Balkin, 2001, p. 30). And they were right. But the challenge of breaking down segregation at the elementary-school level was greater. At first the NAACP goal, expressed in a 1945 Legal Defense and Educational Fund statement, was to attain equal schooling conditions while not attacking segregation: "The NAACP still believes that segregation in public education is unconstitutional. However, in view of the present decisions of the United States Supreme Court, it is believed that an affirmative campaign to compel the Southern states to give absolute equality in its Southern schools will not only give Negro children equal educational facilities but the tremendous cost of maintaining an equal dual school system will eventually destroy segregation" (Greenberg, 1994, p. 63). Thurgood Marshall was quoted as saying, "Those racial supremacy boys somehow think that little kids of six or seven are going to get funny ideas about sex and marriage just from going to school together, but for some equally funny reason youngsters in law school aren't supposed to feel that way. We didn't get it but we decided that if that was what the South believed, then the best thing for the moment was to go along" (Balkin, 2001, p. 30).

But by 1950, Marshall shifted the goal to desegregation.

The Appeals in *Brown I*

As noted earlier, cases from four states were consolidated in the original *Brown* appeal. The lead case challenged school segregation in Topeka, Kansas, claiming it violated the Equal Protection Clause of the Fourteenth Amendment. At that time, high schools in Kansas were desegregated by state law but elementary schools in some of the larger cities were not. The legislature permitted the 12 largest cities to have segregated elementary schools; only 6 cities, including Topeka, actually did. Thurgood Marshall sent his chief deputy, Robert L. Carter, to oversee the litigation in Kansas while Marshall focused on the suit in South Carolina, *Briggs v. Elliott*, which became one of the four consolidated petitions. (It was 1 of 32 cases Marshall argued before the Supreme Court; he won 29 of the 32.)

Thirteen Topeka families joined in the suit against the school board. The first named plaintiff was Oliver Brown, hence "*Brown v. Board of Education*." The name "Brown" will forever be associated with the momentous school desegregation decision, in part because the Supreme Court decided to combine several petitions into one case. Although the specifics of the cases in Kansas, South Carolina, Delaware, and Virginia differed, the basic constitutional issue remained the same, hence the consolidation. Among those separate petitions, the one from South Carolina, first filed in November 1950, was sent back to the trial court for further hearings, as the state legislature had passed a bill promising to equalize school facilities. So the Kansas case replaced it as being the first on the Supreme Court docket and was listed first. Had the South Carolina case not been so treated by the Court, we would be referring to this landmark case as *Briggs v. Elliott*, but instead, "the free state of Kansas not Clarendon County, South Carolina, became identified as the place where public school segregation made its last stand" (Wilson, 2004, p. 158).

Among the 13 aggrieved plaintiffs who sued the Topeka Board of Education, Oliver Brown was listed first, but not for alphabetical reasons; there was another plaintiff named Darlene Brown (not related to Oliver). A variety of possible explanations for this order have surfaced. Richard Kluger (1976), who interviewed many of the participants, believed that Oliver Brown was listed first because of his personal characteristics. He was modest, nice looking, steadily employed, a union member (which protected him if reprisals sought to take away his job), and an assistant pastor to his church. He was not a member of the NAACP, nor was he especially militant. Members of the Brown family believed, however, that Oliver Brown's name was placed first because all the other plaintiffs in the original suit were women, mothers of children denied access to all-white schools.

There remains yet another possible reason. Paul Wilson, the Kansas assistant attorney general who argued the appeal, recalled that Charles Scott, one of the attorneys representing the parents, told him that there was no rational order for the listing of the plaintiffs' names, rather, the secretary who typed the complaint entered their names randomly (Wilson, 1995, p. 24). As Kluger has observed, "It is one of the idiosyncrasies of American constitutional law that cases of profound consequence are often named for plaintiffs whose involvement in the original suit is either remote or entirely fortuitous" (1976, p. 407). Linda Brown later recalled that her father agreed to join with other families in the Topeka lawsuit because he was fed up with the long trip his daughter had to make twice a day (Kluger, 1976). Oliver Brown played an important role in this case, to be sure, but he was only one of many parents and attorneys, spread throughout the country, who contributed to the landmark case we call *Brown v. Board of Education*.

At the trial generated by the Topeka lawsuit, Oliver Brown testified that his daughter had to walk across railroad tracks and Topeka's busiest street to wait for a bus, one that was often late, to take her to her racially segregated school. Monroe School was 21 blocks from her house. As Balkin observed, "walking across the railroad yards was dangerous, and Linda sometimes had to wait in the rain and snow [with no shelter] for the bus to arrive; when the bus deposited her she had to wait another 30 minutes in front of the school until it opened" (2001, p. 32). An all-white school, Sumner School, was only six and one-half blocks away, without the challenge of any railroad tracks or dangerous streets to cross. Linda Brown had to leave for school 1 hour earlier than a white child who lived in the same racially mixed neighborhood, and the white child could come home for lunch, while Linda Brown could not.

The trial was decided by a panel of three federal judges, who ruled unanimously that the facilities of the two schools were substantially equal. Since *Plessy* was still the operative decision when the trial was held in June 1951, there was no denial of equal protection. Similarly, plaintiffs in trials in Virginia, South Carolina, Delaware, and the District of Columbia were unable to overturn the segregation of schools. Hence the losing side in each of these lawsuits appealed to the Supreme Court.

When the 13 parents petitioned the Supreme Court in October 1951, the Topeka Board of Education agonized for months and then finally, a year later, chose not to respond, so the burden fell upon the state attorney general's office to represent Kansas' position. The staff members of that office were conflicted; most felt that "racial segregation in the public schools of any Kansas community was morally, politically, and economically indefensible" (Wilson, 1995, p. 112). And yet there was an obligation to defend a Kansas statute that the attorney general's office felt was constitutional, based on *Plessy v. Ferguson.*

The state dragged its feet in submitting a respondent brief, even as oral arguments were scheduled for 6 weeks away, in December 1952. The Supreme Court sent an ominous order to the Kansas attorney general: "Because of the national importance of this issue and because of its importance to the State of Kansas, we request that the State present its views at oral argument. If the State does not desire to appear we request the Attorney General to advise whether the State's default shall be considered as a concession of invalidity" (Wilson, 1995, p. 118).

The state could not avoid its responsibility. Over the Thanksgiving weekend of 1952, Assistant Attorney General Paul Wilson prepared a brief, with, including an extension granted by the Court, only 12 days remaining before the rescheduled oral arguments. (The brief was delivered to the Court the day before the oral arguments.)

The Oral Arguments in *Brown I*

The Supreme Court held oral arguments for *Brown I* twice, the first being on December 9–10, 1952, while Fred Vinson was still chief justice. The attorneys for each side in each of the five petitions (including the District of Columbia) were permitted 1 hour before the Court; the two sides in the Kansas case went first. The range in professional ability and accomplishment was incredibly widespread. At one end was John W. Davis, described in Chapter 1 as the most renowned advocate before the Court during the first half of the twentieth century. A friend of the governor of South Carolina, James Byrnes, Davis represented that state without charging a fee. At the other extreme was Paul Wilson, the assistant attorney general for the State of Kansas, who, according to Kluger (1976) was "by Eastern standards a hayseed. His background and practice did not seem to qualify him very well" (1976, p. 548). Wilson described his own background as follows: "I was a former county attorney of Osage County,

Kansas....My professional activities had been limited largely to county and district courts in Kansas. I had never argued before any appellate court" (1995, p. 6). He had only joined the state attorney general's staff a year before, and was not the senior assistant attorney general. When Wilson prepared the brief in the case, he had assumed that his boss, the Kansas attorney general, would make the oral argument. On December 4, 5 days before the proceedings, he was told that he would make the argument.

The NAACP lawyers represented the parents of the schoolchildren. Thurgood Marshall argued the South Carolina appeal, and his assistant, Robert Carter, argued the Kansas appeal. Carter spoke first, his focus being to question the constitutionality of the Kansas statute that permitted the maintenance of segregated schools. He also argued that *Plessy v. Ferguson* was wrongly decided because discrimination was inevitable under the separate but equal doctrine (Carter, 2005). Carter's memoirs, published 50 years later, described his goals as follows:

> The heart of my argument was that the separate but equal doctrine had been first applied in a transportation case and therefore applied to a number of school cases without independent analysis to determine whether it could properly govern equal opportunity in school facility cases. [Justice] Frankfurter challenged my analysis, pointing out that over the years very able and distinguished jurists had applied the doctrine to educational cases, even listing the names of some of the justices who had done so. I agreed, but countered that these justices had done no independent analysis of their own. They had assumed that a prior Court had done so, but no prior Court had. This Court now had that opportunity, and when it made its independent analysis, it would agree with me that the doctrine could not provide equal educational opportunity for black children as the Constitution requires.
>
> When Frankfurter could not make me back off my position, he relaxed and I believe he said, "You mean there is no rational basis for classification based on race." Whether he made that concession or by gesture indicated that he was satisfied, he indicated that I had done what he wanted done. Frankfurter did not ask idle questions. They were put to make a point—sometimes, as he would say to me time to time, to explore the implications of the issues and to reveal the full effect of what would result if we prevailed. In this case, since the Court accepted and incorporated my argument in Chief Justice Warren's opinion, Frankfurter's questioning could have been to see whether my argument could be defended or whether he could make me bend.
>
> After completing the constitutional phase of the argument, I spent the rest of my hour giving a factual picture of the Topeka school system. (2005, pp. 122–123)

In response, the state of Kansas argued that the separate but equal doctrine was still the law of the land. Wilson told the Court the following:

> It is our position that the principle announced in the *Plessy* case
> and the specific rule announced in the *Gong Lum* case are abso-
> lutely controlling here. We think it is sheer sophistry to attempt to
> distinguish those cases from the case that is here presented, and we
> think the question before the Court is simply this: Is the *Plessy* case
> and the *Gong Lum* case and the "separate but equal" doctrine still
> the law of the land? We think if you decide in favor of these appel-
> lants, the Court will necessarily overrule the doctrines expressed
> in those cases and, at the same time, will say that the legislatures of
> the seventeen or twenty-one states, that the Congress of the United
> States, that dozens of appellate courts have been wrong for a period
> of seventy-five years, when they have believed and have manifested a
> belief that facilities equal though separate were within the meaning
> of the Fourteenth Amendment. (Wilson, 1995, p. 148)

At this point Justice Harold Burton raised an objection: "Don't you recognize that it is possible that within seventy-five years the social and economic
conditions and the personal relations of the nation may have changed so that
what may have been a valid interpretation of them seventy-five years ago
would not be a valid interpretation of them constitutionally today?" (Wilson, 1995, pp. 148–149). Wilson responded, "We recognize that as a possibility.
We do not believe that this record discloses any such change…We concede
that this Court can overrule the Gong Lum doctrine, the Plessy doctrine, but
nevertheless until those cases are overruled they are the best guide we have"
(Wilson, 1995, p. 149).

Assistant Attorney General Wilson also argued that no substantial in-
equality existed between the all-white and black schools in Topeka. Justice
Frankfurter, who asked more questions than all the other justices combined,
inquired about the possible consequences if the Court overturned *Plessy*
and ordered desegregation. Wilson conceded: "In perfect candor, I must say
to the Court that the consequences would probably not be severe.…Our
Negro population is small [4% of the population]. We do have in our Negro
schools Negro teachers, Negro administrators, that would necessarily be as-
similated in the school system at large. That might produce some administrative difficulties. I can imagine no serious difficultly beyond that" (Wilson,
1995, p. 147).

Paul Wilson did not use all of his allotted hour. Forty years later, in
recounting his experiences, he wrote:

> During the last several minutes of my argument the justices asked
> me no questions. They appeared to listen but I suspected that their
> interest was waning. I had said all that I could honestly say on be-
> half of Kansas. I doubted that more words would add quality to my

argument. To continue would be to invite questions that I might not be able to answer. Although I had used hardly half of my allotted hour, I decided it was time to stop. I sat down. The task that I had anticipated with dread and distress had not been unpleasant. (1995, pp. 150)

After the oral arguments for the Kansas petition were completed, the South Carolina case was argued. In some ways, even for participants in the *Brown* argument, the South Carolina case, pitting Thurgood Marshall against John W. Davis, was the main attraction. The Virginia, District of Columbia, and Delaware cases were argued during the next day.

Kluger described Marshall's presentation this way: "In some of his appearances before the Court he was good; in others, he tended to be on the dull side. On this day he was at his best" (1976, p. 570). Marshall denied that the *Plessy* case had any relevance, leading to a challenge from Justice Frankfurter (1 of the 53 interruptions of Marshall):

Justice Frankfurter: Do you really think it helps us not to recognize that behind this are certain facts of life, and the question is whether a legislature can address itself to those facts of life in despite of or within the Fourteenth Amendment, or whether, whatever the facts of life might be, where there is a vast congregation of Negro population as against the states where there is not, whether that is an irrelevant consideration? Can you escape facing those sociological facts, Mr. Marshall?

Marshall: No, I cannot escape it. But if I did fail to escape it, I would have to throw completely aside the personal and present rights of those individuals.

Justice Frankfurter: No, you would not. It does not follow because you cannot make certain classifications, you cannot make some [other] classifications.

Marshall: So far as the appellants in this case are concerned, I cannot consider it sufficient to be relegated to the legislature of South Carolina, where the record...shows their consideration of Negroes...I think that when an attack is made on a statute on the ground that it is an unreasonable classification, and competent recognized testimony is produced, I think then that the least that the state has to do is to produce something to defend their statutes.

Justice Frankfurter: I follow you when you talk that way. (Kluger, 1976, p. 571)

John W. Davis was also exemplary as an advocate; "he was clear. He was direct. He was cutting. His sentences had beginnings, middles, and endings. And there was a Victorian elegance to his language that added authority to his every assertion" (Kluger, 1976, p. 572). In contrast to its treatment of Thurgood Marshall, the Court interrupted Davis only twice. The first interruption was from Justice Burton, and was the same question he had asked Paul Wilson.

Davis:	My answer is that changed conditions may affect policy, but changed conditions cannot broaden the terminology of the Constitution. The thought is an administrative or political one, and not a judicial one.
Justice Burton:	But the Constitution is a living document that must be interpreted in relation to the facts of the time in which it is interpreted. Did we not go through that with child labor cases, and so forth?
Davis:	Oh, well, of course, changed conditions may bring things within the scope of the Constitution which were not originally contemplated, and of that perhaps the aptest illustration is the interstate commerce clause. Many things have been found to be interstate commerce which at the time of the writing of the Constitution were not contemplated at all... But when they come within the field of interstate commerce, then they become subject to congressional power, which is defined in the terms of the Constitution itself. So circumstances may bring new facts within the purview of the constitutional provision, but they do not alter, expand, or change the language that the framers of the Constitution have employed. (Kluger, 1976, p. 573).

That led Justice Frankfurter to ask the following:

Justice Frankfurter:	Mr. Davis, do you think that "equal" is a less fluid term than "commerce between the states?"
Davis:	Less fluid?
Justice Frankfurter:	Yes.
Davis:	I have not compared the two on the point of fluidity.
Justice Frankfurter:	Suppose you do it now.
Davis:	I am not sure I can approach it in just that sense.
Justice Frankfurter:	The problem behind my question is whatever the phrasing of it would be.

Davis:	That what is unequal today may be equal tomorrow, or vice versa?
Justice Frankfurter:	That is it.
Davis:	That might be. I should not philosophize about it. But the effort in which I am now engaged is to show how those who submitted the amendment and those who adopted it conceded it to be, and what their conduct by way of interpretation has been since its ratification in 1868.
Justice Frankfurter:	What you are saying is that, as a matter of history, history puts a gloss on "equal" which does not permit elimination or admixture of white and colored in this aspect to be introduced?
Davis:	Yes, I am saying that. (Kluger, 1976, p. 573)

Davis closed his argument well before his hour was up, with the level of oratory for which he was famous:

> Is it not the fact that the very strength and fiber of the federal system is local self-government in those matters for which local action is competent? Is it not, of all the activities of government, the one which most nearly approaches the hearts and minds of people—the question of the education of their young? Is it not the height of wisdom that the manner in which that shall be conducted should be left to those most immediately affected by it, and that the wishes of the parents, both white and colored, should be ascertained before their children are forced into what may be an unwelcome contact? I respectfully submit to the Court, there is no reason assigned here why this Court or any other should reverse the findings of 90 years. (Kluger, 1976, p. 574)

The Conference and its Aftermath

After this set of oral arguments, the justices met to discuss the decision, but they could not agree. One group wanted to overturn *Plessy v. Ferguson*, the Southerners on the Court were reluctant to do so, and two justices, Frankfurter and Jackson, opposed segregation but also believed in judicial restraint and were loath to overturn previous decisions. Justice Douglas summarized the difference of opinion in his memoirs:

> Only four of us—Minton, Burton, Black, and myself—felt that segregation was unconstitutional. Vinson was chief justice and he seemed to be firm that *Plessy v. Ferguson* should stand, and that the states should be allowed to deal with segregation in their own way and should be given time to make the black schools equal to those of whites. Justice Reed held that segregation was on its way out

and over the years would disappear, and that meanwhile the states should be allowed to handle it in their own way. Frankfurter's view was that it was not unconstitutional to treat the Negro differently from a white but that the cases should be reargued. Jackson felt that nothing in the Fourteenth Amendment barred segregation and that it "would be bad for Negroes" to be put in white schools, while Justice Clark said that since we had led the states to believe that segregation was lawful, we should let them work out the problem by themselves. It was clear that if a decision had been reached in the 1952 term, we would have had five saying that separate but equal schools were constitutional, that separate but unequal schools were not constitutional, and that the remedy was to give the states time to make the two systems of schools equal. (1980, p. 113)

While it is hard to assess the accuracy of Douglas's assessment of each justice—he and Frankfurter did not speak to each other—it seems likely that the majority of justices wanted to delay any decision, some to avoid a hard decision, others out of concern for the fallout from a divided opinion (Urofsky, 2004). Finally, as the term was coming to an end in the spring of 1953, the Court decided to hold the case over until the next term and reconsider it then.

As the new term approached, the chief justice suddenly died of a massive heart attack, on September 8, 1953. A Kentuckian not especially concerned with social reforms, Vinson had made no effort to reconcile the Court. In fact, critics have concluded that he was quite ineffective in constraining the rampant egos of the prima donnas on the Court, especially Douglas, Black, and Frankfurter. Some even saw Vinson's death as a blessing, coming just before the re-argument of *Brown I*. Justice Frankfurter was quoted by a law clerk as saying, "This is the first indication I have ever had that there is a God" (Kluger, 1976, p. 656).

The Re-arguments

Earl Warren was appointed by President Eisenhower as Vinson's replacement. It is said that the appointment of any new justice to the Court changes its atmosphere, especially when a new chief justice is installed. Earl Warren was charismatic yet modest (he had Hugo Black preside until he gained experience on the Court). He was not a constitutional expert but he knew what his values were; he was collegial but not reluctant to use gentle persuasion with his colleagues. His presence was felt at the re-argument of the cases in December 1953. As Justice Douglas has written, "The new Chief, sensing the deep division in the Court, did not press for a decision but made it clear he thought segregation was unconstitutional" (1980, p. 113).

It is interesting to speculate whether President Eisenhower even considered the upcoming *Brown* re-argument (then scheduled for less than a month away but later postponed for 2 months) when he chose Earl Warren for chief justice. Probably he did not. Eisenhower had promised Warren he would be the first Supreme Court appointment because Warren had swung the California delegates at the 1952 Republican convention away from Robert Taft and to Eisenhower, thus assuring the Eisenhower the nomination. (When the position of chief justice became the first vacancy, however, Eisenhower initially balked at naming Warren, but Warren forced him to do so.)

Back when *Brown I's* initial oral arguments were docketed, the Truman administration had instructed the office of the solicitor general to submit an amicus brief supporting the parents who were challenging segregation, just as it had done in the *Sweatt* and *McLaurin* cases. (As president, Truman had desegregated military and government jobs.) But President Eisenhower's position on desegregation was different. In 1948 he testified before the Senate Armed Services Committee that, in his opinion, racial segregation should be maintained in the military at the platoon level (Kluger, 1976). While it is true that the Department of Justice submitted a brief for the *Brown I* re-argument indicating that school segregation should not be maintained, Eisenhower was not an advocate of massive desegregation. When asked during his election campaign in the spring of 1952 about the added costs of a dual system of schools in 22 states, candidate Eisenhower responded, "You brought up a feature of this thing that I have not even thought about. I did not know that there was an additional cost involved" (Kluger, 1976, p. 665).

For the re-argument, the order of cases was rearranged, and the South Carolina and Virginia appeals were combined. According to observers, the attorney for the NAACP challenging those states, Spottswood Robinson, did a better job than he had a year before (Kluger, 1976). But Thurgood Marshall, who was next, was less impressive; "indeed, he was assaulted so rapidly and steadily that he seemed to come unhinged. It was one of his least creditable performances before the Court" (Kluger, 1976, p. 669). But John W. Davis, representing South Carolina, also had his problems. "At the age of eighty, Davis was making the last of his 140 appearances before the Court. He came in his cutaway, a throwback to a more formal era, and he was reduced by age to consulting his notes more often than he ever had" (Kluger, 1976, p. 671). Toward the end of his argument, he became emotionally overwrought, realizing, perhaps, that his day had passed.

When it came his time to reargue, Paul Wilson repeated his argument from a year before, even though the Topeka school board had begun a school desegregation plan. Robert Carter, arguing for the Topeka parents, "told the justices that Wilson had raised no points they had not heard before and so he would not take their time other than to note that he still had clients with a constitutional grievance" (Kluger, 1976, p. 676).

Between the time of the second set of oral arguments and the announcement of the decision in *Brown I*, President Eisenhower tried to influence Warren. He invited both the chief justice and John W. Davis to a White House stag dinner. "During the dinner, the President went to considerable lengths to tell me what a great man Mr. Davis was," Warren wrote in his memoirs (1977, p. 291). As they left the dining room, the President took the Chief's arm and, referring to whites in the South, urged, "These are not bad people. All they are concerned about is to see that their sweet little girls are not required to sit in school alongside some big overgrown Negroes" (1977, p. 291).

The Second Conference and the Decision

Chief Justice Warren clearly knew how he was going to vote and how the case should be resolved. But he did not push for an immediate resolution of the appeal, or even for a vote. Justice Douglas recalled the immediate developments after the second set of oral arguments:

> On December 12, 1953, at the first conference after the second argument, Warren suggested that the cases be discussed informally and no vote taken. He didn't want the conference to split up into two opposed groups. Warren's approach to the problem and his discussions in conference were conciliatory; not those of an advocate trying to convince recalcitrant judges. Frankfurter maintained the position that history supported the conclusions of *Plessy* that segregation was constitutional. Reed thought segregation was constitutional, and Jackson thought the issue was "political" and beyond judicial competence. Tom Clark was of the opinion that violence would follow if the Court ordered desegregation of the schools, but that while history sanctioned segregation, he would vote to abolish it if the matter was handled delicately. (1980, p. 114)

Douglas's account has been questioned by scholars (Tushnet & Lezin, 1991; Urofsky, 2004), who have suggested that there was less division on the Court than Douglas suggested. But it is true that Frankfurter and Jackson had reservations about overturning *Plessy*, not because they were segregationists (which they decidedly were not; Frankfurter, for example, had been an early supporter of the NAACP and was the first justice to hire an African-American law clerk). Rather, it was because they supported *stare decisis* and judicial restraint. Frankfurter told his colleagues that the Court did not have to "go out and meet problems" (Simon, 1989, p. 217).

It was decided that Warren should try his hand at an opinion. But this draft opinion was not sent to the printing office to have copies distributed to each justice. Rather, the chief justice personally handed his draft to each justice separately so that the justice could express any doubts or uncertainties privately before a formal opinion was circulated (Douglas, 1980). He received approval from four colleagues quite soon, but he realized that a 5-to-4 vote "would not be a decisive decision historically" (Douglas, 1980, p. 114).

From January until May 1954 he set out to convince his recalcitrant colleagues to overturn *Plessy*. Once he was clear that a majority was for that, he worked on the dissenters to ensure that the decision—certainly to be a controversial one—would reflect unanimity on the Court. And he was successful, in the view of Justice Douglas:

> As the days passed, Warren's position immensely impressed Frankfurter. The essence of Frankfurter's position seemed to be that if a practical politician like Warren, who had been governor of California for eleven years, thought we should overrule the 1896 opinion, why should a professor object? The fact that a worldly and wise man like Warren would stake his reputation on this issue not only impressed Frankfurter but seemed to have a like influence on Reed and Clark. Clark followed shortly, Reed finally came around somewhat doubtfully, and only Jackson was left. Jackson had had a heart attack and was convalescing in the hospital, where Warren went to see him. I don't know what happened in the hospital room but Warren returned to the Court triumphant. Jackson had said to count him in, which made the decision unanimous. (1980, pp. 114–115)

The support of Frankfurter was important, as he represented a well-developed position that favored judicial restraint. The new chief justice was fortunate that it was his first term on the bench, and Frankfurter, ever the expert in ingratiation and manipulation, was trying to recruit Warren to his philosophical position. Over the next decade their relationships deteriorated, leading to angry exchanges during oral arguments, as described earlier in this book (Schwartz, 1981).

Along with his law clerks, Warren drafted an opinion that was brief—11 pages long—readable, and free of legal jargon. But he did not submit this opinion for a formal vote until very shortly before the unanimous decision was announced on May 17, 1954. It is perhaps a commentary on his skill that Chief Justice Warren's memoirs downplay the degree of disagreement and give exceptional credit to his colleagues. He wrote:

> Contrary to the speculations of the press, there had not been a division of opinion expressed on the Court at any time. At the weekly conference after arguments in the case, the members, conscious of the gravity and far-reaching effects, decided not to put the case to a vote until we had thoroughly explored the implications of any decision. As a result, we discussed all sides dispassionately week after week, testing arguments of counsel, suggesting various approaches, and at time acting as "devil's advocates" in certain phases of the case, but not stating our final decision until February of 1954. I write this at some length to emphasize that there was no dissension within the Court in connection with the *Brown* case. There was not even vigorous argument. Our decision represented the judgment of every justice independently arrived at in the finest collegiate tradition.

In my entire public career, I have never seen a group of men more conscious of the seriousness of a situation, or with a greater desire for unanimity. To show how desirous we all were to present a united front, Justice Robert Jackson, who had been in the hospital for a month or so as the result of a heart attack, surprised us all by insisting on dressing and coming to the Court for the announcement. I showed concern about the danger of his overdoing, but he insisted that the case was of such importance as to call for a full Court, and he prevailed. (1977, pp. 2–3).

The Social Scientists' Brief in *Brown I*

The decision in *Brown I* angered many white residents of the South and many of the members of Congress who represented Southern states. A total of 101 Southerners in the Senate and the House of Representatives signed a "Southern Manifesto," denouncing the Supreme Court's decision as a "clear abuse of judicial power." (The only Southern Senators who refused to sign the manifesto were Albert Gore, Sr., Estes Kefauver, and Lyndon Johnson.) Senator James Eastland of Mississippi, chair of the Judiciary Committee, in retaliation initiated a requirement that all future nominees to the Supreme Court had to appear before the committee; that requirement continues today. (Ironically, the first nominee so required to do so, John Marshall Harlan II, was the grandson of the one justice who had dissented in the *Plessy* decision in 1896.) Furthermore, members of Congress from the South vented their anger at the NAACP, calling for an inquiry into its tax status, trying to restrict its ability to file lawsuits, and seeking to publicize the names of NAACP members who lived in the South.

But a footnote in the decision angered legal purists, regardless of whether they agreed with the thrust of the decision. Footnote 11 came from the efforts of the NAACP to determine if there was empirical work on the detrimental effects of segregation. Around 1950, Thurgood Marshall and Robert Carter learned of the research on racial identity being done by Dr. Kenneth B. Clark (then an assistant professor of psychology at the City College of New York) and his wife Mamie Clark, also a psychologist. Their research materials were four dolls, each about a foot in length and dressed in diapers. Two were pink and two were brown. (The Clarks had purchased them for fifty cents each at a five-and-ten-cent store in New York City.) The psychologists showed black children, ages 3 to 7 years, the four dolls and gave them instructions. First, "Give me the white doll" and "Give me the Negro doll." Then the instructions shifted: "Give me the doll that is the nice doll" and "Give me the doll that looks bad." Having tested 400 children in a variety of locations (Philadelphia, Boston, Worcester, Massachusetts, and several cities in Arkansas), the Clarks found "an unmistakable preference for the white doll and a rejection of the brown doll" in most of the children, even in the 3-year-olds (Kluger, 1976, p. 318).

The Clarks were disturbed by their findings, writing, "we sat on them for a number of years. What was surprising was the degree to which the children suffered from self-rejection, with its truncating effect on their personalities, and the earliness of the corrosive awareness of cold. I don't think we had quite realized the *extent* of the cruelty of racism and how hard it hit" (Kenneth Clark, quoted by Kluger, 1976, p. 318, italics in original).

Robert Carter approached Clark and asked him to testify in the *Briggs v. Elliott* trial in South Carolina. Clark was also asked to enlist other social scientists in the cause. He did both. But not all the NAACP lawyers shared Carter's and Marshall's enthusiasm over the relevance of the doll study; for some, the dolls were a source of "considerable derision" and other attorneys were skeptical about the impact of the Clarks' research findings on federal judges (Kluger, 1976, p. 321). But Marshall and Carter sought all the help they could get.

The NAACP lawyers asked for a summary of the social-science findings as they prepared for the Supreme Court appeal in December 1952. Clark, working with Stuart W. Cook and Isidor Chein of NYU's psychology department, prepared a 24-page statement that became an amicus brief from 32 "concerned social scientists," including Jerome Bruner, David Krech, Otto Klineberg, M. Brewster Smith, Robert Merton, Gordon Allport, and Hadley Cantrilt.

The statement, accompanied by 35 footnotes, was low-key and authoritative. Its conclusions were the same as Dr. Clark's testimony: minority children developed poor self-esteem and other negative qualities. Furthermore, the institutionalization of segregation by the school system was more deleterious than the expression of prejudice by individuals, as the school system reflected the authority of the state.

In his oral argument, John W. Davis had devoted some of his most scathing criticism to the social scientists' brief. He told the Court, "Much of that which is handed around under the name of social science is an effort on the part of the scientist to rationalize his own preconceptions. They find usually, in my limited observation, what they go out to find" (Kluger, 1976, p. 573).

But when the decision was announced on May 17, 1954, readers found the following statement in it:

> Segregation of white and colored children in the public schools has a detrimental effect upon colored children. The impact is greater when it has the sanction of the law, for the policy of separating the races is usually interpreted as denoting the inferiority of the Negro group. A sense of inferiority affects the motivation of children to learn. Segregation with the sanction of law, therefore, has a tendency to retard the educational and mental development of Negro children and then deprive them of some of the benefits they would receive in a racially integrated school system. Whatever may have

been the extent of psychological knowledge at the time of *Plessy v. Ferguson*, this finding is amply supported by modern authority. (*Brown v. Board of Education*, 1954, p. 494)

Footnote 11 of the opinion is then cited; the footnote simply listed several sources from psychological journals and books.

Why did the Court apparently rely on social-science findings for its decision? Why did the Supreme Court not simply note that school desegregation, on the face of it, induced an assumption of inferiority, leading to a response of humiliation? It may have been "precisely because the Court knew it was bucking a firm precedent and entering a heated debate that it wished to garner *all* the supporting evidence that was available. Without data, there was a danger that the arguments on both sides might merely have become so much moral posturing and empty assertions" (Perkins, 1988, p. 471). As Thurgood Marshall had observed, the earlier separate but equal "doctrine had become so ingrained that overwhelming proof was sorely needed to demonstrate that equal educational opportunities for Negroes could not be provided in a segregated system" (Rosen, 1972, p. 430).

Certainly Chief Justice Warren, in drafting the opinion, capitalized on the social scientists' statement, and several sentences in the opinion echo the conclusions of the social scientists. But it is more likely that the main reason for its inclusion was to broaden the underpinnings of an unpopular decision. This is confirmed by a later comment by Otto Klineberg, one of the signers, who spoke to Chief Justice Warren a few years later:

> He told me that the members of the Court would probably have
> come to the same conclusion in any case, but they (and he in
> particular) felt their position was strengthened by the clear support
> of the present generation of psychologists.... We were all proud that
> the psychological research findings were included in...the legal
> brief...to which Chief Justice Earl Warren made approving reference. (1986, pp. 53, 54)

Did the Oral Arguments Affect the Outcome?

No conclusive evidence exists that the oral arguments played an influential role in the *Brown v. Board of Education* decision. If any one factor was most significant, it was the replacement of Fred Vinson with Earl Warren as the leader of the Court. Warren was steadfast in his conclusions and his goal, and he persuaded his colleagues who were not. Certainly the outspoken liberals on the Court, Douglas and Black, had made their minds up long before the oral arguments. When the justices saw the briefs and heard the oral arguments relying on *Plessy v. Ferguson* as a defense for what everyone recognized as unequal treatment, the allegiance to a states' rights principle faltered.

"Great man" theories of leadership are no longer in favor; the name is obviously sexist but beyond that, the title is seen as a simplification as we try to ascertain the causes for events in history. Would Germany have started World War II if Hitler had been killed while he was a soldier in World War I? Most historians would say that forces were present in Germany between the two wars that led to the militarism and ethnocentrism that Hitler cleverly exploited. Would the Supreme Court have ruled that school segregation was unconstitutional if Fred Vinson had not suddenly died before the re-arguments? At some point, yes. There is even some speculation that Vinson saw the need for such a decision and was moving steadily in that direction but was concerned about its timing and scope (Kurland, 1968; Tushnet & Lezin, 1991). Clearly the placement of Earl Warren in the leadership position accelerated the process. When he announced the decision on May 17, 1954, the outcome, if not the process since the public oral arguments, became known to the world.

7

Predicting Votes from Oral Arguments

The secret for successful advocacy is simply to get the Court to ask your opponent more questions.
> —John Roberts (from a speech given while he was still an advocate before the Court, 2005, p. 25)

A Decision Fraught with Disagreement—Could It Have Been Foretold by the Comments at Oral Arguments?

John G. Roberts, Jr., initiated his service as chief justice of the United States with the term that began on October 3, 2005. By the two-thirds point in that term, late March of 2006, things had progressed incredibly smoothly under the reins of the novice leader: Decisions had been announced in 31 of the cases before the Court, and in 22 of these cases, or 71%, the vote had been unanimous—a rate that was almost twice what was typical in recent terms. Furthermore, as described in Chapter 5 and evaluated in Chapter 8, justices and observers of the Court described it as having a more relaxed and congenial atmosphere. Former Chief Justice Rehnquist had been known for his methodical procedure at case conferences; little discussion was tolerated at these, and votes were taken quite expeditiously. In contrast, it was speculated that the new chief justice was encouraging more exchange of viewpoints.

But on March 22, 2006, a decision was announced that signaled an irrevocable division on the Court. In a 5-to-3 vote (newly confirmed Justice Alito did not participate), the Court ruled in *Georgia v. Randolph* that it is unconstitutional for police without a warrant to search a home if two occupants are present and one person consents but the other objects. The case stemmed from a domestic conflict in 2001 that involved Scott and Janet Randolph of Americus, Georgia. When a police officer responded to the disturbance, Janet Randolph told him that her husband had drugs in the home, and she was amenable to letting the police inside to search for them. Although Scott Randolph objected, the police officer entered anyway, based on Janet Randolph's acquiescence. She led him to drug paraphernalia (actually a straw containing cocaine residue) in an upstairs bedroom. Randolph, a lawyer, was convicted, whereupon he appealed. A trial judge held that the search was valid but the Georgia Court of Appeals and the Georgia Supreme Court both concluded that the search was a violation of the Fourth Amendment's protection against an unlawful search and seizure. Thus the State of Georgia persuaded the Supreme Court to review its petition.

The *Georgia v. Randolph* decision was noteworthy not only because of the disruption from the path of a seemingly amicable Court but also because it generated opinions from six of the eight justices who participated in the decision. Justice Souter wrote the opinion for the Court, and Justices Stevens and Breyer wrote separate concurrences; each of the minority of three, Justices Scalia, Thomas, and Roberts, wrote separate dissents. (For the chief justice, it was his first written dissent.) Only Justices Kennedy and Ginsburg did not write separately. There six different opinions—unusual but not unique—and their tone was in direct contrast to the collegial nature the term had displayed thus far. Writing about the decision in the *New York Times*, Linda Greenhouse described the tone as "pointed, personal, and acerbic" (2006b, p. A1).

Justice Souter's opinion for the Court concluded that the search was unreasonable because of the husband's objections. In previous cases, the Court had permitted a search whenever one party who shared premises with another gave consent, under the "co-occupant consent rule." But Justice Souter noted that this case could be distinguished from the earlier ones because the facts were different. In previous cases the person who later objected was not present when the police were admitted, but in the current case Scott Randolph was. The fact that the objecting person was present changed everything, wrote Justice Souter; it defied "widely shared social expectations" for someone to enter when one occupant acquiesced but the other objected. He wrote, "In sum, there is no common understanding that one co-tenant generally has a right or authority to prevail over the express wishes of another, whether the issue is the color of the curtains or invitations to outsiders.... We have, after all, lived our whole national history with an understanding of the ancient adage that a man's home is his castle.... Disputed permission is thus no match for this central value of the Fourth Amendment" (*Georgia v. Randolph*, 2006, pp. 10–11 of slip opinion).

Justice Breyer's concurrence raised a concern about the implications of the decision. For example, if the call was generated by a claim of domestic abuse, the invitation to enter the home "could reflect the victim's fear about being left alone with an abuser. It could also indicate the availability of evidence, in the form of an immediate willingness to speak, that might not otherwise exist. In that context, an invitation (or consent) would provide a special reason for immediate, rather than later, police entry. And, entry following invitation (or consent) by one party ordinarily would be reasonable even in the face of direct objection by the other" (*Georgia v. Randolph*, 2006, p. 3 of Breyer slip opinion). Justice Breyer noted that family disturbance calls constitute the most frequent type of calls received by police departments each year. Thus he joined the majority with the understanding that the nature of the holding was "case-specific."

Justice Stevens' two-page concurring opinion took "originalists" to task, if they failed to "recognize the relevance of changes in our society" (*Georgia v. Randolph*, 2006, p. 1 of Stevens slip opinion.) Specifically, he noted that in the eighteenth century, when the Fourth Amendment was adopted, only the permission of the husband would matter, but today "each of the partners has a constitutional right that he or she may independently assert or waive" (Stevens p. 2 slip opinion). Justice Scalia's three-page dissent, after indicating support to the much more detailed dissent by the chief justice, spent its entirety on a response to Justice Stevens' critique of originalists.

Justice Thomas's dissent challenged the conclusion that what occurred in this case qualified as a Fourth Amendment search. He noted that no general search occurred; rather, "Mrs. Randolph told police responding to a domestic dispute that respondent was using a substantial quantity of cocaine. Upon police request, she consented to a general search of her residence to investigate her statements. However ... the record is clear that no such general search occurred. Instead, Sergeant Brett Murray asked Mrs. Randolph where the cocaine was located, and she showed him to an upstairs bedroom, where he saw the 'piece of cut straw' on a dresser ... upon closer examination, Sergeant Murray observed a white residue on the straw, and concluded that the straw had been used for ingesting cocaine.... He then collected the straw and the residue as evidence" (*Georgia v. Randolph*, Thomas pp. 1–2, slip opinion.)

The chief justice's dissent was much longer (17 pages) and more developed than the dissents by Justices Scalia and Thomas. He challenged the majority's assumption that an invited guest who encountered two disagreeing co-occupants would leave, and he argued that someone choosing to share space has also chosen to share privacy. He wrote, "Our common social expectations may well be that the other person will not, in turn, share what we have shared with them with another—including the police—but that is the risk we take in sharing. If two friends share a locker and one keeps contraband inside, he might trust that his friend will not let others look inside. But by sharing private space, privacy has 'already been frustrated' with respect to the lockermate" (Roberts, p. 5 slip opinion).

But as Linda Greenhouse commented, the justices revealed their real feelings in their footnotes:

> Justice Souter, usually mild-mannered to a fault, said in Footnote 4 that "in the dissent's view, the centuries of special protection for the privacy of the home are over." By invoking a "false equation" between inviting the police into the home and reporting a secret, he said, the chief justice "suggests a deliberate intent to devalue the importance of the privacy of a dwelling place." Chief Justice Roberts responded in turn. The majority had mischaracterized his position on privacy and "seems a little overwrought," he said in a footnote. In a concluding paragraph of his dissent, he said: "The majority reminds us, in high tones, that a man's home is his castle, but even under the majority's rule, it is not his castle if he happens to be absent, asleep in the keep or otherwise engaged when the constable arrives at the gate. Then it is his co-owner's castle." Justice Souter also attacked as a "red herring" a warning by Chief Justice Roberts that the rule the Court was adopting would hamper the ability of the police to protect victims of domestic violence. Justice Souter said the law was clear on the right of the police, despite any objection, to enter a home to protect a crime victim. But that issue "has nothing to do with the question in this case," he said. (Greenhouse, 2006b, p. A18)

Given these strong feelings, was there anything in the questions and judicial comments during the oral arguments that anticipated the written opinions? Psychologists and, for that matter, people in general often engage in what has come to be called "postdiction," that is, we take an outcome and then try to identify the circumstances in an earlier event that led to the outcome. "Post-dictions" are fraught with limitations, and later in this chapter I will describe efforts at genuine prediction, or at least examining antecedent events to see if they are related to outcomes. But the case of *Georgia v. Randolph* led to such emotional comments that it is worth examining in detail the contents of its oral arguments. (These were held on November 8, 2005; the split decision was announced on March 22, 2006. This interval of 4 1/2 months is not unusual, given the record in past terms.)

Recall that Justices Souter, Breyer, Stevens, Ginsburg, and Kennedy were in the majority; Chief Justice Roberts and Justices Scalia and Thomas dissented. Justice O'Connor participated in the oral arguments but was no longer on the Court (and hence did not vote) when the decision was announced. Some of the votes by justices were predictable from their questions, but a few were not. Based on questions and comments during the oral arguments, Justice Breyer's vote was the most surprising. He aimed many of his questions at the ubiquitous Thomas Goldstein, the maverick advocate described in Chapter 3 who represented Scott Randolph. Justice Breyer was concerned that a ruling in favor of the respondent "would prevent the many, many cases of spousal abuse from being investigated" (*Georgia v. Randolph*, oral argument transcript, p. 37). His comments anticipated those that he wrote in his concurrence, as noted before, in which he described the Court's decision as "case-specific."

As noted in earlier chapters, Justice Thomas rarely speaks during oral arguments, but on this occasion he had a question: would the case have been different if Randolph's wife had run upstairs, retrieved a straw with cocaine residue, and handed it to the police? This question anticipated the content of his dissent.

From Predisposition to Final Disposition

People reveal their feelings, their preferences, and their biases by what they say as well as how they behave. Do justices consistently reveal their eventual votes on appeals by the kinds of questions and statements they make during oral arguments? The previous chapters have shown that the questions posed by the justices are varied. Some may straightforwardly seek information; others may reflect a distrust or skepticism about an advocate's position. Taken as a whole, a justice's questions should reflect the position of the devil's advocate: they should tap into the weaknesses of each side's position. But how often do they do this? Or is it more common for the predominance of questions to reflect a predisposition toward one side by the justice?

Newspaper and magazine accounts indicate that, at least in some appeals, justices' comments appear to reflect their predispositions. In a case challenging a law that required cable television systems to carry the signals of most broadcast stations (*Turner Broadcasting v. Federal Communications Commission*, 1997), the headline in the *New York Times* described the oral argument by concluding, "Justices Skeptically Review Law on Cable System Access" (Greenhouse, 1996a, p. A10). The same newspaper boldly (and correctly) presented the outcome in a partial-birth abortion case (*Stenberg v. Carhart*, 2000) by the headline "Justices Appear Set to Reject Law on Abortion Procedure" (Greenhouse, 2000, p. A1). More recently, after the oral arguments were given regarding the constitutionality of a Vermont law that severely limited how much political candidates could spend (*Randall v. Sorrells*, 2006), the *New York Times* bore the headline "Vermont Campaign Limits Get Cool Reception in Court" (Greenhouse, 2006a, p. A14). Magazines also anticipate outcomes; in describing the oral argument in a physician-assisted suicide case, *Newsweek* captioned the story, "Whose Right Is It? The Justices Seem Eager to Let the States Resolve the Issue of Assisted Suicide for Themselves" (Reibstein, 1997).

Not every case's oral arguments generate such headlines, but those journalists who cover the Supreme Court as their full-time activity are not reluctant to make predictions based on the oral arguments when they believe the pattern of interactions warrants it. For example, Linda Greenhouse, who has reported on the Court for more than 25 years, did so regarding the constitutional challenge to the Solomon Amendment, which withheld federal grants to those universities that did not permit the military to recruit at their law schools. With respect to the oral argument for the case of *Rumsfeld v. Forum for Academic and Institutional Rights* (2006), she wrote, "The result was a lopsided argument during which the justices appeared strongly inclined to uphold . . . the Solomon Amendment" (2005b, p. A1). She was prescient; less than 3 months later the Court announced its decision in this case, and it was a unanimous one supporting the constitutionality of the law.

Can Votes Be Predicted? The Experts Say "Yes"

The purpose of this chapter is to determine empirically the degree to which individual justices' questions and the general thrust of their questions predict the individual justices' votes and the overall decisions in cases. These questions would appear to be capable of being answered in a straightforward manner, but before providing detailed answers, some methodological issues must be considered. These will be described in the next section. First, it is helpful to review the basic conclusions of those experts who have considered the content of the oral arguments as predictive tools. By "experts" I refer here to a journalist who covers the Supreme Court, a former advocate before the Court, and a researcher who has observed a number of oral arguments.

Linda Greenhouse

The Supreme Court reporter for the *New York Times* has acknowledged the journalist's tendency to be bold enough to anticipate votes. At a symposium that focused on various predictive devices, she said, "I frequently make predictions in my accounts of oral arguments, part of my effort to raise the story above the level of the formulaic: 'The Supreme Court heard argument today on whether . . .' and to give the reader my best judgment on what is likely to happen next—the oral argument, after all, being only a snapshot of the decisional process" (2003, p. 25). In preparing her comments for the symposium, she decided to assess the quality of her own predictions, based solely on oral arguments, using cases from the October 2002 term. In only about one third of the cases, or 27 cases, had she prepared an article on the oral arguments. She included some form of prediction in 17 cases (although one of these later ended in a dismissal and so couldn't be counted) and avoided making a prediction in the other 10. So of 16 cases for which her story implied a particular outcome, in 12, or 75%, her predictions were correct. (Two were wrong and two had a "mixed" outcome.)

Interestingly, one of her self-labeled "mixed" outcome cases was *Virginia v. Black* (2003), described in Chapter 5 because of Justice Thomas's reaction during the oral argument. Greenberg wrote at that time, "While the justices had earlier appeared somewhat doubtful of the Virginia statute's constitutionality, they now seemed [after Justice Thomas's emotional outburst] quite convinced that they could uphold it consistent with the First Amendment" (2002, p. A1). As she noted in her talk on prediction, "In fact, while the Court did affirm the notion of criminalizing cross-burning, it struck down the Virginia statute as not meeting the appropriate evidentiary test for intentional intimidation" (2003, p. 27).

John Roberts

A success rate of 75% accuracy, while not perfect, is above the rate of chance, and indicates that justices' questions often signal their eventual votes. Can other approaches match it? As described in Chapter 1, before becoming chief justice, John Roberts addressed the Supreme Court Historical Society at its annual meeting. Although most of his talk dealt with the reemergence of a Supreme Court bar, he did report on an analysis he had conducted. He took the first and last cases in each of the 2-week argument sessions for the October 1980 term and for the October 2003 term. He determined, for each case, the number of questions directed toward the petitioner and the number directed toward the respondent. Then he examined which side won. He reported: "In the 28 cases I looked at, 14 from the 1980 term and 14 from 2003, the most-questions-asked 'rule' predicted the winner—or, more accurately, the loser—in 24 of those 28 cases, an 86 percent prediction rate" (2005, p. 25).

Thus, we have an even higher success rate than that of Linda Greenhouse, and even better, it appears on first blush to be a highly accessible and reliable measure—all that is involved is counting up the number of questions. But, as will be shown later in this chapter, determining what constitutes a "question" is not so simple.

Sarah Shullman

While a law student at Georgetown University, Sarah Shullman undertook an innovative study. Unfortunately, it is a study impossible to replicate, but her results are nonetheless provocative. Perhaps their allure is best reflected by a statement she makes in her report: "My research indicates that by keeping track of the number of questions each justice asks, and by evaluating the relative content of these questions, one can actually predict before the argument is over which way the justice will vote" (2004, p. 272). This is an astounding claim; is it legitimate, and on what grounds is it based?

Shullman attended 10 oral arguments during the term that began in October 2002. She recorded each question and noted which justice asked it. While doing so, she assigned a score to each question based on its intent, using a scale of 1 (most helpful) to 5 (most hostile). In addition, she made notes about the justices' tone of voice, their use of jokes and hypothetical questions, and other relevant occurrences. Later, for each justice, she tabulated the number of questions the justice asked for each case, the number asked of the party that later received the justice's vote, and the number asked of the party that later lost the justice's vote.

After doing this for seven cases, she used the results from these to predict the outcome in three cases. It is unclear from her report how many of the first seven cases led to greater questioning of the eventual losing side than of the eventual winning side. She reported, "All nine justices seemed to ask fewer questions of whose party they would ultimately decide" (2004, p. 278). This is, at best, an ambiguous statement; it can be read to mean *each justice* did so, which obviously is untrue (for example, Justice Thomas did not ask any questions at all). But even if it refers to the combined questions by any of the justices, the report of results is incomplete. She mentions two cases in which the justices asked more questions of the losing side (*United States v. Bean* and *Federal Communications Commission v. NextWave Personal Communications, Inc.*) and then states, "the one exception" was *Moseley v. V Secret Catalogue,* "in which the justices asked slightly fewer questions of the respondent, but unanimously held for the petitioner" (2004, p. 278). Thus, apparently the number of questions predicted outcomes correctly in six of these seven cases, or 86%.

Then she made predictions about three subsequent cases, and in each of these found that more questions were directed toward the losing side. Adding these to the previous seven, her accuracy rate is 9 out of 10, or 90%. Her conclusion was the following:

> This analysis brings me back to the original question: Do the justices use oral argument to play devil's advocate by posing questions designed to elicit the strongest and weakest arguments of each side, or do they use oral argument to do some advocacy of their own? My limited research suggests that the answer is a little of both. Many of the justices pose hostile or argumentative questions to both sides, but it seems that more often they go easy on the lawyer for the party they support and only play devil's advocate to the lawyer for the party they oppose. Essentially, whether they do it by asking more questions or by asking questions that are more hostile in content, the justices simply give the side they disagree with a harder time. And, regardless of whether the justices actually intend to do their own advocating, this information suggests that one might profitably use an analysis of their questions to predict what was previously thought to be unpredictable. (Shullman, 2004, pp. 292–293)

Implied in Shullman's comments and findings is the conclusion that justices have already made up their mind before the oral argument begins. Shullman raised this issue briefly in her introduction but did not resolve it. Instead, she moved to what she stated was what most advocates believe, that the advocates cannot discern from the justices' questions just how they will vote.

But Shullman's results have several methodological limitations. First is the problem of lack of inter-rater reliability. Only one observer classified the questions; it is regrettable that a second coder was not there to independently record and categorize questions. Even if one later used audiotapes of the oral arguments as an independent check, the opportunity to observe would be missing. The chance to be in the courtroom to watch these cases has passed. The presence of a second observer would give credence to the feasibility of the typical observer being able to do what Shullman reported that she did: to decide on the spur of the moment (without instant replay) what *is* a question, how many questions are embedded in one exchange, and whether each is helpful or hostile (or neither). Recall that the typical 30-minute oral argument by one side produces anywhere from 30 to 100 questions, plus an equal number of responses by the advocate.

Science relies on replicability in order to be confident that an empirical finding has validity. Other researchers must be able to find the same effect using the same procedures. Later in this chapter I will describe an effort by my research team to replicate Shullman's findings, but we had to use a different procedure. Shullman should be commended for her innovation, but her specific procedure needs to be replicated using two or more coders in the courtroom, not only to determine the generalizability of her findings but also to assess the feasibility of the method.

A concern with feasibility of coding on the spur of the moment is also reflected in our second problem: What *is* a question? Just like Justice Roberts in his article, Shullman gives us no guidance here. The reader may assume that it is obvious what is classified as a question and that is easy to assign a question to the "helpful" or "hostile" category, but neither of these assumptions is true. In an attempt to replicate the impressive conclusions of Shullman's and Roberts's studies, Jacqueline Austin and I discovered some of the difficulties. We could not attend oral arguments as Shullman did but used transcripts, as Justice Roberts did. These transcripts, available on the Supreme Court's Web site (http://www.supremecourtus.gov/) and prepared by the Alderson Reporting Company of Washington, D.C., range from 45 to 60 pages in length. They list the names and affiliations of every attorney representing the petitioner and the respondent, and the transcripts since October 2004 identify the name of the justice asking the question or making a comment. Thanks to the efforts of Chief Justice Roberts, beginning with the October 2006 term, transcripts were made available on the Supreme Court Web site the same day as the oral argument, rather than 1 to 2 weeks later.

The transcripts generally appear to be free of errors, although occasionally the recorder makes a mistake. For example, on page 11 of the transcript for the oral argument in *Dodd v. United States* (2005), there is the word "movant," which is not a word and perhaps intended to be "movement," clearly a transcription error. Another difficulty occurs when the transcriber apparently does not understand the reference made by a justice. For example, in *Dodd v. United States*, the transcript has Justice Breyer saying, "but if you don't—aren't—I mean the language is open, and it's sort of like the virtue of this—suddenly it's like tinkers to Everest chance" (p. 25). This appears to be a reference by Justice Breyer to the double-play combination many years ago of

"Tinker to Evers to Chance," but the transcriber apparently was not a fan of old-time baseball.

Determining what is a question is difficult because, as noted earlier in the book, interactions between advocates and justices do not flow in a discrete manner; two justices may begin to speak at the same time, a justice may interrupt an advocate, and justices make elongated statements that may contain several questions. As shown in Justice Breyer's comment, both justices and advocates may make statements that begin with a thought and then pause and start all over.

Following is an example of a typical exchange, from the case *Small v. United States* (2005). Gary Small had been convicted of a crime while in Japan and had served time there in prison. After his return to the United States he purchased a gun; to do so, he had to answer the question if he had ever been convicted of a crime "in any court." He said no. He was later arrested and charged with violating the law. The question before the Supreme Court was whether Congress, when it wrote "in any court," meant any court in the United States or any court anywhere in the world.

In the excerpt below, Paul Boas of Pittsburgh, representing Gary Small, has just told the Court that certain offenses in the United States carry less than a 1-year penalty, whereas in France or England, conviction for the same crime carries a penalty of more than 1 year.

Justice Breyer:	Are there any such cases? I mean, I never heard actually—
Mr. Boas:	No.
Justice Breyer:	—when people—no. I mean, are there any cases in which France or England has convicted people of an antitrust violation punishable by imprisonment for more than a year? I—I didn't know that their antitrust laws had a criminal aspect, though I haven't looked it up.
Mr. Boas:	Nor have I—
Justice Breyer:	Fine. Well, I—I've never heard if anyone in any foreign country, other than ours, though I gather my law clerk found that in Japan, in fact, Japan does have a criminal antitrust law. They may be the only ones outside the United States, and I don't know that anyone has ever been convicted under it because they're not too—or they didn't used to be too fierce on antitrust enforcement.
Mr. Boas:	Well, 921(20) or—
Justice Breyer:	I'm just wondering how anomalous...your anomaly is.
(Laughter.)	
Mr. Boas:	Well, the—the limitation not only excludes antitrust offenses, it excludes any business regulatory offense.
Justice Breyer:	And are there such?

Mr. Boas:	Of course. I think—
Justice Breyer:	I mean, maybe.
Mr. Boas:	Yes.
Justice Breyer:	I don't—I don't—but I just—are we sure there—that, you know, that this anomaly exists?
Mr. Boas:	I—I'm certain there are business regulatory crimes throughout the world. (*Small v. United States*, 2005, transcript of the oral argument, pp. 6–7)

Using a transcript rather than listening, Austin and I initially discovered that it was not clear just what was a question. We had to develop a set of ground rules, and only then were the two of us, working independently, able to come up with a very similar number of questions.

An Attempt to Replicate the Earlier Findings

In a 2006 senior honors thesis done at the University of Kansas, Jacqueline Austin, under my supervision, sought to replicate the findings that the number of questions asked was related to votes and decisions. We also sought to broaden the number of cases used by Shullman and to use a procedure that increased the reliability of coding.

Our Hypotheses

It made sense to us to expect that justices would ask somewhat more questions to the advocate whose side they disagreed with, *if* the justices had already formed an opinion. But that's a big *if*. It is conceivable that some justices have a tendency to prematurely form irrevocable judgments prior to oral arguments. Justice Thomas's statement at the beginning of Chapter 2 indicated that, in his view, "most justices" do. Our position is that individual differences exist—not only are some justices predisposed, but some types of cases elicit a predisposition more often than others. As Chief Justice Rehnquist wrote, he was more likely to be influenced during oral argument in those cases in which he was less familiar with the topic. So what is the nature of a case that leads to a premature judgment?

Austin and I made a distinction between ideologically related cases and those that are not ideologically related. As first mentioned in Chapter 2, by "ideological" we mean cases whose issues trigger a value-laden bias in a justice, cases dealing with abortion, rights of minorities, and federalism for instance. The terms "conservative" and "liberal" probably do a better job of describing these value-laden biases than any other set of terms.

With this distinction as background, we hypothesized that justices' questions are more likely to be predictive in those cases where ideology is central; in nonideological cases, frequency of questions is less likely to predict votes.

Our theory on the rationale for justices asking questions and making statements reflects two main functions of this activity: to seek support for their own positions by asking questions that emphasize one side and to play devil's advocate by asking questions that test the weaknesses of the other side.

Our Procedure

Of the 74 cases for which there were signed opinions in the October 2004 term, we selected 24 for analysis—12 that we believed to reflect a possible ideological bias and 12 that did not. To determine if a case was ideological or not, we independently rated the degree to which the issue dealt with value-related matters, using a five-point scale (5 = very ideological, 4 = somewhat ideological, 3 = unclear, 2 = somewhat nonideological, and 1 = definitely nonideological). After doing our ratings separately, we compared our ratings and selected for our analysis only those cases for which our ratings were in complete agreement: 12 cases in which we had both rated each them a 5 (very ideological) and 12 cases in which we had rated each of them a 1 (definitely not-ideological). Hence our ratings reflected 100% agreement.

We wanted the two groups of cases to be as similar as possible on other variables, to eliminate confounds that would serve as other explanations for any differences in results. For example, it would not be desirable to compare ideological cases that had been decided by 9-to-0 votes with nonideological cases decided by 5-to-4 votes. We were able to select two sets of cases that had similar variability in vote splits. One variable for which we were not able to exert any control was whether the original case was civil or criminal. Criminal cases are inherently more likely to generate ideology-related reactions; all but one of the cases we selected for this category were criminal (the one that was not was *Kelo v. City of New London*, dealing with eminent domain). All the nonideological cases were civil in origin.

The 12 ideological-related cases were the following:

1. *Deck v. Missouri*, on whether it was a constitutional violation to force a capital murder defendant to appear in court in chains and shackles for the penalty phase of his jury trial
2. *Brown v. Payton*, on the relevance of an alleged religious conversion by the defendant as a consideration by the jury in determining its sentence of death versus life in prison
3. *Bradshaw v. Stumpf*, on whether the constitutional rights of a capital murder defendant were compromised by inconsistent arguments by the prosecutor
4. *Roper v. Simmons*, on the constitutionality of a sentence of death for a defendant who committed the crime when he was a minor
5. *Florida v. Nixon*, on the constitutionality of the sentence of death to a defendant after his lawyer had pleaded him as guilty without his consent

6. *Halbert v. Michigan,* which questioned the lower court's affirmation of the defendant's sentence after he had appealed without the assistance of an attorney
7. *Johnson v. California,* on what constitutes racial bias in jury selection
8. *Miller-El v. Dretke,* on what constitutes racial bias in jury selection in a capital murder trial
9. *Wilkinson v. Austin,* on the acceptability of an Ohio law determining when prisoners could be sent to a maximum-security prison
10. *Small v. United States,* on the interpretation of being convicted "in any court," which prohibits citizens from owning guns
11. *Illinois v. Caballes,* on the use of drug-sniffing dogs for checking cars even without reasonable cause
12. *Kelo v. City of New London,* on the constitutionality of local government taking people's homes against their wishes, for private development

The 12 nonideological cases were the following:

1. *ExxonMobil v. Saudi Basic,* on whether the Rocker-Feldman doctrine applies to federal jurisdiction
2. *Grable v. Darue,* which asked if U.S. tax-code issues involving state property and the IRS should be decided by the federal courts
3. *National Cable and Telecommunications Assn. v. Brand X Internet Service,* on whether cable television companies that offer Internet services should be regulated as information providers or telecommunications providers
4. *American Trucking Association v. Michigan,* on whether Michigan's $100 annual trucking fee for commercial trucking companies discouraged interstate commerce
5. *Mid-Con Freight v. Michigan,* on the applicability of a $100 fee on trucks with Michigan license plates preempting legal authority
6. *Granholm v. Heald,* on the possibly discriminatory and anticompetitive nature of state laws barring customers from ordering out-of-state wines
7. *Cooper Industries v. Aviall Services,* on the right of a company to sue to recover costs when it cleaned up pollution on land it bought, even without a direct order to do so
8. *Merck KGaA v. Integra Life Sciences,* on the right of drug companies starting research on competing medications to have freedom under FDA rules to ignore rivals' patents
9. *MGM Studios v. Grokster,* on the legality of downloading music and movies over the Internet
10. *Kansas v. Colorado,* on a dispute over water rights for the Arkansas River
11. *Alaska v. United States,* on the rights to ownership of submerged lands in a national park

12. *Norfolk Southern Railway v. Kirby*, on the limits of federal maritime law on the liability for damage caused by a derailment

In seeking to replicate the procedure of the earlier studies, we encountered several methodological problems. The first was determining what the unit was. Initially, we chose to classify each sentence by a justice separately. However, using *Dodd v. United States* as a test case, we found this to be unworkable, because there were too many interrupted statements and unfinished thoughts. Thus we decided to use each statement by a justice, whether it was a brief question or several sentences, as one "question."

The second problem came in trying to classify the content of the statements and questions. We began with a six-point rating scale: 6 for a statement intended to hinder agreement and using a negative tone, 5 for a hindering statement without a negative tone, 4 for a statement or question used to clarify, 3 for a helpful statement but with a negative tone, 2 for a question or statement intended to help the argument along and shine light on the good aspects of it, and 1 for an irrelevant question or statement. This procedure proved to be unreliable.

Our next attempt to develop a classification scheme was to classify each statement as sympathetic, unsympathetic, or neutral. But once more, too many statements were hard to classify or possessed both friendly and unfriendly aspects. We finally opted for a more global approach. Each of us read the entire transcript and identified the justices whose overall pattern of questions was unsympathetic to one side or the other. For example, in the oral argument for *Small v. United States*, on page 29 of the transcript Justice Ginsburg says, "Congress thinks about the United States, our country, and if it means to say something will take place in other places in the world, it says so clearly." She is arguing here for the side of Small, so both of us rated this statement as unsympathetic to the federal government's position in this case. We found that this procedure provided a high degree of reliability between raters. We used it to identify specific justices who we felt would vote one way or the other. As an example, in *Small v. United States,* Justices Ginsburg and Souter were unsympathetic to the United States and Justice Scalia was unsympathetic to Small. (And in a 5-to-3 decision favoring Small, each of these justices voted as we expected them to.)

We also counted the number of questions asked of each side, much like Shullman did. (Unfortunately, Shullman not only failed to define a "question," but she also presented no tables with the number of questions directed toward each side in each case. This is regrettable, because if she had, we could have compared our results, using our system for defining a "question.")

Our Results

First, we found that those justices who expressed unsympathetic questions toward one side were much less likely to vote for that side. In 79 of 109 times, justices voted against the side to which they addressed unsympathetic questions. In examining the total number of unsympathetic justices in the 12 ideological cases, we found 60 instances, or exactly an average of 5 per case. A total of 52 of these 60 questions reflected unsympathetic comments against the side that eventually lost that justice's vote, or 87%. In the nonideological cases, there were 49 unsympathetic comments or questions, or about 4 per case. Of these, 34, or 69%, were unsympathetic to the side failing to gain the justice's vote. The ideological nature of the case seemed to be a determinant; with five-sixths of the classifiable questions going against the side that the justice eventually voted against, it is plausible to conclude that in these cases the justice had a predisposition before the oral arguments began. But in the nonideological cases, this relationship occurred less often, though still more than half the time.

Our second analysis followed Shullman's procedure, by examining the total number of questions directed toward the winning and losing side. Among the 12 ideologically related cases, in 7 cases the eventual losing side received more questions. Among the 12 nonideological cases, by contrast, the losing side received more questions in only 3 cases. While ideology made some difference, it was not strong, and the basic finding is that of the 24 cases, the more-questions-asked rule prevailed in only 10 cases, or 42%, much below the results in the studies by Shullman and by Roberts. In fact, 42% is not significantly different from an outcome by sheer guessing, of 50%.

Does the Number of Questions Predict Outcomes?
—An Attempt to Resolve the Inconsistency

While we have demonstrated that individual justices' questions seem to be related to their eventual votes, the findings on the validity of the more-questions-asked rule is in doubt. In summary, we have three sets of findings:

1. Shullman's findings for the October 2002 term, which found that the side that received the most questions tended to lose
2. Roberts' findings for the October 1980 and 2003 terms, which had similar results
3. Our findings for the October 2004 term, which found that in only about half of the cases were more questions directed at the eventual losing side

How does one account for these differences? Each study dealt with different terms of the Court, and each study only sampled the cases, using anywhere from 10 to 24 cases per term. It seems unlikely that the specific term would account for such large differences in the relationship. A second potential cause centers on the matter of what constitutes a "question." Neither Shullman nor Chief Justice Roberts indicated how they defined a question, whereas Austin and I had some specific ground rules. Could this be the source of the discrepancy? To determine this, we analyzed the cases from the October 2003 term used by Chief Justice Roberts. He chose the first and last oral arguments in each of the seven 2-week sessions of the Court; these 14 cases were the following:

1. *Frew v. Hawkins*, on whether a consent degree by a federal agency filed under a Medicare entitlement program was enforceable
2. *Castro v. United States*, which dealt with a prisoner's right to file a second habeas petition
3. *Kontrick v. Ryan*, on the timeliness of a bankruptcy petition
4. *Olympic Airways v. Husain*, on whether a foreign carrier could be sued for liability for a passenger's death
5. *United States Postal Service v. Flamingo Industries*, on whether the Postal Service is subject to liability under antitrust laws
6. *Vieth v. Jubelirer*, on the reapportioning of congressional district boundaries in Pennsylvania
7. *United States v. Galletti*, on an interpretation of the tax code with regard to the assessment of employment taxes
8. *Iowa v. Tovar*, on a defendant's claim that he had not knowingly waived his right to counsel
9. *Household Credit Services v. Pfennig*, on an interpretation of the federal Truth in Lending Act when applied to credit card interest charges
10. *Grupo Dataflux v. Atlas Global Group*, which dealt with the rights of a partnership involved in diversity litigation to change the nature of its partnership
11. *Tennard v. Dretke*, on the applicability of a low IQ as a mitigating factor in determining a sentence for murder
12. *Thornton v. United States*, on the limits of the search of a car after the arrest of a suspect standing outside the car
13. *Central Laborers' Pension Fund v. Heinz*, on post-employment procedures and the receipt of post-employment benefits
14. *Rumsfeld v. Padilla*, on the designation of the proper respondent when a detainee sues for habeas relief

The decision to choose the first and last cases argued in each 2-week session does not produce a random sample of cases, but it certainly would seem to be a valid procedure to select a representative group. Slightly more than half deal with civil matters, so in our terminology they would be mostly non-ideological cases. The rest, on criminal issues, are ideological—a fortuitous split. One problem with using cases from this term (and earlier ones) is that the justices are not identified by name in the transcript, thus there is a little uncertainty in determining where one question stops and another starts.

Using our definition of what constitutes a question, we found that in 11 of the 14 cases the losing side was asked more questions, and in 3 of the 14 cases the losing side was asked fewer questions, leading to a 79% predictability. This compares with Chief Justice Roberts' 86% prediction rate. (This figure is a combined figure for the two terms Justice Roberts surveyed; he did not report separate figures for the two terms.) The three cases that did not support the hypothesis that the winning side receives fewer questions were *Kontrick v. Ryan*, *Vieth v. Jubelirer*, and *Grupo Dataflux v. Atlas Global Group*. All three of these cases stemmed from civil suits and were, in our terminology, nonideological cases. We also used a separate measure of a "question"—specifically, any uninterrupted utterance by a justice. Using this method, the number of questions is always larger than that with our method, but the ratio of questions to petitioner and to respondent was the same as in our method. (For example, in *Frew v. Hawkins* our method identified 44 questions to the petitioner and 54 to the respondent; with the other method, these numbers increased to 68 and 79, respectively.) If, indeed, John Roberts used this method, he too found in the October 2002 sample that the more-questions-to-the loser rule applied in 11 of the 14 cases. But in those cases that were ideologically related, the rule predicted the outcome correctly in all of them.

We did the same analysis with the 10 cases used by Shullman. These cases, from the October 2002 term, were the following:

1. *Yellow Transportation, Inc. v. Michigan*, on the application of a federal law to fees collected by a state
2. *Federal Communications Commission v. NextWave Personal Communications*, on whether the FCC could revoke licenses under the Bankruptcy Code
3. *Barnhart v. Peabody Coal Co.*, which dealt with the eligibility of retired coal miners to benefits
4. *Eldred v. Ashcroft*, on whether the Copyright Term Extension Act of 1998 violated First Amendment rights
5. *Miller-El v. Cockrell*, which dealt with jury-selection procedures that excluded minorities
6. *United States v. Bean*, on convicted felons possessing firearms
7. *Moseley v. V Secret Catalogue*, a case dealing with the issue of trademark infringement
8. *Ewing v. California*, on the constitutionality of California's three-strikes law
9. *Lockyer v. Andrade*, also on the constitutionality of California's three-strikes law (although in this case the petitioner was the state, whereas in the above case the petitioner was the prisoner)
10. *Norfolk & Western Railway Company v. Ayers*, on claims of employees of a railroad of emotional distress

Four of the 10 cases dealt with defendants' rights or prisoners' rights and two dealt with a suit of employees or ex-employees against a large organization.

From her report it appears that Shullman found the rule of more questions to the losing side to apply in 9 of the 10 cases. Using our definition of questions, we found that the rule applied in only 7 of these 10 cases. So we applied the broader definition of a "question," assuming that perhaps this was Shullman's criterion; that is, we went through the transcript and strictly counted the number of times that "QUESTION" was located on the left side of the page. Thus, this is a tally of each time a justice spoke, including interrupted statements and continued thoughts as separate "questions."

There are three cases of greatest concern: *Moseley v. V Secret Catalogue*, *Eldred v. Ashcroft*, and *Norfolk & Western Railway v. Ayers*. Shullman reported that the one case that did not conform to the rule was *Moseley v. V Secret Catalogue*; as she noted, "the justices asked slightly fewer questions of the respondent, but unanimously held for the petitioner" (2004, p. 278). Our original method showed that the petitioner received 54 questions and the respondent, 50. In the method using a more broadened definition the petitioner got 77 questions and the respondent got 74. So both methods show more questions for the winning side, and according to both methods there were, in Shullman's words, "slightly fewer questions of the respondent." So far, perhaps our expanded definition is what Shullman used.

But problems surface in two discrepant cases. Like *Moseley v. V Secret Catalogue*, *Eldred v. Ashcroft* was a copyright case. Specifically, it dealt with whether the Copyright Term Extension Act of 1998 violated First Amendment rights. The Court upheld the lower court's decision and ruled in favor of Attorney General Ashcroft in a 7-to-2 decision. Using our method, the petitioner received 43 questions and the respondent, 46, which is close in number, but against the loser-gets-more rule. By simply counting the number of times "QUESTION" was listed, the petitioner had 62 questions and the respondent had 66. Our reading of Shullman's article leaves the impression that this was one of the cases that, according to her system, fit the rule. But in a footnote she stated, "Note that these findings do not account for oral arguments in which the Solicitor General (or a Deputy or Assistant Solicitor General) argued on behalf of the United States. However, it is important to note that the justices' questions often increase in number and hostility when they are addressed to the Solicitor General. My numbers may in consequence be skewed in cases in which the United States was a party or an amicus" (2004, p. 278, Footnote 41). In *Eldred v. Ashcroft*, a federal law had been challenged by the petitioner, and so the solicitor general of the United States (at that time, Theodore Olson) was the only attorney who represented the respondent (John Ashcroft, who was then attorney general) at the oral argument. It may be true that attorneys from the solicitor general's office induce more questions, as Shullman says, but we are bewildered by her characterization that these are "hostile." If they are, why does the party represented by the solicitor general win so often? At any rate, this analysis causes a revision in the initial impression that Shullman's rule was as effective as she claimed.

The remaining bothersome case, *Norfolk & Western Railway v. Ayers*, involved the claims by railroad employees of emotional distress. The Court ruled in favor of the respondent in a unanimous decision. The petitioner received 53 questions and the respondent, 54, according to our original method. Using the broader method, the petitioner was asked 77 questions and the respondent, 83. Thus, regardless of the method, there is no verification of the loser-gets-more rule. Although Shullman did not explicitly say that the rule applied to this case, later in her report she singled out this case as an example of her ability to predict the vote correctly, even though it is based on the average hostility content of the questions to each side, not the sheer number. "In *Ayers*, the justices asked the respondent questions with an overall score of 2.93, whereas the petitioner faced questions with an average score of 3.71" (Schullman, 2004, p. 290). On her scale, 1 = most helpful and 5 = most hostile.

We also returned to Greenhouse's conclusion that her report was generally accurate in those cases where her story indicated that the Court was leaning in one direction or the other, based on the oral arguments. She had 16 decided cases where this applied, and in 12 of the cases "leaning" predicted the outcome. Six of these cases were also studied by Shullman, the other 10 came later in the term. Do her predictions reflect a predominant questioning toward one side?

We tabulated the questions in these 12 cases and found that only in 8 cases, or 67%, did the Roberts' rule of more questions to the loser hold up. While the number of questions may have entered into Greenhouse's prediction, doubtless she also processed the content of the questions and the side that received the brunt of hostile questions.

So, where do we stand with regard to the validity of measurements of the more-questions-asked rule? First, as a methodology, simply counting on the transcript each instance of a justice saying anything, even an interrupted comment, seems to produce the same relative difference between petitioners and respondents as that produced by our more time-consuming procedure of scrutinizing the transcript and collapsing interruptions and other variances into single questions. In our analysis of each counting method, using the 14 cases studied by Chief Justice Roberts and 10 cases studied by Shullman, we found no case in which the *relative* numbers of questions to each differed; this occurred even in arguments where the questions for each side were similar. For example, in *Tennard v. Dretke*, our original system found 42 for the petitioner and 43 for the respondent; in the "complete" system, the numbers were 50 and 51, respectively.

Second, the validity of the rule, as it applies to all types of cases, still remains in doubt. We find it difficult to use Shullman's findings because of the problems in coder reliability mentioned earlier. It does appear that Shullman used the ratio of friendly to hostile questions as well as the sheer number directed to each side in making her predictions of votes. Chief Justice Roberts' findings for the October 2003 term (based on 14 cases) differ widely from ours for 24 cases in the next term. However, the difference between ideological and nonideological cases is consistent: the rule applies more in ideological cases—this was found in both Roberts' sample and in ours.

The most fruitful prediction would seem to be based on both the relative number of questions and the number of hostile questions to each side. Using both these measures I replicated the procedure, using all the oral arguments in several different terms. For the October 2001 term, the eventual losing side was asked more questions in 29 of 41 ideological cases, or 70.7%; in contrast, in nonideological cases, the eventual losing side was asked more questions in 8 of 16 cases, or only 50%. For those cases that were difficult to classify as ideological or nonideological, the eventual losing side was asked more questions in 6 of 14 cases, or 42.8%. Thus the rule of more questions to the loser applied more often in ideological cases.

For the October 2002 term, the same distinction applied; the eventual losing side was asked more questions in 21 of the 33 ideological cases (63.6%), in 9 of 16 borderline cases, or 56.2%, and in only 11 of 23 ideological cases, or 47.8%. For the October 2005 term, the results were consistent with those of the October 2001 and 2002 terms, although the differences between types of cases were smaller. More questions were asked the losing side in 28 of 43 ideological cases (65.1%), in 9 of 14 borderline cases (64.3%), and 9 of 15 nonideological cases.

In analyzing the results of the October 2006 term, I chose a different procedure. This term was highly unusual in its case outcomes, as 24 of the decisions, or one third of the total, were decided by a 5-to-4 vote. Most of these were ideological cases, dealing with abortion, the death penalty, affirmative action, sex discrimination, and environmental concerns, along with the typical cases on prisoners' rights and defendants' rights. For this term, I examined the record of each justice in these 24 oral arguments, specifically the number of questions asked by the justice to each side and the justice's eventual vote. The results were surprising. In these 24 highly contested cases, Chief Justice Roberts had 96 questions or comments for the side he eventually supported and 382 questions or comments for the side he eventually voted against. In 23 of these 24 cases, he eventually voted against the side that he questioned most extensively. His ratio of almost 4 to 1 was the highest; second was Justice Souter, who had 90 and 276 questions, respectively, or a ratio of about 3 to 1; third was Justice Breyer, who had 141 questions or comments for his eventual winning side and 262 for his eventual losing side, a ratio of 1.84. In fact, every justice who spoke during the oral arguments spoke more often to the advocate for the side that justice voted against. However, among them, Justice Kennedy, reflecting his open-minded characterization from Chapter 5, had the smallest ratio. He had 116 comments or questions for his winning advocate and 160 for the losing advocate, a ratio of only 1.37. In these 24 cases, Justice Kennedy voted against the side to which he directed the most questions in only 13 cases, compared to Roberts' 23, Stevens' 20, and Souter's 19 cases.

What are we to make of this imbalance? It could be argued, as Tony Mauro (2007b) has suggested, that the justices are giving that side more opportunities to convince them. Or it could be that they have predispositions to rule against that side in these highly ideological cases.

8

Contentious Issues

The day may come when television will have become so commonplace an affair in the daily life of the average person as to dissipate all reasonable likelihood that its use in courtrooms may disparage the judicial process.

> —Justice John Marshall Harlan II, concurring opinion in *Estes v. Texas* (1965, pp. 595–596)

Unresolved Issues

The oral argument is the one constant throughout the more than 200 years of the Supreme Court. Yes, there have been changes in the procedure. Briefs were not available at the beginning of the Court's existence, only a few advocates argued all the cases before the Court, and the courtroom moved from the basement of the Capitol building to its present distinguished facility. It is true that in early times the oral arguments for one case might range over several days, but even today, as it did 200 years ago, the oral argument draws attention from the media and awe from its onlookers.

Despite its enduring nature, not all issues involving the operation of the oral argument have been resolved. The purpose of this chapter is to examine several of these and then provide some final conclusions about the place of oral arguments in the Court's decision-making process. Currently the most salient of these issues is that of televising the oral arguments. Issues of fairness of the process also need to be considered.

Televising Oral Arguments

For years the possibility of televising oral arguments of the Court has been discussed. The speeches and press conferences of the president are often carried by the television networks; C-SPAN routinely televises the sessions of the Senate and the House of Representatives and occasionally televises committee hearings. Even the confirmation hearings of Supreme Court nominees before the Senate Judiciary Committees are televised by CNN and C-SPAN. And the Supreme Court has permitted state courts to televise their trials and appellate arguments. But the Court has steadfastly refused to permit cameras in its own courtroom.

Action by the Senate Judiciary Committee

The issue of television simmered for years but became active in September 2005, when Senator Arlen Specter submitted a bill (S. 1768) to permit televising of Supreme Court proceedings. Specifically, the bill proposed an amendment to the United States Code, as follows:

> In general, Chapter 45 of title 28, United States Code, is amended by inserting at the end the following:
>
> Sec. 678 Televising Supreme Court proceedings
>
> The Supreme Court shall permit television coverage of all open sessions of the Court unless the Court decides, by a vote of the majority of the justices, that allowing such coverage in a particular case would constitute a violation of the due process rights of one or more parties before the Court.

The bill's sponsors, beyond Senator Specter, were Senators Leahy, Cornyn, Allen, Grassley, Schumer, and Feingold, a bipartisan group. The bill was referred to the Committee on the Judiciary (which was then chaired by Senator Specter).

In a letter to the editor of the *Washington Post*, published on April 25, 2006, Senator Specter expressed his animosity toward the Supreme Court. He began by noting that no cameras were allowed to cover the oral arguments in *Bush v. Gore* in 2000, "a momentous event." He observed the irony that the Court, in 1980, in *Richmond Newspapers v. Virginia*, had concluded that "a public trial belongs not only to the accused but to the public and press as well." Observing that "so far the justices have steadfastly rebuffed all efforts to get them to open their public proceedings to electronic coverage," he cited as examples of Congress's legislative authority to decide procedures basic to the operation of the Supreme Court such matters as the beginning date of each term, the number of justices, and the number of justices that constitutes a quorum (six). (Senator Specter did not mention the notorious tinkering the Congress did in reducing the number of justices in the late 1860s to prevent President Andrew Johnson from nominating a replacement justice, or Congress abolishing a term in 1802 so as to prevent the Court from acting on certain petitions.)

He concluded that the Supreme Court does not "respect" Congress. He interpreted the reaction of Justices Kennedy and Thomas at a House appropriations subcommittee hearing as telling Congress that it "should mind its own business and respect the court's autonomy." Claiming that the present Court is acting as a "super-legislature," he cited several recent Supreme Court decisions in which, in Specter's view, it invalidated legislation it disliked. (While William Rehnquist was chief justice, the Court overruled more than 30 acts of Congress [Mauro, 2003c].) The Senator concluded that "congressional procedures and authority have been severely diminished by the court." In his view, public airing of the oral arguments would permit the public to see what the Court is doing.

This letter truly was a remarkable document, reflecting the animosity of one branch of the federal government toward another. In the letter Specter consistently referred to the Supreme Court as "the court" (i.e., a lower-case "c," while normal style capitalizes "the Court," as recognition of its eminence. Whether this was an intended slight or an editing decision is unknown.) The assumption that a public airing of the Court's oral arguments would somehow mobilize the public to pressure the president to nominate justices who would "do right" seems a little disingenuous.

But the letter reflects Senator Specter's persistence. At a hearing on the bill on November 9, 2005, he said, "It's a question of when, in my judgment, not if" (Mauro, 2005b, p. 13). Several witnesses at this hearing cited the intensified public interest in the workings of the Court, spurred by the *Bush v. Gore* decision and the confirmation hearings for new justices. "Nominees for the Supreme Court are widely seen in televised hearings conducted by this committee, only to disappear from view the moment they are sworn in as justices," stated Barbara Cochran, president of the Radio-Television News Directors Association (Mauro, 2005b). Brian Lamb, chief executive officer of C-SPAN, promised that if the bill were to become law, C-SPAN would provide gavel-to-gavel coverage of all the Supreme Court proceedings that were public. Lamb stated that a need for more awareness by the public was made more evident to him when a student recently asked him "where they put the jury in the Supreme Court" (Mauro, 2005b).

The Judiciary Committee's hearing took an ironic turn when Peter Irons, a political-science professor, testified and played an audiotape of an excerpt from the oral argument that Thurgood Marshall made in the important 1958 civil-rights case of *Cooper v. Aaron*. The Court has made audio recordings of all its oral arguments for the last 50 years, and 15 years ago Professor Irons made excerpts from the arguments in some classic cases commercially available, both on cassette tape and in book form. Since the late 1960s tapes of the complete oral arguments have been stored at the National Archives, which permitted access to them if they were to be used for "serious scholarly and legal research." Professor Irons was required to sign an agreement that the tapes would be used only for such purposes and that he would not reproduce them. But he made copies of the arguments in 23 cases, including the major cases of the last half of the twentieth century, such as *Roe v. Wade*, the *Gideon* case, and a major death penalty case. After obtaining endorsements from many of the prominent lawyers whose voices he planned to reproduce, he even wrote Chief Justice Rehnquist, asking for his blessing. Rehnquist did not reply, but his administrative assistant, Robb Jones did, apparently without Rehnquist's knowledge: "I applaud the concept and your efforts," Jones wrote (Mauro, 1995, p. 276). Only when the book-and-tapes package was being distributed to bookstores, in August 1993 did the Court officially respond, with a terse statement condemning Irons' actions: "in light of this clear violation of Professor Irons' contractual commitments, the Court is considering what legal remedies may be appropriate" (Mauro, 1995, p. 277). But it did nothing, and Irons subsequently published two more compilations of audiotapes. At the hearing in November 2005, Irons argued that since audiotapes are available, "I can't see any reason not to add pictures to the audio" (Mauro, 2005b, p. 13).

Also discussed at the Judiciary Committee's hearing was another bill (S. 829), intended to give federal appellate and trial judges the option of opening their courtrooms to cameras. (Trials in state courts can now be televised but federal trials cannot; however, two circuit courts of appeals, the Second and the Ninth Circuits, permit televising of their oral arguments if the media requests it and the judicial panel agrees. C-SPAN has occasionally televised oral arguments from these two circuit courts.) At the hearing a judge from the Ninth Circuit, Diarmuid O'Scannlain, testified that few if any problems had surfaced since permission was first granted in 1991, but objections were raised by witnesses to allowing cameras into federal trials. The Judicial Conference, which establishes policy for the federal courts, announced its opposition, a federal trial judge from Pennsylvania warned of intimidation of juries and witnesses, and the National Association of Criminal Defense Lawyers opposed the bill.

But in March 2006, the Senate Judiciary Committee passed, by a vote of 12 to 6, each of these two bills. In contrast to the committee's votes on recent presidential appointments to the federal courts, this was not a party-line vote, as several Democrats voted with the majority. As of this writing (early 2008) the Senate as a whole has taken no action on these bills.

The Supreme Court's Decisions on Televising Trials

Before considering how the justices might react to the idea of televising their own oral arguments, I believe it is instructive to review the Supreme Court's decisions regarding the general legitimacy of the use of cameras in the courtrooms. The Supreme Court has agreed to decide appeals regarding the use of cameras in the courtrooms in trials because their use is relevant to a basic conflict between the First and Sixth Amendments to the Constitution. As the Supreme Court itself has recognized, "the authors of the Bill of Rights did not undertake to assign priorities as between First Amendment and Sixth Amendment rights ranking one as superior to the other" (*Nebraska Press Association v. Stuart,* 1976, p. 561). The First Amendment provides freedom to the press, the Sixth, the rights of defendants to receive a fair trial. Or as the preface of a book authored by a journalist and a trial attorney put it, "Journalists feel strongly that they should be able to report the news as they see fit. Many criminal defense attorneys fear that once cameras are allowed into courtrooms, they will change the very proceedings they try to depict, to the detriment of their clients" (Cohn & Dow, 1998, p. 1).

With the advent of television after World War II, some states began to permit limited television coverage inside the courtroom. Oklahoma is considered to be the first, in a trial in December 1953, with Colorado, Kansas, and Texas soon following suit (Cohn & Dow, 1998). At first, the procedure was to film some testimony in the courtroom and, after editing, show some excerpts on the evening newscasts. The first live telecast took place in Waco, Texas, in 1955, with the television equipment operating unobtrusively from a balcony.

Two Supreme Court decisions were important in setting a standard about legality of such activities, *Estes v. Texas* (1965) and *Chandler v. Florida* (1981).

Estes v. Texas (1965)

Billie Sol Estes, a Texas wheeler-dealer and friend of then-President Lyndon Johnson, was brought to trial for fraud, for swindling farmers of their money. A jury convicted him in a trial that lasted just 3 days. Following Texas law, the trial judge had permitted still cameras and television cameras at both a 2-day pretrial hearing and at the trial itself. Ironically, the preliminary hearing dealt with a motion by Estes's lawyers to prohibit cameras at the actual trial. The judge denied the motion. The procedures differed in the hearing and the trial:

> Twelve television cameramen and still photographers were admitted to the pretrial hearing. Cameras snaked across the courtroom floor. Almost everyone conceded it was a disruptive scene. When the actual trial began, all the photographers were restricted to a booth in the back of the courtroom, constructed and painted to blend in with the room's permanent decor. (Cohn & Dow, 1998, p. 19)

Estes appealed his conviction, claiming that these procedures had denied him a fair trial. By a 5-to-4 vote the Supreme Court overturned his conviction, concluding that even the limited television violated the defendant's Fourteenth Amendment guarantee of due process. Justice Tom Clark, who wrote the opinion for the Court, acknowledged that no empirical evidence existed that could lead to a conclusion that the use of cameras had prejudiced the case against Estes. But he concluded that the presence of television cameras had a detrimental psychological effect on jurors, witnesses, the judge, and the defendant. A concurring opinion by Chief Justice Warren (joined by Justices Douglas and Goldberg) went even further:

> The prejudice of television may be so subtle that it escapes the ordinary methods of proof, but it would gradually erode our fundamental conception of a trial. A defendant may be unable to prove that he was actually prejudiced by a televised trial, just as he may be unable to prove that the introduction of a coerced confession at his trial influenced the jury to convict him. (*Estes v. Texas,* 1965, p. 578)

Justice Potter Stewart dissented; while acknowledging that confusion existed in the courtroom during the pretrial hearing, he noted that nothing bearing on Estes's guilt or innocence was discussed, only procedural matters. He challenged the assertion that the presence of cameras influenced courtroom participants in subtle ways.

In the *Estes* decision, justices in both the majority and the dissent held out hope for those who sought greater free-speech accommodations. Justice Clark's opinion for the Court included, "When the advances in these arts permit reporting...by television without their present hazards to a fair trial we will have another case" (p. 540). And Justice Brennan, in dissent, wrote, "Today's decision is *not* a blanket constitutional prohibition against the televising of state criminal trials" (p. 617, italics in original).

But it took 16 years for the Court to change its mind. In the interim there were developments both broad and specific. The emerging improvements in the technology of television provided detailed coverage of the war in Vietnam; the Senate Watergate hearings were televised live, and these and other developments led to demands for "new openness" in government (Cohn & Dow, 1998). The specific development happened in Florida. In 1975 a chain of television stations petitioned the Florida Supreme Court to rescind the prohibition against television coverage of trials. While the court refused to permit a wholesale overturning of the prohibition, it did eventually agree to a 1-year test of the procedure. Thus television viewers were permitted to watch the trial of Ronny Zamora, a 17-year-old charged with murdering an elderly neighbor. Only one television camera was permitted in the courtroom. After the trial was completed, the judge met with the jurors and later sent an evaluation to the Florida Supreme Court. In it he reported that jurors believed that the television camera, while being a minor distraction, did not affect their ability to concentrate on the testimony or the instructions. Both the prosecutor and the defense attorney agreed about the lack of intrusion from the camera. In response, the Florida Supreme Court decided to permit television coverage of trials in its state, if the presiding judge agreed.

Chandler v. Florida (1981)

In December of 1977 two Miami Beach police officers, Noel Chandler and Robert Granger, went on trial for conspiracy to commit burglary of a well-known Miami Beach restaurant; they were convicted. At the trial the main prosecution witness was a ham radio operator who, by chance, overheard and recorded the conversations between the police officers on their police walkie-talkie radios during the burglary. Portions of the trial were televised, specifically the testimony of the radio operator and the closing arguments. The two police officers appealed their conviction to the Supreme Court. In the case of *Chandler v. Florida*, decided by the Court in 1981, the officers' attorney claimed that the use of a television camera prevented his clients from receiving a fair and impartial trial. In doing so, he relied on Chief Justice Warren's concurring opinion in the *Estes v. Texas* decision, in which he wrote:

> While I join the Court's opinion and agree that the televising of criminal trials is inherently a denial of due process, I desire to express additional views on why this is so. In doing this, I wish to emphasize that our condemnation of televised criminal trials is not based on generalities or abstract fears. The record on this case presents a vivid illustration of the inherent prejudice of televised criminal trials and supports our conclusion that this is an appropriate time to make a definitive appraisal of television in the courtroom. (1965, p. 552)

But the Court in 1981 did not rely on Justice Warren's position from 1965. Instead, it voted 8 to 0 to uphold the conviction of the Florida police officers (Justice Stevens did not participate in the decision.) Chief Justice Burger wrote the opinion for the Court, and Justices Stewart and White each prepared a concurrence. (It is worth noting that only three justices who decided the *Estes* case were still on the Court 16 years later; Justices Stewart, White, and Brennan all had dissented in the original opinion and now served as a core of the majority that reversed the ruling in *Estes*.) The majority opinion in *Chandler v. Florida*, rather than concentrating on Warren's concurrence in *Estes*, put its emphasis on another of the concurrences, a more hospitable one by Justice Harlan. He had written:

> Permitting television in the courtroom undeniably has mischievous potentialities for intruding upon the detached atmosphere which should always surround the judicial process. Forbidding this innovation, however, would doubtless impinge upon one of the valued attributes of our federalism by preventing the states from pursuing a novel course of procedural experimentation. (*Estes v.* Texas, 1965, p. 591)

The majority opinion in *Chandler v. Florida* then concluded:

> Parsing the six opinions in *Estes*, one is left with a sense of doubt as to precisely how much of Justice Clark's opinion was joined in,

and supported by, Justice Harlan....Nonetheless, it is fair to say that Justice Harlan viewed the holding as limited to the proposition that "*what was done in this case* infringed the fundamental right to a fair trial assumed by the Due Process Clause of the Fourteenth Amendment" (*Chandler v. Florida*, 1981, pp. 572–573, italics in original).

Thus, Chief Justice Burger ruled that "*Estes* is not to be read as announcing a constitutional rule barring still photographic, radio, and television coverage in all cases and under all circumstances" (1981, p. 573). While the *Chandler* decision did not declare that television cameras had a constitutional right to be in American courtrooms, it did give state legislatures and state courts permission to develop rules and procedures (Cohn & Dow, 1998). Currently, all 50 states permit some access, although restrictions are often present. Some states limit access to only civil trials or to appellate courts. When access is permitted, the presiding judge has discretion to consider the circumstances and deny permission in a specific case.

But no cameras are permitted in federal trials. A 3-year pilot program, begun in 1990, was not extended, hence the introduction of Senate Bill 829. In summary, current thinking is that "the Constitution doesn't necessarily prohibit cameras in the courtroom, but it does not require they be allowed in either" (Cohn & Dow, 1998, p. 43).

Research Findings

When Justice Clark wrote the opinion for the Court in the *Estes* case in 1965, he observed that he could present no empirical evidence that Billie Sol Estes had received prejudicial treatment because of the camera in his courtroom. In the 40 years since then, extensive research has found, in general, that the presence of cameras has no major effects. Two types of studies have been done: surveys of judges and jurors, and laboratory studies in which respondents role-play witnesses or jurors. The surveys of judges have more often found support for television than not; for example, a survey of New York judges found that 90% felt that the cameras were not distracting. Surveys of jurors found an almost unanimous reaction that the cameras had not affected the fairness of their verdicts (Goldfarb, 1998). Goldfarb concluded that in state after state, "initial skepticism was replaced by general acceptance" (1998, p. 76). The experimental studies found that an awareness of the presence of a camera may distract jurors initially, but this effect diminished over time, leading to no significant loss of information retained (Kassin, 1984). This adaptation to the presence of the camera is also supported by interviews with actual trial witnesses and jurors. Marjorie Cohn and David Dow, authors of a book on cameras in the courtroom, interviewed a number of judges, lawyers, witnesses, and jurors and asked them: Did the television camera make a difference? The problem with such self-report studies is that respondents are tempted to offer a favorable response. However, the authors noted the following:

> But many who did admit to a difference had a common response: they felt the camera's impact initially and soon forgot about it. Even a seasoned "professional" witness, Beverly Hills police detective Leslie Zoeller, admitted feeling "nervous" when he took the stand to testify in California's Billionaire Boys Club murder case in 1987, his first encounter with a courtroom camera. "Once I started testifying," he recalls, "my attention was drawn to the attorneys asking the questions or the judge. I really didn't notice the camera." (Cohn and Dow, 1998, p. 67)

Arguments for and against Televising Oral Arguments at the Supreme Court

Especially since the introduction of the Senate bill to televise oral arguments, commentators have come forward with a number of viewpoints on the issue, some favorable, some unfavorable.

Arguments Favoring the Televising of Oral Arguments

Former U.S. Attorney General Dick Thornburgh and lawyer Donald Fine have argued that a democracy champions open government, "that prohibition is never a good idea" (2005, p. 26). They wrote:

> Allowing television coverage of the Supreme Court's oral arguments would help to counter [the public's] skepticism about the judicial [system] in ways both actual and symbolic. The public could see and hear the arguments the lawyers make and the questions the justices ask. Americans could better understand the issues and why they are often more complex and difficult than brief and sometimes simplistic press summaries might suggest. Even if they did not have time to watch, they would at least know that the process was open to them. (Thornburgh and Fine, 2005, p. 26)

Dahlia Lithwick, a columnist for *Slate* magazine and the *American Lawyer*, offered a different argument:

> If the justices knew, for instance, that they were being watched by millions of eyeballs, they might be less inclined to giggle among themselves at oral arguments.... Supreme Court justices are beholden to no one. They hold their seats for life; we have no effective means to remove them. So why shouldn't we be entitled to monitor their job performance? Should they choose not to perform—to stare fixedly at the ceiling throughout oral argument, as Justice

Thomas has been known to do—they suffer no consequences. And having a camera trained on them might just induce them to work harder. (2006, pp. 36–37)

Law Professor Ann Althouse, on her blog, amplified Lithwick's concern. Televising oral arguments would, she wrote, "institute a valuable check on the life tenure provision, which has, in modern times, poured too much power into the individuals who occupy the Court" (2005, p. 3). Last but not least, Tony Mauro, who earlier covered the Court for *USA Today* and now does so for *Legal Times* and *American Lawyer Media*, is a strong advocate of televised sessions, arguing that the First Amendment and an open democracy require informing the public of the Court's procedures.

Arguments against the Televising of Oral Arguments

One of the most striking features of the arguments against televising is the eminence and experience of their adherents. Nina Totenberg of National Public Radio, who, like Tony Mauro, is one of the journalists whose sole topic is the Court, told a meeting of defense lawyers, "After more than 25 years of covering the Court, I have concluded it's a rotten idea to have television there" (Cohn & Dow, 1998, p. 1). Professor Barbara Perry, author of a book on the Supreme Court's public image, has written:

Perhaps TV would reveal the best elements of the judicial process at the Supreme Court level (civility, reasoned deliberation, impartiality, professionalism), but television would also denigrate those virtues by overexposure and trivialization. My suggested line of media access to the Supreme Court thus stops at the televising of oral arguments. Journalists already have access to the building, the oral arguments, the justices (on an individual basis), and officers of the Court. Although broadcasting oral argument sessions would fulfill a unique educative function, that benefit would come with an unacceptably high cost, that is, the risk of undermining the Court's image through sound biting, simple overexposure, or unknown problems introduced by the presence of television cameras. (1999a, p. 154)

The Justices on Televised Arguments

The justices of the Supreme Court have not been reluctant to express their opinions about televising their proceedings, and almost always their opinions have been negative. Even back before the current controversy, Justice Douglas, in 1960, unequivocally disparaged the use of television in the courts, fearing, among other things, that it would cheapen and vulgarize government by tarnishing the dignity of the courts. Both the chief justices prior to the current one expressed concern about this possibility; Chief Justice Burger stated that there would be "no cameras in the Supreme Court of the United States while I am there" (Goldfarb, 1998, p. 166).

During the 2000 presidential election dispute, Chief Justice Rehnquist rejected the requests of television networks to televise the oral arguments in *Bush v. Gore*. He wrote a letter to C-SPAN that a "majority of the Court" agreed that to do so would be an intrusion (Lithwick, 2006). His response was frustrating to media advocates. When, as an associate justice, he testified at confirmation hearings in 1986 on his nomination as chief justice, he stated: "If I were convinced that coverage by television of the Supreme Court would not distort the way the Court works at present, I certainly would give it sympathetic consideration. But if it meant a whole lot of lights that would distort the present relationship between lawyers and judges and arguing cases, I don't think I would be for it" (Goldfarb, 1998, p. 167). But once confirmed, Rehnquist refused a request by the ABC Radio Network to provide live coverage of the oral argument for an important abortion case; he did so without even consulting his colleagues (Goldfarb, 1998).

Among current justices the most explicit in his opposition is Justice Souter, who, at a legislative hearing on the Supreme Court budget, told members of the House of Representatives, "The day you see a camera coming into our courtroom, it's gonna roll over my dead body" (Perry, 1999b, p. 88). Supporters among the justices are fewer and less public. In a book published in 1998, Ronald L. Goldfarb reported that "two journalists who cover the Supreme Court told me that they have been told in private conversations with a few justices that they favored the idea" (p. 168). Among the few who have made public comments is Justice Ginsburg, who stated during her confirmation hearings that "if it's gavel to gavel then I don't see any problem at all in an appellate court" (Mauro, 1995, p. 272). And at the confirmation hearings, both Chief Justice Roberts and Justice Alito appeared to be open to the idea. In a speech to a bar association Alito said, "Some ordinary viewers who are today unable to name a single member of the Supreme Court would become familiar with the justices and would form opinions, favorable or unfavorable" (Mauro, 2006c, p. 10). But he also cautioned, "some lawyers arguing before the Court in televised cases would use the occasion to address the television audience for political or other purposes" (Mauro, 2006c, p. 10).

Justice Breyer, while not expressing an opinion, has stated that it is "almost inevitable" that the Court will televise its proceedings. However, in an interview televised on C-SPAN on December 4, 2005, he had concerns that the presence of cameras would affect the behavior of the advocates and the justices and ultimately affect the image of the Court.

Why are a majority of justices opposed to television within their courtroom? The possible reasons range from the public-spirited to the self-centered. Frequently, they mention the image of the Court, as well as expressing concerns that 30-second "sound bites" on the evening news would not convey the complexity of the issues the Court faces. In a 1990 speech, Justice Scalia spoke of the Court's work being difficult for the public to understand. "That is why the *University of Chicago Law Review* is not sold at the Seven-Eleven," he quipped (Mauro, 1995, p. 264). A. E. Dick Howard, a University of Virginia law professor, expressed it well: "The Court's mystique has its place. It probably enhances the public's view of them for the Court to be perceived as a little different from everyone else" (Mauro, 1995, p. 264). Even Chief Justice Rehnquist acknowledged that cameras "would lessen to a certain extent some of the mystique and moral authority of the Court" (Lithwick, 2006, p. 37).

But some observers are not so complimentary about the justices' motivations. The real objection, according to Dahlia Lithwick, is that the justices want their privacy. "Of course they don't want cameras to televise their jobs any more than I want cameras to televise mine" (Lithwick, 2006, p. 37). On rare occasions the justices publicly acknowledge how much they value their privacy, as noted by Tony Mauro:

> At an Eighth Circuit conference in August, 1993, retiring Justice Byron White candidly offered one reason why he is glad that television cameras, ubiquitous in the world of the other two branches of government, have been kept out of the nation's highest court. "I'm very pleased to be able to walk around, and very seldom am I recognized," White said. "It's very selfish, I know." (1995, p. 264)

And the justices do have privacy, as the example in Chapter 5 of Justice Breyer's being called for jury duty illustrates. Barbara Perry describes another example: "On several occasions, I have seen current and retired justices stroll through the crowded public areas of the Court unrecognized, and I once saw the Chief Justice [Rehnquist] walk through Washington's National Airport utterly unnoticed by the public" (1999a, p. 154). At a memorial service for Chief Justice Rehnquist in June 2006, his former administrative assistant told an anecdote reflecting how the chief justice could be amused by his anonymity, Rehnquist had given a speech in New Orleans and on Sunday morning attended a church service. The pastor asked any visitor to stand up and when the chief justice did, the pastor asked him his name.

"Bill Rehnquist."

"And where are you from?"

"Washington, D.C."

"And what do you do there?"

"I'm a government lawyer."

The Justices' Reactions to Senate Bill 1768

Each year, two of the justices appear before the subcommittee on appropriations of the House of Representatives to justify the Supreme Court's budget requests and to answer a variety of often pointed questions from subcommittee members. At the April 4, 2006, session to discuss the Court's $76 million request, predictably the subcommittee brought up Senate Bill 1768. Justice

Kennedy said it raised a "sensitive point" about the separation of powers. He said, "We feel very strongly that we have intimate knowledge of the dynamics and the needs of the Court, and we think that proposals mandating and directing television in our Court in every proceeding are inconsistent with the deference and etiquette that should apply between the branches" (Mauro, 2006c, p. 11). Justice Thomas agreed: "It runs the risk of undermining the manner in which we consider cases," he said, adding there are security concerns—"members of the Court who now have some degree of anonymity would lose their anonymity" (Mauro, 2006c, p. 11). The two justices repeatedly used the term "we," implying that they felt they were speaking for the entire Court. (It was these comments that were mentioned in Senator Specter's previously described letter to the *Washington Post*.)

What's in the Future?

At present (early 2008), Senate Bill 1768 has not come before the entire Senate for adoption. Were it to pass in the Senate, it would then go to the House of Representatives for consideration. (In the fall of 2005, the full House passed a bill that would give the chief judge or justice in each federal court broad jurisdiction to allow or bar television cameras.) Let us assume that the bill passes, essentially in its original form, and is signed into law by the president. What would happen next? One of several scenarios could take place.

One option would be for the Supreme Court to acquiesce. Perhaps in a spirit of conciliation, Chief Justice Roberts could persuade his colleagues to go along. If this occurred, the question would become an operational one: How and when does the Court decide that the oral argument for a particular case should not be televised because of a violation of due process rights of one or more parties? Probably, this decision would best be made at the conference when the petition is granted *certiorari*. Or, perhaps, the Court might give a blanket permission at the beginning of each term, with the proviso that any justice could raise a concern about televising a particular oral argument. And what would be a "due process violation?" The Court would have to decide that.

Another option would be for the Supreme Court to simply ignore the law. It is often noted that the Supreme Court has no enforcement powers. Here the question is how do the other branches enforce a rule about the Court's procedures?

Finally, the Court could strike down the law as unconstitutional, as a violation of the separation of powers, as implied in Justice Kennedy's concerns before the House subcommittee on appropriations. But to do so, a petitioner would have to come forward claiming that his or her oral argument was unfair because of the new law.

Many issues of implementation would have to be settled. If television cameras were to be admitted, how many would that include? Would there be only one, facing the justices in a panorama? Or would it be allowed to pan in on the justice asking a question (or on another justice who is dozing, as Justice Ginsburg did during a rare afternoon session in early 2006)? Or would there be a second camera, facing the advocate at the lectern? If television cameras are permitted, would still photographers demand equal access? And if granted, how many? Would they clog the small space between the lectern and the bench, just as they inundated the area between the nominated justice and the Senators during confirmation hearings? Who decides these procedural problems?

Are Parties before the Court Treated Fairly?

It is worth asking if the oral arguments serve the purpose of permitting parties before the Court to get their points across as they wish, as well as the purpose of permitting justices to gain the information they want and need. In this section, these goals are evaluated.

Do Advocates Do an Effective Job?

Chapters 1 and 3 described the nature of advocates before the Court. From what we know, advocates during the first 50 years of the Court were quite effective, and in the most recent 50 years the reemergence of a Supreme Court bar has improved the quality of advocacy. Although no current advocate is approaching the hundreds of cases argued by Daniel Webster and other luminaries of the early 1800s, in the last decade the emergence of a talented group of appellate advocates is reflected by the frequent appearances of many of these advocates. By the end of the 2005–2006 term, Carter Phillips had argued 50 cases before the Court; Seth Waxman, 47; and Theodore Olson, 43. Waxman, now with the firm Wilmer Cutler Pickering Hale & Dorr, argued five cases during one term, and Phillips argued four (Mauro, 2004b, 2005a). Phillips has reported, "It's clearly true that more and more sophisticated clients are looking to the lawyers who have been there time and time again" (Mauro, 2004b). As Tony Mauro has put it, "Lawyers who have been litigating before the Court for years know the dynamics among the justices and the arguments and style that will appeal to each of them at both the petition and oral argument stages" (2004b, p. 10).

However, as is true throughout the levels of the legal system, there is a danger that powerful corporations and affluent individuals get more effective representation than, for example, criminal defendants. In a *Legal Times* article published in May 2006, Tony Mauro highlighted the issue: the frequent presence of novice criminal-defense attorneys before the Court. The problem is that "solo newbies hold on to the romantic notion that if they can conquer a hometown jury, they can work the same charm on the nine justices of the nation's highest court" (Mauro, 2006d, p. 1). The term ending in June 2006 saw an unusually high number of state criminal cases. Of these, the petitioner in 20 cases was represented by a relatively inexperienced attorney from the petitioner's home locale, and some of these "were not argued or briefed well from the defense side" (Mauro, 2006d, p. 1). As noted in Chapter 3, sometimes it is difficult for the attorney who initiated the action to relinquish the role of advocate if the petition is granted *certiorari* by the Supreme Court. These lawyers operate out of "a fierce tradition of independence.... There is a lone-wolf quality to the culture" of criminal-defense lawyers, stated one of the officers of the National Association of Criminal Defense Lawyers (Mauro, 2006d, p. 1). Some of these advocates reject offers of help from larger firms or from the National Association for Criminal Defense Lawyers (NACDL) when their cases have been accepted for review. (And some of these rejections are justified, as, on occasion, a larger firm will try to take over the case completely.) Mauro describes one example:

> One recent case that caused concern among the defense bar was *Brigham City v. Stuart* [2006], in which three residents of Brigham City, Utah, challenged a police search on Fourth Amendment grounds. Responding to a late-night noise complaint, police entered a home without knocking, after they saw a fight underway inside. Their original lawyer won before the Utah Supreme Court, but he ended his representation at that point. So when Utah appealed the case to the U.S. Supreme Court, the defendants went to the Internet and hired Michael Studebaker of Ogden, Utah, who has been a lawyer for four years and whose only appellate experience was arguing once before a Kentucky appeals court as a legal aid lawyer. He filed an opposition to *certiorari* that ran only six pages long. The high court granted review, and Studebaker, 37, filed a merits brief that raised eyebrows. It was 13 pages long, far short of the 50-page maximum that most other lawyer exploit.... Concern in the defense lawyer community mounted as Studebaker struggled through two difficult moot courts in Washington. But Studebaker improved, and when he finally argued, on April 24 [2006], his performance was not as bad as some had feared. Still, he seemed at a loss when asked several key questions, and at one point his answer to a justice's question was, "Personally, yes; legally, no." (2006d, p. 8).

Studebaker lost the case; the Court ruled unanimously, in an opinion written by the chief justice, that police do not need a warrant to enter a home in which a fight is taking place and injuries have occurred or could soon occur.

Local lawyers, according to veteran Supreme Court advocate Jeffrey Fisher, "don't know that the Supreme Court is totally different from any other court, even any other appellate court" (Mauro, 2006d, p. 1). Fisher, who as a sole practitioner has argued several Supreme Court cases during each recent term, is now at the Stanford University Law School, where he assists criminal defense attorneys prepare briefs and arguments. Even with help, local attorneys who represent criminal defendants or prisoners before the Court face a great obstacle. In contrast to earlier times,when a state would be represented by its attorney general (who often had more political than legal skills), 31 states now have solicitors general whose proficiency is appellate advocacy. (Four of the 31 are former Supreme Court law clerks.) These attorneys provide professionalism and exposure that state attorney generals lack. As Mauro has noted:

> Some state attorneys general don't get where they are because of their appellate advocacy skills. But many used to argue before the Supreme Court anyway—often to burnish their resumes on the road to running for governor. The problem was, some would try to charm the justices the same way they would woo a crowd at a campaign cookout: with empty rhetoric, folksy humor, and a minimum of preparation. A North Dakota attorney general, for example, once tried to bolster an argument by joking about the tie he was wearing. That earned him a glowering look from Justice Kennedy, who asked, "Do you have any better reason?" When an Arkansas AG fumbled for an answer for an awkward few minutes and mentioned his fallback position, a justice interjected, "It's time to fall back." Such performances are still seen at the high court, but much more rarely. In a growing number of states, the attorney general can—and usually does—turn to the state solicitor general to argue before appeals courts. (2003b, p. 8)

Beyond the advantage of recent state appellate specialists, in many cases the office of solicitor general sides with the state and is granted some time at the oral arguments. (Of the 22 state criminal cases in the 2005–2006 term, the office of solicitor general was a participant in 16.) "It's not a case of defense lawyers getting worse, it's just that the state's side is getting so much better," said Richard Lazarus, director of the Supreme Court Institute at the Georgetown University Law Center (Mauro, 2006d, p. 8). If it is accurate to say that most appeals by criminal defendants have on one side a sole practitioner who is not an appellate specialist presenting his or her first Supreme Court argument, and on the other side two experienced advocates, then this scenario is unfair. In the view of some, this unfairness hurts the image of the Court. Thus the Court should make efforts to assist inexperienced advocates to avoid writing a poor brief or making a poor oral argument.

Are Some Justices so Biased in Some Cases as Not to Be Fair?

In Chapter 2, I reported Justice Scalia's statements prior to the *Hamdan v. Rumsfeld* oral arguments, held on March 28, 2006, justifying his decision not to recuse himself from the case. As indicated, this was not the only case in which Justice Scalia has had a conflict of interest or an apparently irrevocable prejudgement. His decision not to recuse himself in the 2004 case involving Vice President Cheney resurfaced in April 2006. At a question-and-answer session after a speech at the University of Connecticut Law School, Scalia told the group that he had no regrets about his decision not to recuse himself: "I think the proudest things I have done on the bench is not allow myself to be chased off that case" (Associated Press, 2006a). He went on to tell the students, "For Pete's sake, if you can't trust your Supreme Court justice more than that, get a life." He did acknowledge that he would have recused himself if the case had involved Cheney personally, but he viewed the situation as different because the vice president was acting in his official capacity. (The case dealt with Cheney's efforts to keep private the details of a closed-door White House committee on energy policy.)

At the Supreme Court level, judges have a great degree of discretion as to whether they should abstain from participation in a particular case for reasons of potential bias. Chief Justice Rehnquist was quite resistant to claims that, in a certain cases involving certain justices, he should intervene. It is not yet clear what Chief Justice Roberts' stance will be. (As the oral argument for *Schaffer v. Weast* was called on October 5, 2005, observers were surprised to see Chief Justice Roberts—on only his second day on the bench—get up and leave, a sign that he was recusing himself. His reasons were unclear to court watchers, and he declined to offer any. But perhaps it will act as a signal to his colleagues that he intends to take concerns about propriety seriously.)

It is doubtful that the problem of justices failing to restrain themselves will go away by itself. Justice Scalia appears to be increasingly willing to make bombastic remarks or take provocative actions in public. In a short span of 6 weeks in the spring of 2006, he first made what some considered to be an obscene gesture in response to a Boston reporter's question (he fanned his fingers of one hand under his chin), he then expressed his proud defense of his behavior in the Cheney case, and, in a speech on Capitol Hill, he told Congress to mind its own business if it was tempted to pass legislation directing the Supreme Court to avoid using foreign law in its decisions. (At the time a bill introduced by Representative Tom Feeney, with 83 co-sponsors, said judges should generally not rely on foreign rulings or laws, and in the Senate, Richard Shelby introduced a bill that would forbid federal judges from relying on "any constitution, law, administrative rule, executive order, directive, policy, judicial decision, or any other action of any foreign state or international organization or agency, other than English constitutional and common law up to the time of the adoption of the Constitution of the United States" [Mauro, 2006e, p. 1].) Justice Scalia told the audience, which included some legislators, "As much as I think that it is improper to use foreign law to determine the meaning of the Constitution, I don't think it's any of your business" (Associated Press, 2006b, p. A4). He went on to say, "If you can tell us not to use foreign laws, you can tell us not to use certain principles of logic.... Let us make our mistakes, just as we let you make yours." He seems to enjoy his role, telling one recent audience, "Part of my charm is that I always tell people things they don't want to hear" (Biskupic, 2006b, p. 4A).

Do Advocates Get a Fair Shot at Getting Their Points Across?

The oral argument is obviously a challenging task for any advocate, whether novice or veteran. The advocate can expect to be interrupted and the justices to be ever vigilant for errors or loose thinking. Would a different atmosphere improve the quality of discussion? Midway through John Roberts' first term as chief justice, observers began to note that the Court seemed more relaxed; it was claimed that there were fewer interruptions and more laughter. We set out to assess some variables empirically; these variables at least indirectly could indicate the atmosphere in the Court. Specifically, we compared the 78 oral arguments in Chief Justice Roberts' first term with those in the two immediately preceding terms. (We used two terms for two reasons, not only for reliability purposes but also because Chief Justice Rehnquist was ill and did not chair 44 of the 74 oral arguments during the 2004–2005 term. For this term we separated the 30 oral arguments chaired by the chief justice from the 42 oral arguments chaired by Justice Stevens, the senior associate justice, and the 2 cases chaired by Justice O'Connor, when Justice Stevens also had to miss the Court's proceedings.)

We assessed the following variables, which we considered to be indirect indications of the general atmosphere of the Court:

1. The number of words expressed at the beginning of his or her appearance, before being interrupted by a justice, by the petitioner's lead attorney and the respondent's lead attorney
2. The number of times the official transcript of the oral argument indicated "(Laughter)" in response to a statement by either an advocate or a justice

To compare the terms with regard to uninterrupted opening statements, we used the median rather than the mean as the average number of words uttered before interruption, because the distribution is skewed instead of being bell-shaped. Most initial interruptions occur well before 200 words are spoken, but on occasion the advocate will get to utter 400, 500, or more words. The range is impressive; in the 2003–2004 term, 7 of the 74 respondents got out fewer than 40 words (or, two or three sentences) before being interrupted. But of the three terms we studied, the middle one had the most variation; as mentioned in Chapter 5, in *Dodd v. United States*, Justice O'Connor interrupted the respondent's attorney before he uttered a single word, while the justices permitted the respondent for *Brand X* to speak 862 words without interruption.

Our results indicate that the Rehnquist Court, in the earlier term, was more relaxed in its willingness to let advocates speak before an initial interruption. The median number of words spoken by petitioners before an initial interruption was as follows:

For the 2003–2004 term, 111 words
For the 2004–2005 term, also 111 words
For Justice Roberts's first term, 149 words, or a 38% increase

The results for interruptions to respondents showed a similar difference, although across the three terms respondents were interrupted somewhat more quickly than petitioners. For the 2003–2004 term, respondents' initial interruption came after 82 words; for the next term, after 77 words; and for Chief Justice Roberts's first term, 110 words.

Can these differences be attributed solely to the change at the helm? No, one factor is that Justice O'Connor participated fully in the first two terms assessed here, but in only 40 of the 78 oral arguments in the last term. (Her retirement took effect at the end of January 2006, as Justice Alito had been confirmed by the Senate and sworn in that month.) As mentioned in Chapter 5, Justice O'Connor was well known for being the first justice to ask a question, particularly of the petitioner; for example, in her 40 oral arguments of her last term, she initiated questioning to 14 of the petitioners and 5 of the respondents. In contrast, Justice Alito, who took part in 38 oral arguments, perhaps reflecting freshman reticence, did not initiate the questioning to *any* petitioner or respondent. Did this substitution affect interruption times? Yes, when O'Connor was present, the median (for petitioners) was 137 words; with Alito, it was 155 words, so this change did make a difference, but it did not account for all the change. (The 137-word average was still substantially higher than the 111 words in the two earlier terms.) Interestingly, with regard to initial interruptions of the respondent, the change from O'Connor to Alito made no difference, but, as mentioned earlier, O'Connor's "first-question" behavior was directed to petitioners much more than to respondents.

Frequency of laughter showed consistent results with the measure of latency of initial interruptions. For the first two terms, on average there were about three exchanges that elicited enough of a reaction from the audience to cause the court reporter to note "(Laughter)." In the first term with Roberts as chair, the average number increased to about 3.5. So, in general, it does appear that observations of a more relaxed Court are confirmed by these empirical measures.

Does the Procedure Work?

The final contentious issue returns to the theme of the first chapter of this book: Has the oral argument outlived its usefulness? At the beginning of the Republic it was essential—the English tradition had downplayed written materials and left it up to justices to hear arguments and decide on the basis of what they heard. Has the oral argument become only window-dressing? The only book other than the current one to use an empirical approach to oral arguments, by Timothy Johnson (2004), concludes that "justices use oral arguments to seek information about their policy options, other actors' preferences, and institutional rules that may constrain their ability to make certain decisions" (2004, p. 125). In analyzing the contents of oral arguments, Johnson found that 40% of their questions dealt with policy considerations. More impressive is his finding that almost 80% of all the justices' questions referred to matters not raised by the litigants' briefs or amicus briefs. As he noted, "This is compelling evidence that Supreme Court justices use oral arguments to gain information beyond the briefs that they believe will help them make decisions in line with their preferred goals" (2004, p. 126).

Johnson suggested that "there is also convincing evidence that oral arguments begin the coalition formation process as the justices move toward final decisions" (2004, p. 126). He acknowledged that this conclusion was based on Justice Powell's notes, but showed that Powell listened to his colleagues' questions, "especially those who would most likely help him secure majority coalitions" (p. 126).

Oral arguments appear to perform the function of pruning and narrowing the issues raised in the briefs. Johnson found that 90% of all the justices' comments during their merit conferences dealt with issues that were discussed during oral arguments. Furthermore, he found that "almost 30 percent of all the legal and policy points made in majority opinion syllabi refer to issues that the opinion writer obtained directly from oral argument" (2004, p. 127).

Clearly the oral arguments serve more than a window to the public to observe the Court in action; they play a vital role in the decision making of the Court.

References

Alaska v. United States, 125 S. Ct., 2137 (2005).

Allport, G. W., & Odbert, H. S. (1936). Trait-names, a psychological study. *Psychological Monographs, 47* (1, Whole No. 211).

Althouse, A. (2005, December 12). Why Congress should impose TV cameras on the Supreme Court. http://althouse.blogspot.com/2005/12/12/why-congress-should-impose-TV-camera.html

American Trucking Association v. Michigan, 125 S.Ct. 2419 (2005).

Associated Press. (2006a, April 13). Scalia says he's proud he heard '04 case involving Cheney. *USA Today,* p. 7A.

Associated Press. (2006b, May 19). Scalia suggests Congress butt out. *Kansas City Star,* p. A4.

Austin, J. (2006, May). *Do Supreme Court justices' questions during oral arguments predict their decisions?* Lawrence, KS: Senior Honors Thesis, Department of Psychology, University of Kansas.

Balkin, J. M. (Ed.). (2001). *What Brown v. Board of Education should have said: The nation's top legal experts rewrite America's landmark civil rights decision.* New York: NYU Press.

Barnhart v. Peabody Coal Co., 123 S.Ct. 748 (2003).

Barth, A. (1974). *Prophets with honor: Great dissents and great dissenters in the Supreme Court.* New York: Random House.

Bashman, H. J. (2006, June 5). Just call him 'Your Honor.' *Legal Times,* p. 70.

Bauer, W. J., & Bryson, W. C. (1983, Spring). The appeal. *Docket,* pp. 12–13.

Baum, L. (1997). *The puzzle of judicial behavior.* Ann Arbor, MI: University of Michigan Press.

Baum, L. (2007). *The Supreme Court* (9th ed.). Washington, DC: CQ Press.

Beard v. Banks, 126 S.Ct. 2572 (2006).

Bennett, R. (Chair). (1997). *How to argue a case before the Supreme Court* [video-cassette]. C-SPAN video.

Biskupic, J. (1995, February 27-March 5). Disorder in the Court. *Washington Post National Weekly Edition*, p. 34.

Biskupic, J. (2003, May 16). Lawyers emerge as Supreme Court specialists. *USA Today*, p. 6A.

Biskupic, J. (2005). *Sandra Day O'Connor: How the first woman on the Supreme Court became its most influential justice.* New York: HarperCollins.

Biskupic, J. (2006a, May 19). Scalia tells Congress not to meddle. *USA Today*, p. 4A.

Biskupic, J. (2006b, October 6). Justices make points by questioning lawyers. *USA Today*, p. A7.

Board of Education v. Pico, 457 U.S. 853 (1982).

Bolling v. Sharpe, 347 U.S. 497 (1954).

Bradshaw v. Stumpf, 125 S.Ct. 2398 (2005).

Bradwell v. Illinois, 83 U.S. 130 (1873).

Breyer, S. (1997, January 18). C-SPAN television interview, *America and the Courts.*

Briggs v. Elliott, 193 F.Supp. 920 (1952).

Brigham City v. Stuart, 126 S.Ct. 1943 (2006).

Brown v. Board of Education of Topeka, 98 F. Supp. 797 (1953).

Brown v. Board of Education of Topeka, 347 U.S. 483 (1954).

Brown v. Board of Education of Topeka, 349 U.S. 294 (1955).

Brown v. Payton, 125 S.Ct. 2248 (2005).

Burger, W. (1984). Conference on Supreme Court Advocacy (October 17, 1983). *Catholic University Law Review, 33,* 525–527.

Bush v. Gore, 121 S.Ct. 525 (2000).

California v. Deep Sea Research, Inc., 118 S.Ct. 1464 (1998).

Camps Newfound/Owatonna v. Town of Harrison, 520 U.S. 564 (1997).

Caplan, L. (1987). *The tenth justice: The solicitor general's office and the rule of law.* New York: Random House.

Carey v. Musladin, 127 S.Ct. 649 (2007).

Carter, R. L. (2005). *A matter of law: A memoir of struggle in the cause of equal rights.* New York: The New Press.

Casto, W. R. (1995). *The Supreme Court in the early republic: The chief justiceships of John Jay and Oliver Ellsworth.* Columbia, SC: University of South Carolina Press.

Castro v. United States, 124 S.Ct. 786 (2004).

Central Laborers' Pension Fund v. Heinz, 124 S.Ct. 2230 (2004).

Chandler v. Florida, 449 U.S. 560 (1981).

Cheney v. U.S. District Court for the District of Columbia, 124 S.Ct., 2576 (2004).

Clary, B. G., Paulsen, S. R., & Vanselow, M. J. (2004). *Advocacy in appeals* (2nd ed.). St. Paul, MN: West Publishing.

Cleary, E. J. (1994). *Beyond the burning cross: A landmark case of race, censorship, and the First Amendment.* New York: Random House.

Clinton v. Goldsmith, 119 S.Ct. 1538 (1999).

Cohn, M., & Dow, D. (1998). *Cameras in the courtroom: Television and the pursuit of justice.* Jefferson, NC: McFarland.

Colby, W. H. (2002). *Long goodbye: The deaths of Nancy Cruzan.* Carlsbad, CA: Hay House.

Cooper, P. J. (1995). *Battles on the bench: Conflict inside the Supreme Court.* Lawrence, KS: University Press of Kansas.

Cooper v. Aaron, 358 U.S. 1 (1958).

Cooper Industries v. Aviall Services, 125 S.Ct. 577 (2005).

Coyle, M. (1996, April 29). Justices query lawyer on excessive awards review. *National Law Journal,* p. A12.

Coyle, M. (1997, December 15). Alaska budgets $1 M for Supreme Court lawyers. *National Law Journal,* p. A12.

Coyle, M. (2006, December 18–December 25). For a high court battle, two words: Get Carter. *National Law Journal,* p. 18.

Craig v. Boren, 429 U.S. 190 (1976).

Cruzan v. Director, Missouri Department of Health, 447 U.S. 261 (1990).

Cullinan, K. (2004, September 6). Just imagine it's the Supremes. *Legal Times,* p. 10.

Cushman, C. (2001). Women advocates before the Supreme Court. *Journal of Supreme Court History, 26,* 67–88.

DaimlerChrysler v. Cuno, 126 S.Ct. 1854 (2006).

Dartmouth College v. Woodward, 17 U.S. (4 Wheat) 518 (1819).

Davis v. Washington, 126 S.Ct. 2206 (2006).

Deck v. Missouri, 125 S.Ct. 2007 (2005).

Deen, R. E., Ignagni, J., & Meernik, J. (2003). The solicitor general as amicus 1953–2000: How influential? *Judicature, 87,* 60–71.

Denniston, L. (2005, November 7). Court to rule on military tribunals. http://www.scotusblog.com/movabletype/archives/2005/

Denniston, L. (2006, March 27). Scalia asked to step aside. http://www.scotusblog.com/movabletype/archives/2006

Dixon v. United States, 126 S.Ct. 2437 (2006).

Dodd v. United States, 125 S.Ct. 2478 (2005).

Dolan v. United States Postal Service, 126 S.Ct. 1252 (2006).

Douglas, W. O. (1960). The public trial and the free press. *American Bar Association Journal, 46,* 840–844.

Douglas, W. O. (1980). *The Court years, 1939–1975: The autobiography of William O. Douglas.* New York: Random House.

Dred Scott v. Sandford, 60 U.S. (19 Howard) 393 (1857).

eBay, Inc. v. MercExchange, LLC, 126 S.Ct. 1837 (2006).

Eldred v. Ashcroft, 123 S.Ct., 769 (2003).

Elk Grove Unified School District v. Newdow, 124 S. Ct. 2301 (2004).

Epstein, L., & Knight, J. (1998). *The choices justices make.* Washington, DC: CQ Press.

Estes v. Texas, 381 U.S. 532 (1965).

Ewing v. California, 123 S.Ct. 1179 (2003).

ExxonMobil v. Saudi Basic, 125 S.Ct, 1517 (2005).

Federal Communications Commission v. NextWave Personal Communications, 123 S.Ct., 832 (2003).

Finley, S. W. (1979). Daniel Webster packed 'em in. *1979 Supreme Court Historical Society Yearbook,* pp. 70–78, 83.

Florida v. Nixon, 125 S.Ct. 551 (2005).

Frank, J. (1930). *Law and the modern mind.* New York: Coward-McCann.

Frederick, D. (2003a). *The art of oral advocacy.* St. Paul, MN: West Publishing.

Frederick, D. (2003b). *Supreme Court and appellate advocacy.* St. Paul, MN: West Publishing.

Frederick, D. C. (2005a). Advocacy before the Supreme Court: 1791 to the present. In C. Tomlins (Ed.), *The United States Supreme Court: The pursuit of justice* (pp. 382–397). Boston: Houghton Mifflin.

Frederick, D. C. (2005b). Supreme Court advocacy in the early nineteenth century. *Journal of Supreme Court History, 30,* 1–16.

Freeman, L. M. (2006). Mr. Jay rides circuit. *Journal of Supreme Court History, 31,* 18–27.

Frew v. Hawkins, 124 S.Ct., 899 (2004).

Georgia v. Randolph, 126 S.Ct. 1515 (2006).

Gibbons v. Ogden, 22 U.S. (9 Wheat) 1 (1824).

Gideon v. Wainwright, 372 U.S. 335 (1963).

Ginsburg, R. B. (1999). Remarks on appellate advocacy. *South Carolina Law Review, 50,* 567–571.

Ginsburg, R. B. (2003). Foreword. In D. Frederick (Ed.), *The art of oral advocacy* (pp. ix–x). St. Paul, MN: West Publishing.

Goldfarb, R. L. (1998). *TV or not TV: Television, justice, and the courts.* New York: NYU Press.

Goldman, J. (1975). *Attitude of United States judges toward limitation of oral argument and opinion-writing in the United States Court of Appeals.* Washington, DC: Federal Judicial Center.

Goldman, T. R. (2006, July 31). Katyal's crusade. *Legal Times,* pp. 1, 17–18.

Gong Lum v. Rice, 275 U.S. 78 (1927).

Grable v. Darue, 125 S.Ct. 2363 (2005).

Granholm v. Heald, 125 S.Ct. 1885 (2005).

Greenberg, J. (1994). *Crusaders in the courts: How a dedicated band of lawyers fought for the civil rights revolution.* New York: Basic Books.

Greenhouse, L. (1996a, October 8). Justices skeptically review law on cable system access. *New York Times,* p. A10.

Greenhouse, L. (1996b, October 10). High Court raises issue of stripping charities of exemptions. *New York Times,* p. A12.

Greenhouse, L. (1996c, December 12). 'Easy' outing for Reno backfires at Supreme Court. *New York Times,* p. A20.

Greenhouse, L. (2000, April 26). Justices appear set to reject law on abortion procedures. *New York Times,* pp. A1, A18.

Greenhouse, L. (2002, December 12). An intense attack by Justice Thomas on cross-burning. *New York Times,* pp. A1, A17.

Greenhouse, L. (2003, September 17). Press room predictions. *Forecasting U.S. Supreme Court decisions.* Symposium, Lee Epstein, Chair. St. Louis, MO: Washington University.

Greenhouse, L. (2005a). *Becoming Justice Blackmun: Harry Blackmun's Supreme Court journey.* New York: Times Books.

Greenhouse, L. (2005b, December 7). Justices weigh military's access to law schools. *New York Times,* pp. A1, A26.

Greenhouse, L. (2006a, March 1). Vermont campaign limits get cool reception at Court. *New York Times,* p. A14.

Greenhouse, L. (2006b, March 23). Roberts dissent reveals strain beneath the Court's placid surface. *New York Times,* pp. A1, A18.

Greenhouse, L. (2006c, May 3). In the Roberts Court, more room for argument. *New York Times,* pp. A1, A17.

Grupo Dataflux v. Atlas Global Group, 124 S.Ct. 1920 (2004).

Grutter v. Bollinger, 123 S.Ct. 2325 (2003).

Halbert v. Michigan, 125 S.Ct. 2582 (2005).

Hamdan v. Rumsfeld, 126 S.Ct. 2749 (2005).

Hamdi v. Rumsfeld, 124 S.Ct. 2633 (2004).

Harlan, J. M., II. (1955). What part does oral argument play in the conduct of an appeal? *Cornell Law Quarterly, 41,* 6–11.

Henniger, D. (2006, April 28). Scalia floats and Breyer rocks for a day in court. *Wall Street Journal,* p. A14.

Hobson, C. F. (2005). The Marshall Court: 1801–1835. In C. Tomlins (Ed.), *The United States Supreme Court: The pursuit of justice* (pp. 47–79). Boston: Houghton Mifflin.

Holt, W. W., Jr. (2005). The establishment of the federal court system, 1787–1791. In C. Tomlins (Ed.), *The United States Supreme Court: The pursuit of justice* (pp. 3–25). Boston: Houghton-Mifflin.

Hope v. Pelzer, 536 U.S. 730 (2002).

House v. Bell, 126 S.Ct. 2064 (2006).

Household Credit Services v. Pfennig, 124 S.Ct. 1741 (2004).

Hudson v. McMillian, 503 U.S. 1 (1992).

Hughes, C. E. (1928). *The Supreme Court of the United States.* New York: Columbia University Press.

Hull, A. (1997). *Strategic interaction and schema: An integration and study of judicial decision-making models.* Lawrence, KS: Unpublished manuscript, Department of Political Science, University of Kansas.

Illinois v Caballes, 125 S. Ct. 834 (2005).

Iowa v. Tovar, 124 S.Ct. 1379 (2004).

Isikoff, M. (2006, April 3). Detainees' rights: Scalia speaks his mind. *Newsweek, 147*(14), 6.

Jackson, R. H. (1951). Advocacy before the Supreme Court: Suggestions for effective case presentations. *American Bar Association Journal, 37,* 801–804.

John, O. P. (1990). The "Big Five" factor taxonomy: Dimensions of personality in the natural language and in questionnaires. In L. A. Pervin (Ed.), *Handbook of personality: Theory and research* (pp. 66–100). New York: Guilford Press.

Johnson v. California, 125 S.Ct. 2410 (2005).

Johnson, T. R. (2004). *Oral arguments and decision making in the United States Supreme Court.* Albany: State University of New York Press.

Kane, G. (2000, December 24). Thomas's silence betrays supporters. *Lawrence Journal-World*, p. 7B.

Kansas v. Colorado, 125 S.Ct. 944 (2005).

Kansas v. Marsh, 126 S.Ct. 2516 (2006).

Kassin, S. M. (1984). TV cameras, public self-consciousness, and mock jury performance. *Journal of Experimental Social Psychology, 20,* 336–349.

Kelo v. City of New London, 125 S.Ct. 2655 (2005).

Klineberg, O. (1986). SPSSI and race relations, in the 1950s and thereafter. *Journal of Social Issues, 42,* 53–59.

Kluger, R. (1976). *Simple justice.* New York: Knopf.

Kmiec, D. W. (2006, March 13). United against al Qaeda. *Legal Times,* p. 54.

Kontrick v. Ryan, 124 S.Ct. 906 (2004).

Koons Buick Pontiac v. Nigh, 125 S.Ct. 460 (2005).

Kunda, Z. (1990). The case for motivated reasoning. *Psychological Bulletin,108,* 480–498.

Kurland, P. B. (1968). Earl Warren, the "Warren Court," and the Warren myth. *Michigan Law Review, 67,* 353–358.

Laboratory Corp. of America Holdings v. Metabolite Laboratories, Inc., 126 S.Ct. Per curiam (2006).

League of United Latin American Citizens v. Perry, 126 S.Ct. 2594 (2006)

Lee v. Weisman, 505 U.S. 577 (1992).

Lederman, M. (2006, March 23). Justice Scalia announces opposition to trials in civil courts for alien military detainees. http://www.scotusblog.com/movable type/archives/2006

Lindquist, S., & Klein, D. (2006). The influence of jurisprudential considerations on Supreme Court decision making: A study of conflict cases. *Law and Society Review, 40,* 135–161.

Liptak, A. (2005, December 31). So, guy walks into the bar, and Scalia says....*New York Times,* p. A17.

Lithwick, D. (2004). A high court of one: The role of the "swing voter" in the 2002 term. In N. Devins & D. M. Douglas (Eds.), *A year at the Supreme Court* (pp. 13–31). Durham, NC: Duke University Press.

Lithwick, D. (2006, January 2). Let's put on the show. *Legal Times,* pp. 36–37.

Lockyer v. Andrade, 123 S.Ct. 1166 (2003).

Maltzman, F., Spriggs, J. F., II, & Wahlbeck, P. J. (2000). *Crafting law on the Supreme Court: The collegial game.* New York: Cambridge University Press.

Marbury v. Madison, 1 Cranch 137 (U.S. 1803).

Marshall v. Marshall, 126 S.Ct. 1735 (2006).

Maryland v. Pringle, 124 S.Ct. 795 (2004).

Maryland v. Wilson, 519 U.S. 408 (1997).

Mauro, T. (1995). The Court and the cult of secrecy. In R. A. Smolla (Ed.), *A year in the life of the Supreme Court* (pp. 263–279). Durham, NC: Duke University Press.

Mauro, T. (2003a, May 19). Lessons from a lifetime at the lectern. *Legal Times,* p. 8.

Mauro, T. (2003b, August 11). Stating their case. *Legal Times,* pp. 1, 8.

Mauro, T. (2003c, August 18). High Court post-mortem. *Legal Times,* pp. 24, 26–31.

Mauro, T. (2003d, October 13). The first time: Jitters and all-nighters. *Legal Times,* p. 10.

Mauro, T. (2003e, November 3). Mrs. Malaprop returns. *Legal Times,* p. 8.

Mauro, T. (2004a). Apprentice appellants. *American Lawyer, 26,* 75–76.

Mauro, T. (2004b, July 12). At the Supreme Court, the chosen few. *Legal Times,* pp. 1, 10.

Mauro, T. (2004c). Glasnost at the Supreme Court. In N. Devins & D. M. Douglas (Eds.), *A year at the Supreme Court* (pp. 193–208). Durham, NC: Duke University Press.

Mauro, T. (2004d, September 13). Speaking wisely at the Supreme Court. *Legal Times,* p. 8.

Mauro, T. (2005a). Strength in numbers. *American Lawyer, 27,* 71–72.

Mauro, T. (2005b, November 14). Senate pushes for cameras in high court. *Legal Times,* p. 13.

Mauro, T. (2005c, December 19). The other side of Sam Alito. *Legal Times,* pp. 1, 10.

Mauro, T. (2006a, March 6). Tax incentives mulled. *Legal Times,* p. 10.

Mauro, T. (2006b, March 20). Holding forth on the Supreme Court. *Legal Times,* p. 11.

Mauro, T. (2006c, April 10). Justices push back on cameras in court. *Legal Times,* p. 10.

Mauro, T. (2006d, May 8). Help offered for high court criminal cases. *Legal Times,* pp. 1, 8.

Mauro, T. (2006e, May 19). Scalia tells Congress to stay out of high court business. http://www.law.com/jsp/article.jsp?id=1147943135671

Mauro, T. (2006f, December 4). Schoolyard bullies. *Legal Times,* p. 3.

Mauro, T. (2007a, February 12). After a year on the Court, Alito holds forth. *Legal Times,* pp. 12–13.

Mauro, T. (2007b, July 9). Doubting Roberts. *Legal Times,* p. 10.

McAdams, D. P., & Pals, J. L. (2006). A new Big Five: Fundamental principles for an integrative science of personality. *American Psychologist, 61,* 204–217.

McCloskey, R. G. (1994). *The American Supreme Court* (2nd ed.). Chicago: University of Chicago Press.

McCulloch v. Maryland, 17 U.S. (4 Wheat) 316 (1819).

McGuire, K. T. (1993). *The Supreme Court bar: Legal elites in the Washington community.* Charlottesville, VA: University Press of Virginia.

McLaurin v. Oklahoma State Regents for Higher Education, 339 U.S. 629 (1950).

Merck KGaA v. Integra Life Sciences, 125 S.Ct. 2372 (2005).

Meredith v. Jefferson County Board of Education, 127 S.Ct. 2738 (2007).

Merida, K., & Fletcher, M. A. (2007). *Supreme discomfort: The divided soul of Clarence Thomas.* New York: Doubleday.

Merrill Lynch, Pierce, Fenner, & Smith, Inc. V. Dabit, 126 S.Ct. 1503 (2006).

MGM Studios v. Grokster, 125 S.Ct. 2764 (2005).

Michel, P. R. (1998). Effective appellate advocacy. *Litigation, 24,* 19–23.

Microsoft v. AT&T, 127 S.Ct. 1746 (2007).

Mid-Con Freight v. Michigan, 125 S.Ct. 2427 (2005).

Miller-El v. Cockrell, 123 S.Ct. 1029 (2003).

Miller-El v. Dretke, 125 S.Ct. 2317 (2005).

Missouri ex rel. Gaines v. Canada, 305 U.S. 337 (1938).

Moseley v. V Secret Catalogue, Inc., 537 U.S. 418 (2003).

Muehler v. Mena, 125 S.Ct. 1465 (2005).

National Aeronautics and Space Administration v. Federal Labor Relations Authority, 527 U.S. 229 (1999).

National Cable and Telecommunications Assn. v. Brand X Internet Service, 125 S.Ct. 2688 (2005).

Nebraska Press Association v. Stuart, 427 U.S. 539 (1976).

New Jersey v. New York, 118 S.Ct., 1726 (1998).

Newton, J. (2006). *Justice for all: Earl Warren and the nation he made.* New York: Henry Holt.

Norfolk and Western Railway v. Ayers, 538 U.S. 135 (2003).

Norfolk Southern Railway v. Kirby, 125 S.Ct. 385 (2005).

Norgren, J. (2007). *Belva Lockwood: The woman who would be president.* New York: NYU Press.

O'Brien, D. M. (2000). *Storm center: The Supreme Court in American politics.* New York: Norton.

Olympic Airways v. Husain, 124 S.Ct. 1221 (2004).

Oregon v. Guzek, 126 S.Ct. 1226 (2006).

Pace v. DiGuglielmo, 125 S.Ct. 2931 (2005).

Pennsylvania v. Mimms, 434 U.S. 106 (1977).

Peppers, T. C. (2006). *Courtiers of the Marble Palace: The rise and influence of the Supreme Court law clerk.* Stanford, CA: Stanford University Press.

Perkins, D. D. (1988). The use of social science in public interest litigation: A role for community psychologists. *American Journal of Community Psychology, 16,* 465–485.

Perry, B. A. (1999a). *The priestly tribe: The Supreme Court's image in the American mind.* Westport, CT: Praeger.

Perry, B. A. (1999b). *"The Supremes": Essays on the current justices of the Supreme Court of the United States.* New York: Peter Lang.

Pervin, L., & John, O. P. (2001). *Personality: Theory and research* (8th ed.). New York: Wiley.

Pillard, N. (2005). Women as Supreme Court advocates: Part One. *Supreme Court Historical Society Quarterly, 26,* 10–14.

Pillard, N. (2006). Women as Supreme Court advocates: Part Two. *Supreme Court Historical Society Quarterly, 27,* 10–13.

Plessy v. Ferguson, 163 U.S. 537 (1896).

Posner, R. A. (2001). *Breaking the deadlock: The 2000 election, the Constitution, and the Courts.* Princeton, NJ: Princeton University Press.

Posner, R. A. (2006, February 6). Wire trap. *New Republic, 234,* 15–16.

Prettyman, E. B., Jr. (1978). Supreme Court advocacy: Random thoughts in a day of time restrictions. *Litigation, 4,* 16–20.

Prettyman, E. B., Jr. (1984). The Supreme Court's use of hypothetical questions at oral argument. *Catholic University Law Review, 33,* 555–591.

Randall v. Sorrell, 126 S.Ct. 2479 (2006).

R.A.V. v. City of St. Paul, 505 U.S. 377 (1992).

Regents of the University of California v. Bakke, 438 U.S. 265 (1978).

Rehnquist, W. H. (1984). Oral advocacy: A disappearing art. *Mercer Law Review, 35,* 1015–1028.

Rehnquist, W. H. (1986) Oral advocacy. *South Texas Law Review, 27,* 289–303.

Rehnquist, W. H. (1987). *The Supreme Court: How it was, how it is.* New York: William Morrow.

Rehnquist, W. H. (2001). *The Supreme Court* (revised and updated). New York: Random House.

Reibstein, L. (1997, January 20). Whose right is it? *Newsweek,* p. 36.

Richmond Newspapers, Inc. v. Commonwealth of Virginia, 331 U.S. 374 (1980).

Roberts, J. G., Jr. (2005). Oral argument and the re-emergence of a Supreme Court bar. *Journal of Supreme Court History, 30,* 68–81.

Roe v. Wade, 110 U.S. 113 (1973).

Rohde, D. W., & Spaeth, H. J. (1976). *Supreme Court decision making.* San Francisco: W. H. Freeman.

Rombeck, T. (2002, October 30). Justice takes time for Q&A. *Lawrence Journal-World,* p. 5B.

Roper v. Simmons, 125 S.Ct. 1183 (2005).

Rosen, J. (1996, November 11). The agonizer. *New Yorker,* pp. 82–90.

Rosen, P. (1972). *The Supreme Court and social sciences.* Urbana, IL: University of Illinois Press.

Rumsfeld v. Forum for Academic and Institutional Rights, 126 S.Ct. 1297 (2006).

Rumsfeld v. Padilla, 124 S.Ct. 2711 (2004).

Savage, D. G. (1997, September). Say the right thing. *American Bar Association Journal, 83,* 54–60.

Savage, D. G. (2004). Anthony M. Kennedy and the road not taken. In N. Devins & D. M. Douglas (Eds.), *A year at the Supreme Court* (pp. 33–54). Durham, NC: Duke University Press.

Schaffer v. Weast, 126 S.Ct. 528 (2006).

Scheiber, N. (2006, April 10). The hustler. *New Republic, 234,* 14–19.

Schwartz, B. (1981). Felix Frankfurter and Earl Warren: A study of a deteriorating relationship. In P. B. Kurland & G. Casper (Eds.), *The Supreme Court review, 1980* (pp. 115–142). Chicago: University of Chicago Press.

Schwartz, B. (1997). *A book of legal lists: The best and worst in American law.* New York: Oxford University Press.

Schwartz, E., & Mauro, T. (2006, March 20). Firms buying their way into an exclusive club. *Legal Times*, pp. 1, 22.

Segal, J. A, & Cover, A. D. (1989). Ideological values and the votes of Supreme Court justices. *American Political Science Review, 83*, 557–565.

Segal, J. A., & Spaeth, H. J. (1993). *The Supreme Court and the attitudinal model.* New York: Cambridge University Press.

Segal, J. A., & Spaeth, H. J. (2002). *The Supreme Court and the attitudinal model revisited.* New York: Cambridge University Press.

Severn, B. (1969). *John Marshall: The man who made the Court supreme.* New York: David McKay.

Shalala v. Whitecotten, 514 U.S. 268 (1995).

Shapiro, S. M. (1988). William Pinkney: The Supreme Court's greatest advocate. *1988 Supreme Court Historical Society Yearbook*, pp. 40–45.

Shapiro, S. M. (2005). Rebels at the Supreme Court bar. http://www.appellate.net/article/rebels799.asp

Shullman, S. L. (2004). The illusion of devil's advocacy: How the justices of the Supreme Court foreshadow their decisions during oral argument. *Journal of Appellate Practice and Process, 6*, 271–293.

Simon, J. F. (1989). *The antagonists: Hugo Black, Felix Frankfurter, and civil liberties in modern America.* New York: Simon & Schuster.

Small v. United States, 125 S.Ct. 1752 (2005).

Smolla, R. A. (2004). Cross burning: *Virginia v. Black.* In N. Devins & D. M. Douglas (Eds.), *A year at the Supreme Court* (pp. 153–173). Durham, NC: Duke University Press.

Sorrell v. Randall, 126 S.Ct. 2479 (2006).

Specter, A. (2000). *Passion for truth.* New York: William Morrow.

Specter, A. (2006, April 25). Hidden justice(s). *Washington Post*, p. A23.

Stansell, C. (2007, April 2). Madame candidate. *New Republic, 236*, 56–61.

Starr, K. W. (2002). *First among equals: The Supreme Court and American life.* New York: Warner Books.

State Farm Mutual v. Campbell, 123 S.Ct. 1513 (2003).

Stenberg v. Carhart, 68 U.S.L.W. 4702 (2000).

Stewart v. Dutra Construction, 125 S.Ct. 1118 (2005).

Stone, I. (1958). *Clarence Darrow for the defense.* New York: Bantam Books.

Sweatt v. Painter, 339 U.S. 629 (1950).

Taylor, S. (2005, September 12). The Roberts court will decide. *Legal Times*, pp. 60–61.

Tenet v. Doe, 125 S.Ct. 1230 (2005).

Tennard v. Dretke, 124 S.Ct. 2562 (2004).

Thimsen, S. (2003, May). *A psychological analysis of United States Supreme Court voting patterns.* Lawrence, KS: Unpublished senior honors thesis, Department of Psychology, University of Kansas.

Thornburgh, D., & Fine, D. R. (2005, December 19–December 26). Allow television coverage. *National Law Journal*, p. 26.

Thornton v. United States, 124 S.Ct. 2127 (2004).

Toyota Motor Manufacturing v. Williams, 122 S.Ct. 681 (2002).

Turner v. Safely, 482 U.S 78 (1984).

Turner Broadcasting v. Federal Communications Commission, 520 U.S. 180 (1997).

Tushnet, M. (2005). *A court divided: The Rehnquist Court and the future of constitutional law.* New York: W.W. Norton.

Tushnet, M., & Lezin, K. (1991). What really happened in *Brown v. Board of Education. Columbia Law Review, 91,* 1867–1950.

United States v. Bean, 123 S.Ct. 584 (2003).

United States v. Galletti, 124 S.Ct. 1548 (2004).

United States v. Gonzalez-Lopez, 126 S.Ct. 2557 (2006).

United States Postal Service v. Flamingo Industries, 124 S.Ct. 1323 (2004).

Urofsky, M. I. (1993, September 26). Justice on tape. *New York Times Book Review,* p. 33.

Urofsky, M. I. (2004). "Among the most humane moments in all our history": *Brown v. Board of Education* in historical perspective. In C. Cushman & M. I. Urofsky (Eds.), *Black, white, and* Brown: *The landmark school desegregation case in retrospect* (pp. 1–45). Washington: CQ Press.

Van Orden v. Perry, 125 S. Ct. 2854 (2005).

Vermont Republican Party v. Sorrell, 126 S.Ct. 2479 (2006).

Vieth v. Jubelirer, 124 S.Ct. 1769 (2004).

Virginia v. Black, 123 S.Ct. 1291 (2003).

Wachovia Bank, N.A. v. Schmidt, 126 S.Ct. 941 (2006).

Warren, E. (1977). *The memoirs of Chief Justice Earl Warren.* Garden City, NY: Doubleday.

Wasby, S. L. (1981). Oral argument in the Ninth Circuit: The view from the bench and bar. *Golden Gate University Law Review, 11,* 21–79.

Wasby, S. L. (1982). The functions and importance of oral argument: Some views of lawyers and federal judges. *Judicature, 65,* 340–353.

Washington v. Oregon, 29 S.Ct. 47 (1908).

White, G. E. (1988). The Marshall Court and cultural change, 1815–1835, Vols. 3 & 4 of *History of the Supreme Court of the United States.* New York: Macmillan.

Wiener, F. B. (1958). Oral advocacy. *Harvard Law Review, 62,* 56–75.

Wilkinson v. Austin, 125 S.Ct. 2384 (2005).

Wilson, P. E. (1995). *A time to lose.* Lawrence, KS: University Press of Kansas.

Wilson, P. E. (2004). A time to lose. In C. Cushman & M. I. Urofsky (Eds.), *Black, white and* Brown: *The landmark school desegregation case in retrospect* (pp. 157–170). Washington, DC: CQ Press.

Wisconsin Public Intervenor v. Mortier, 111 S.Ct. 2476 (1991).

Wisconsin Right to Life v. Federal Election Commission, 542 U.S. 1305 (2004).

Woodward, C. V. (1955). *The strange career of Jim Crow.* New York: Oxford University Press.

Wrightsman, L. S. (2006). *The psychology of the Supreme Court.* New York: Oxford University Press.

Yarbrough, T. E. (2005). *David Hackett Souter: Traditional Republican on the Rehnquist Court.* New York: Oxford University Press.

Yellow Transportation Inc. v. Michigan, 123 S.Ct. 371 (2003).

Zuckerman, M. (1986, August). *What lies beyond E and N?* Paper presented at the meetings of the American Psychological Association, Washington, DC.

Index